The Power of
Personal
Storytelling

ALSO BY JACK MAGUIRE

Creative Storytelling

Your Guide to a Better Memory

Care and Feeding of the Brain

Night and Day: The Power of Your Dreams
to Transform Your Life

THE POWER OF PERSONAL STORYTELLING

Spinning Tales to Connect with Others

JACK MAGUIRE

JEREMY P. TARCHER / PUTNAM
a member of Penguin Putnam Inc. *New York*

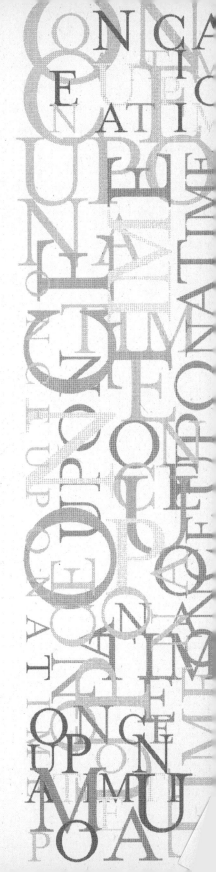

Most Tarcher/Putnam books are available at special quantity discounts
for bulk purchases for sales promotions, premiums, fund-raising, and
educational needs. Special books or book excerpts also can be created to fit
specific needs. For details, write Putnam Special Markets,
375 Hudson Street, New York, NY 10014.

Jeremy P. Tarcher/Putnam
a member of
Penguin Putnam Inc.
375 Hudson Street
New York, NY 10014
www.penguinputnam.com

First Trade Paperback Edition 1998

Library of Congress Cataloging-in-Publication Data

Maguire, Jack, date.
    The power of personal storytelling : spinning tales
to connect with others / by Jack Maguire.
        p.   cm.
    Includes bibliographical references.
    ISBN 0-87477-930-8 (alk. paper)
    1. Interpersonal communication.   2. Interpersonal
relations.   3. Storytelling.   I. Title.
BF637.C45M284   1998   98-21250 CIP
302.3'4—dc21

Printed in the United States of America

12 13 14 15 16 17 18

This book is printed on acid-free paper. ∞

Book design by Lee Fukui

ACKNOWLEDGMENTS

This book grew from the ideas, encouragement, and guidance of my agent, Faith Hamlin, and my editors at Jeremy P. Tarcher, Irene Prokop and Wendy Hubbert, and I very much appreciate their contribution, as well as the excellent help of Jocelyn Wright, assistant editor at Tarcher. I'm also obliged to Robert Smyth of Yellow Moon Press, publisher of my book *Creative Storytelling*, for his ongoing support.

Among the many wonderful storytellers who helped me directly or indirectly to create this book, I am especially indebted to Donald Davis. His life and work testify to the full beauty and power of the storyteller's path. As he says, storytelling "is not what I do for a living . . . it is how I do all that I do while I am living."

Others who inspired me to delve more bravely into the world of personal tales are Judith Black, Elizabeth Ellis, Bill Harley, Jim May, Lee Pennington, and Jackie Torrance. I also feel very lucky to have the influence of Rafe Martin in my storytelling life. Although not best known professionally as a teller of *personal* stories—at least not yet—he communicates traditional and fictional tales with such feeling, commitment, and integrity that they become everyone's personal stories.

I am deeply grateful to my buddies in the Visions Story and Art Center of Poughkeepsie, New York, for their tales, ideas, support, fellowship, and ears, among them Deborah Arnouts; Laurie Baratta; Jeri Burns and Barry Marshall (aka the Storycrafters); Jane Gregory; Lorraine Hartin-Gelardi; Jonathan and Barbara Heiles; Muriel Horowitz; Bill and Pat Joel; Jonathan

Kruk; Allelu Kurten; Tracy Leavitt; Gail McGlinchey; Karen Pillsworth; Rachel Pollack; Mary Summerlin; and Richard Witt.

I would also like to thank all my friends in the League for the Advancement of New England Storytelling (LANES), in particular Marni Gillard; Barbara Lipke; and Mike, Bonnie, and Jesse Myers.

I am blessed to have John Daido Loori Roshi, a wonderful yarnspinner, as my teacher.

I say a million thanks to Tom Cowan, whose wisdom, compassion, humor, and uncommon sense illuminate all my storytelling ventures.

Gene Wilson deserves the highest praise as my stepfather and an especially fine promoter of my career. And in the end, as in the beginning, I acknowledge the good fortune I've had all my life to swap tales with my mother, Becky Wilson.

This book is dedicated to
Tracy Leavitt, who blesses her
friends, family, and neighbors
with her stories and her self.

CONTENTS

Introduction   xiii

PART I
WHY TELL PERSONAL STORIES?   1

1.   Listening: The Telling Difference   3
2.   The Blessings of Personal Storytelling   13

PART II
RECLAIMING YOUR STORYLOVING SELF   35

3.   Your Inner Storyteller   37
4.   Reading Your Own Mind   49
5.   The Quest for the Past   58
6.   Your Hero, Your Self   65

PART III
GETTING STORY IDEAS   75

7.   Lifelines and Storylines   77
8.   Memory Legwork   89
9.   Roving Reporter for the Family News   98
10.   From Abstraction to Reality   104
11.   Getting the Picture   110
12.   Stories Within Stories   115
13.   Making Stories Happen   121

PART IV

BRINGING YOUR STORIES TO LIFE   125

14. Out Loud and Proud   127
15. Crossing the Stream   137
16. Storyboarding   146
17. Enlivening Ways and Means   157

PART V

YOUR STORYTELLING POWERS IN ACTION   167

18. Embodying a Story   169
19. The Voice of Your Being   179
20. The Many Worlds of Personal Storytelling   190
21. Family Storytelling   195
22. Storytelling at Work   201
23. Storytelling in the Community   206
24. Taking the Telling Leap   215

       Appendix   229
       Bibliography   243
       Index   247

The city sleeps and the country sleeps,

The living sleep for their time, the dead sleep for their time,

The old husband sleeps by his wife and the

young husband sleeps by his wife;

And these tend inward to me, and I tend outward to them,

And such as it is to be of these more or less I am,

And of these one and all I weave the song of myself.

WALT WHITMAN, "Song of Myself"

INTRODUCTION

Once upon a time, when people made more of their own things, they created more stories about their life experiences. They told these tales to each other regularly, gracefully, and productively. They did it to give each other insights, to entertain each other, and to engage each other in times of celebration, trial, mourning, or reverence. But primarily they did it to connect with each other. Sharing real-life stories was an essential element in forging friendships, alliances, families, and communities. It brought individuals a greater intimacy with each other and, simultaneously, a stronger sense of self.

Since that time, for all the wonderful progress made in communication technology, social welfare, education, and health care, the world has grown alarmingly less personal. People have given over much of their individual power to the collective, and have let themselves be increasingly distracted from personal storytelling by flashier but ultimately less gratifying activities that compete for their attention. As a result, we citizens of today's world have each lost some of our core vitality—our feeling of having direct contact with the lives we lead, of relating meaningfully with others, and of being individuals in our own right, with our own clear identities.

Now it's time for you to start rekindling that vitality for yourself and the people around you by learning to tell your own personal stories more easily, more skillfully, more enjoyably, and, above all, more often. It's not a matter of turning yourself into an actor, public speaker, or stand-up comic, although each of these roles has roots in storytelling. I'm referring to something

We're all storytellers. We all live in a network of stories. There isn't a stronger connection between people than storytelling.
JIMMY NEIL SMITH

much simpler and much more natural. I'm encouraging you to become better at shaping and expressing true stories about your own life, about the lives of others you've known, and even about the fictional tales that have influenced your reality—and to do all this in a manner that suits who you are, how you live, and whom you encounter.

Human beings are a story; they are living a story and anyone open to this story is living a part—perhaps all—of themselves.

P. L. TRAVERS

Like our ancestors, we are each personal storytellers to some degree, whether or not we think of ourselves that way. Telling personal tales is an intrinsic part of being human. On a daily basis, as we interact with others, we inevitably wind up talking about our present or past experiences. Some of us carry this first-person narrative beyond our own homes and the places where we visit, work, and play, into classrooms, boardrooms, chat rooms, pulpits, therapy sessions, talk shows, rap concerts, or storytelling festivals.

To be a person is to have a story to tell. . . . Within each of us there is a tribe with a complete cycle of legends and dances, songs to be sung.

SAM KEEN

And then there's the speaking we do to ourselves. Throughout our waking hours, we conduct a virtually nonstop interior monologue, much of it weaving and reweaving personal storylines, and we continue this tale-spinning in our dreams at night.

So, both publically and privately, we already lead a storytelling life. But how effectively do we lead it? How satisfying is it to ourselves? To our listeners? How do we recapture the thoughtfulness, dignity, beauty, and sheer delight that once upon a time went into sharing personal tales? How do we break through all our compulsive, mechanical, awkward ego-chatter to the stories that really matter, and to the tellings that are genuinely worthwhile?

This book helps you answer these questions as they apply to your own life. Drawn from my twenty-five-year career as a storyteller, educator, and workshop leader, as well as from the wonderful world of storytellers, educators, and workshop leaders I've been privileged to inhabit, it offers skill-building ideas and activities for anyone involved in personal storytelling—from the good friend or neighbor to the concerned parent or child to the personal-growth quester or facilitator to the professional speaker or storyteller.

Specifically, this book is designed to achieve these goals:

- To inspire you to listen more dynamically to stories—the ones others share with you, the ones you share with others, and the ones you spin for yourself—so that you derive more wisdom and pleasure from them, as well as gain a better sense of what you want to accomplish as a teller

A story is a way to say something that can't be said any other way.

FLANNERY O'CONNOR

- To guide you in reviving and exploring your memories more successfully for story ideas

- To give you methods for building your initial story ideas into fully alive personal tales

- To help you learn these tales—and make them your own—through imaginatively absorbing them rather than memorizing them by rote

- To coach you in communicating a story well, no matter what the situation may be, using your own natural voice and expressive style

- To help you to plan, seek, and recognize opportunities to tell personal tales in a manner that well serves yourself, your listeners, and your causes

The greater hope behind this book is that you will use it not just to gain strategies for developing and telling personal stories but also to help yourself pursue more consciously a storytelling way of life. Storytelling can be much more than merely a leisure activity, a form of entertainment, or a medium of information. It can evolve into a creative practice that enriches every aspect of your existence: private and public, physical and emotional, intellectual and spiritual.

Becoming a more committed storyteller involves having keener insight into the stories that you generate, that you participate in, and that exist all around you. It also means taking these tales to heart, embodying them more creatively as you go about

The stories that people tell are the container that holds their world together and gives meaning to their lives.

ANDREW RAMER

the busy-ness of living, and working to become a better communicator on their behalf.

The five parts of this book follow the complete process of personal storytelling, so that you can, if you want, use the book as a self-instructional course at your own chosen pace. Parts I and II help you develop the ambition, motivation, and courage to tell stories. Parts III and IV chart the adventure of crafting individual personal stories. Part V examines the art of sharing your stories with others.

The chapters within each part focus on key themes or skills relating to that stage of the storytelling process. Each chapter ends with a specific activity that enables you to apply what you've just read to your own situation.

The best way you can take advantage of this book to deepen your personal storytelling practice is to read at least one chapter at each sitting and do the activity in a given chapter as soon as you've finished reading it. Immersing yourself wholeheartedly in each chapter and activity will make the succeeding chapter and activity more meaningful because the book is organized to help you build on the understandings and skills you acquire as you go along.

I urge you to spend a certain amount of time and effort conducting each activity instead of quickly perusing it or skipping it altogether. Taking even small steps of participation will ultimately make it easier for you to overcome any inertia or fear that hinders your progress as a storyteller.

Because some of the activities ask for a written response, I recommend keeping a notebook or scrap paper close at hand as you read. If you choose not to do an activity in writing, go through it mentally as best you can. Remember that any effort you expend, even the most minimal response to a question, will be well worth your while.

Although I've just suggested that you do some of the activities in writing, one of this book's underlying objectives is, ironically, to help you wean yourself from overdependence on the written word. Personal storytelling is a mouth-to-ear transmission of memories shaped by our intelligence, imagination, spirit, and soul—aspects of ourselves that we tend to underestimate, under-value, and undertrust. Using written models or notes to develop or remember personal stories is frequently a way of avoiding re-liance on our own best internal capabilities. Often it can inter-fere with the natural rhythm, charm, and pleasure of the storymaking and storytelling processes as they were meant to be conducted.

Partly for these reasons, I don't include many full text ver-sions of told stories in this book. Instead, I offer summaries, de-scriptions, and snippets of personal tales from a variety of sources. I believe this strategy provides a wide range of point-by-point illustrations and idea triggers without misleading you into thinking that any one story in its entirety represents a standard to imitate.

Another reason I don't include many complete text versions of told stories is that the former can never accurately or fairly re-flect the latter. A word-for-word transcript of a told story misses the gestures, facial expressions, vocal tones, and rhythm that give a told story so much of its content, meaning, and liveliness. In-deed, a word-for-word transcript almost always makes a told story seem dull and awkward (I'm tempted to say "prosaic") in comparison to how it actually sounds, looks, and feels in a live presentation.

Ultimately, the only way to find out how a well-told story re-ally takes shape and sounds is to listen to others and to yourself in action, so that you experience both the tale *and* the teller si-multaneously. This book will help you to do this rewarding kind of storylistening—as well as your own best kind of storytelling—more effectively.

The appendix, "Other Personal Storytelling Activities," of-fers additional projects and experiments to conduct at every stage of the storymaking and telling process. After you've read each part of the book, I recommend that you consult the correspond-ing part of this appendix. Whether or not you choose to do any of the additional activities right away, you will at least have given yourself more ideas for the future.

When you finish this book, you'll want to customize your own

There is no substitute . . . for the story told aloud . . . for the living gesture that interprets human understanding.

D. M. DOOLING

The grace to be a beginner is always the best prayer for an artist. The beginner's humility and openness lead to exploration. Exploration leads to accomplishment. All of it begins at the beginning, with the first small and scary step.

JULIA CAMERON

ongoing personal storytelling practice. You may therefore want to keep track of passages and activities in the book that you find especially helpful or challenging, so that you can return to them easily whenever you want. Throughout the book I propose ways to maintain a storytelling life, but, ultimately, it's something that you need to do on your own, and that only you can do. Deena Metzger, in her book *Writing for Your Life*, makes this point beautifully clear: "There is a fundamental difference between the creative practice and other spiritual disciplines. Following the creative is a path, but it is not a known path. It has to be carved out by each individual practitioner."

May you use this book to illuminate your own unique path of storytelling, and may you tell personal tales happily every after!

PART I

WHY TELL PERSONAL STORIES?

Tell your tales; make them true.
If they endure, so will you.
JAMES KELLER

LISTENING: THE TELLING DIFFERENCE

Call her Harriet: in the early 1980s, the harridan of my daylight hours and an all too frequently recurring harpy in my nightmares. During those years, I was scripting video programs for a large communications company. She was my immediate supervisor, and her management style was driving me crazy. At staff meetings she appeared to be democratic, good-natured, and supportive, but on a one-to-one basis she proved to be exceptionally autocratic, abrasive, and undermining.

One of Harriet's most irritating habits was to communicate her orders or complaints by surreptitiously leaving a typewritten memo on the seat of her intended recipient's empty chair. My office was not visible from hers. It was far away, through a maze of corridors. But many times I would step out of it for just a few minutes only to return and sit down unwittingly on a fresh Harriet dropping. I couldn't help but picture her lurking behind some wall or cabinet near my door, clutching a newly drafted memo, ready to pounce the moment I vacated the premises.

Then one afternoon I was in Harriet's office reporting on the day's taping. A discussion of camera angles somehow prompted her to begin talking about the first time she thought she might need eyeglasses. She was in the second grade, she told

The sine qua non of storytelling is human mutuality, human connection, and the wish for that. When people lose those things, they lose themselves.

ROBERT COLES

A good story has the same effect on me that I suppose a good drink of whiskey has on an old toper—it puts new life in me.

ABRAHAM LINCOLN

Whenever stories are told, stillness falls. We cease our restless frittering. During these times of concentrated devotion to alternative realms we may reconnect with the power of creation. Through such resting we are renewed. Renewal inspires the courage to change.

ALIDA GERSIE

me. From her seat at the back of the classroom she couldn't see her teacher's lips move, and the white *a*'s, *e*'s, and *o*'s on the blackboard all looked the same. She confessed her problem to her parents, and the three of them nervously consulted an eye doctor. It was a dark, clear night when she rode home in the back seat of the car after picking up her new glasses. She stared out the rear window, and for the first time in her life she saw the stars burning white in the black sky.

That three- or four-minute incident in Harriet's office continues to stand out in my memory—thankfully, much more vividly than anything else about her. As most people do, she would occasionally drop a reminiscence or two into workplace conversations; but that afternoon, there was a significant and valuable difference. She was actually taking the time and effort, consciously or not, to go one step further and tell a story that meant something special to her.

I now recognize her extra step as a magical turning point in our relationship. It not only made *Harriet* more human, it also humanized *me*. I was being gifted by her, enlivened with a glimmer of her life. She was according me the privileged role of being an out-of-the-ordinary listener, a witness to human testimony, a secret sharer.

But most important, Harriet's story humanized the *situation*. It subtly transformed the whole atmosphere surrounding us. For at least a few moments, we were no longer enclosed in a corporate setting where employees were laboring against interpersonal odds to assemble products to market. Instead, we were inhabiting a flesh, blood, and soul environment where people's lives were naturally intersecting—a palpably vital, if small, arena in the grand universe of human affairs.

In the months to come, Harriet's management style didn't change, but my response to it did. Because she had shared a meaningful experience with me, we had a real connection as people. At the office, I ceased to recoil so painfully from her offensive behaviors, which had once struck me as downright demonic. And she never again haunted my nightmares.

I begin this book about *telling* personal stories with an anecdote about *listening* to them because listening is, in fact, at the heart of the matter. Like perfecting the gift of speaking intelligibly—something we all do as children—evolving into better storytellers proceeds from listening and relistening, and not only to the people who talk to us, but also to ourselves, to what our deep memories and creative voices have to say to us once we've silenced our mind's surface chatter.

Then, after we've listened to our inner selves, we have to imagine our future audience's experience of our story. How can we make our story as "listenable" as possible? What are the right circumstances for someone else to take it in? How might a particular listener or group of listeners respond to it?

Next, we must listen to ourselves as we actually tell our story, savoring and moderating it with the same ecstatic, total attentiveness that we often slip into automatically when we sing, dance, or play a sport we like.

Finally, in each of these different types of self-listening activities, we must—and, to some degree, inevitably do—draw guidance and inspiration from our most memorable past experiences of listening to other people.

I don't know how consciously Harriet engaged in these listening processes in order to create and spin her eyeglasses yarn, but I'm certain that she did go through each of them at some level, however swiftly and superficially. One of the missions of this book is to assist you to make all your listening endeavors more conscious—and, therefore, richer and more rewarding—in your own storytelling life. Right now, I invite you to consider carefully your most memorable past experiences of listening to others. At the least, this kind of second hearing can help us recall good tales to pass along to others. At its best, it can motivate us to tell and help us to hone our telling style better than anything else can.

When I was in college, for example, I once felt a self-transforming, human-to-human communion, similar to the kind that Harriet's story engendered, when I listened to a local politician speak at a sports banquet about the physical fitness program he had designed for himself as a twelve-year-old. It wasn't so much his words that carried me beyond myself. It was his gen-uinely human, simply personal manner. Guided by his voice, gestures, and facial expressions, I, too, sneaked out of the house in the middle of the night to run around the streets of the city, until I was stopped and questioned by the police. I, too, forced myself to eat a pound of raw hamburger per day. I, too, walked backward at every opportunity to build up weak calf muscles, much to the fiendish delight of witnessing peers.

I experienced the same special communion one day when I asked my mother how my grandparents met, and she recon-structed the evening when a short, black-haired, strong-willed girl was first introduced to a tall, shy, blond-haired boy with a beautiful tenor voice at a pre—World War I house dance. And I've felt it countless times inside huge, packed tents at the annual Na-tional Storytelling Festival in Jonesborough, Tennessee—for ex-ample, in 1996, when Kathryn Windham from Alabama, the unofficial matriarch of the post-1970 American storytelling re-vival, recalled her decision to go naked underneath her robe at her college commencement because of the heat, only to discover at the end of the ceremony that graduates were expected to hand in their robes as they filed out of the assembly hall.

Sometimes a personal story that stirs us as listeners isn't drawn entirely from the teller's own life but also involves the teller's re-counting of a favorite folktale, fairy tale, myth, legend, histori-cal incident, or other "established" story. In this type of personal story within a story, the teller sets the established story within a personal framework. In other words, besides communicating the established story itself, the teller describes how it came into his or her life and, directly or indirectly, why it has personal meaning.

For instance, a friend named David once shared with me a personal story that revolved around the legend of the mysterious aristocrat Bluebeard, who forbids his new bride to enter a cer-tain locked room in his mansion. One day when he's away, her curiosity gets the better of her, and she breaks into the room. To her horror, she finds it filled with the bodies of previous wives he has apparently murdered.

David led up to his retelling of "Bluebeard" by describing his

This feeling, an inexplicable renewal of enthusiasm after storytelling, is familiar to many people.

BARRY LOPEZ

Every story you tell is your own story.

JOSEPH CAMPBELL

6

first visit as a child to the home of a sophisticated adult neighbor he knew as Mr. Philips. To discourage his young visitor from messing up his den, Mr. Philips had told him the ghoulish saga as a cautionary tale about going into forbidden rooms. David had never heard it before, but Mr. Philips's hoary rendition left such a strong, inhibiting impression on him that he's still prone to envision the ghostly image of Bluebeard (who, in his imagination, resembles Mr. Philips) whenever he's tempted to invade someone else's private domain.

By using personal material to introduce and cap his retelling of "Bluebeard," David was fashioning a personal tale *about and around* a traditional one. As I listened to him, I was first drawn into his experience (a child in awe of an adult neighbor) and then guided beyond that experience to the larger world of human legend. In this way David gave me not only a special glimpse of something unique to him but also a deep appreciation of a tale that transcends any particular teller or listener and, therefore, could belong equally to both of us.

Every noteworthy teller I've recalled in this chapter—from Harriet to Kathryn to David—has contributed to the way I share stories and to the joy it gives me. So have many other tellers. We all learned to speak, think, and imagine by listening to others, so it's only natural that our most memorable story*listening* experiences have the power to be the best inspirations and models for our story*telling* ventures. Most of the time, we may not apply much conscious effort to these ventures, but, let's face it, we do make them quite frequently.

We tell personal stories when we're gossiping with our friends and family members or filling them in on what happened to us since we last saw them.

We tell them when we're giving some sense of who we really are to our favorite young people or to intriguing new acquaintances.

We tell them when we're rendering something we've witnessed more vividly to an audience of colleagues.

Some of us even tell them in front of strangers to earn a living!

So if we're going to tell personal stories anyway, as part of our

The tales we cherish . . . are tools for making sense of our journey.

DAN YASHINSKY

To speak is to sow; to listen is to reap.

TURKISH PROVERB

7

everyday lives, why not go further toward making these story-telling occasions even more memorable and satisfying for both ourselves and our listeners? Why not work—or, even better, play—toward becoming the most effective communicators of our personal experience that we can be?

I've briefly described what it feels like to *listen* to a good personal story; but, even more germane to the purposes of this book, what does it feel like to *tell* one?

Communion between mortals is immortal.

BORIS PASTERNAK

That feeling begins deep inside with the thrilling, nerve-tingling, magically self-affirming recognition that we have, in fact, experienced something worth telling. If we leave it at that, and never go ahead and forge that story possibility into a working tale, our initial feeling of excitement can easily flip over into its sinister opposite: fear. And fear can take many forms to pester us into giving up on our story and ourselves.

Life shrinks or expands in proportion to one's courage.

ANAÏS NIN

We may wonder, "How can I possibly make a coherent story, much less an interesting one, out of a bunch of memory fragments that aren't very clear?" Thus we belittle our innate talents to "re-member" or "re-story" those fragments in our imagination.

We may discourage ourselves by thinking, "How can I ever bring myself to talk about something so private, so trivial?" Thus we override our need and desire to do exactly that.

We may fret, "What if my story doesn't really mean anything to anyone else?" Thus we deny the initial jolt of enthusiasm that signalled a story worth telling, and negate our own power (literally "response-ability") to invest the story with meaning for our listeners.

We may worry, "What if I botch the story while I'm telling it?" Thus we choose to torture ourselves with an unlikely, worst-case scenario, instead of reassuring ourselves that we can, should, and want to tell the tale.

If we do manage to overcome these fears and follow through on our initial delight about having a story to tell, we can then enter into the wondrously rich, passionate, all-absorbing creative process of giving form to a story. During that process, we re-energize our finest powers of being and making. We discover that as we revive any part of our personal past, we renew our entire self.

When we finally tell a personal story that we've shaped with skill and love, we can experience a feeling of communion with others similar to the one we get from listening to a good story. But that feeling is additionally charged with the half-visceral sensation of giving to others, and of releasing ourselves into something greater.

We feel as if we are doing something that we are naturally meant to do, like a bird trilling, a coyote howling, or a spider weaving. It's what the Germans call *Funktionlust*, the sheer pleasure an animal takes in doing what it does best. To some degree, we experience a sense of rightness, of living up to ourselves, and of extending ourselves into the world that is unobtainable in any other way. The Minnesota-based storyteller Michael Cotter, a third-generation farmer, uses an organic metaphor to describe this dynamic: "The storyteller is the soybean . . . the audience is the sun."

I've felt this expanded sense of aliveness in many different kinds of telling situations—some impromptu and rough, others involving a great deal of preparation and polish. Once, as a college English instructor, I found myself departing from my talk on the literary merits of Charles Dickens's *Bleak House* to tell about how I, personally, came to love the book. It happened midway through my junior year in college. I spent an entire weekend reading the huge novel cover to cover, curled deep within a brown beanbag chair in the living room of a small apartment I shared with several friends. As the hours ticked by on a clock with a busted cuckoo, the familiar flesh-and-blood people wandering around my chair miraculously started displaying as much eccentricity and drama as the characters in the book. I began to appreciate quite tangibly that *Bleak House* was transforming the way I was perceiving the outside world.

While I was sharing the specific circumstances of that long-ago realization with my students, I could feel them opening up to what I was saying in a way they never had before. I sensed they were "right" with me, and I was "right" with them. And I'm confident that my story helped lure some of the more resistant students into actually reading the assigned novel!

During one of my more formal storytelling endeavors—the

Where do stories come from? Listeners have hundreds of hands and they pull them out of you.

JAY O'CALLAHAN

much-rehearsed delivery of my first personal story in a concert setting—I felt for a few, precious moments that same, special sensation of oneness and aliveness with an audience of more than three hundred strangers. I know in my heart that this feeling arose within me and, perceptibly, spread to include many of my listeners not because of the story itself or any particular skill I exercised in telling it. What made the critical difference between merely feeling that I'd done a good job and experiencing a heightened state of consciousness was the fact that I became totally involved in expressing something that was true to myself as a human being, and, in so doing, prompted me and many of my listeners to realize simultaneously our common humanity.

In other words, the sensation was not a matter of my performance but a matter of course—as it is in any sincere, committed personal storytelling exchange. Our spirits rise to the clear tune of a personal tale, whether we're telling it or hearing it, because we all lead lives that are filled with, and shaped by, stories.

He who knows others is learned. / He who knows himself is wise.

LAO-TSE

ACTIVITY
Listening to Others and Yourself

A. Listening to Others

Our memories of what we've heard in the past tend to be vague and impressionistic. We rarely recall whole conversations word for word or even point by point. Often, however, the gist of a particular story we've heard leaves a lasting imprint. This phenomenon is yet more evidence of the power of a narrative—and a narrator—to compel our attention.

The more we ponder aspects of memorable times when others told us their tales, the better sense we get of what we value as listeners. We can then apply this sensitivity in creating the kinds of storytelling occasions that we most want to occur, and that we're best equipped by our past experience to offer.

Consider some highlights of your personal story*listening* life by answering the following questions. You may find it helpful to record your answers in writing.

1. Recall an occasion when you were particularly moved by, or enjoyed listening to, a personal story that someone (a family member, friend, colleague, even a stranger) told you during a *casual conversation*. Ask yourself:

   - What was the subject matter of the story?

   - How, more specifically, did I feel as I was listening to it, and then afterward?

   - What aspects of the telling itself—such as the teller's voice, tone, style, or body language—helped make the listening experience memorable?

   - What circumstances relating to the time, place, or situation added to the story's special impact?

2. Recall an occasion when you were particularly moved by, or enjoyed listening to, a personal story that was told in a more *formal context*, such as during a speech, a sermon, or a storytelling performance. Ask yourself:

   - What was the subject matter of the story?

   - How, more specifically, did I feel as I was listening to it, and then afterward?

   - What aspects of the telling itself—such as the teller's voice, tone, style, or body language—helped make the listening experience memorable?

   - What circumstances relating to the time, place, or situation added to the story's special impact?

B. Listening to Yourself

As natural storytellers from the time we learned to speak, we have each already tried out a variety of different narrative subjects, styles, and strategies. Most of this experimentation has been conducted with little fore- or afterthought. We have simply seized, flowed with, or been grabbed by the moment. Nevertheless, if only on a subconscious level, we have registered what we have liked and not liked in telling stories about ourselves, and what has seemed to work or not work for our listeners.

Now, at the start of a concerted effort to become a better teller of personal tales, you need to bring that subconscious learning to a more conscious level. Identifying the elements that have most pleased you in telling personal stories will motivate you to do it more effectively and more often. It will also help you to focus on the specific aspects of telling personal stories that are likely to be the most rewarding.

Consider some highlights of your personal story*telling* life by answering the following questions. You may find it helpful to record your answers in writing.

1. Recall an occasion when you especially enjoyed or appreciated telling a personal story to someone else (a family member, friend, colleague, even a stranger) during a *casual conversation*. Ask yourself:

   • What was the subject matter of the story?

   • How, more specifically, did I feel as I was telling it, and then afterward?

   • What indications did I have of the listener's feelings as I was telling it, and then afterward?

   • What circumstances relating to the time, place, or situation added to the story's special impact?

2. Recall an occasion when you enjoyed or appreciated telling a personal story in a more *formal context*, such as during a family gathering, a meeting at work, a speaking engagement, a workshop, or a storytelling concert. Ask yourself:

   • What was the subject matter of the story?

   • How, more specifically, did I feel as I was telling it, and then afterward?

   • What indications did I have of my listeners' feelings as I was telling it, and then afterward?

   • What circumstances relating to the time, place, or situation added to the story's special impact?

THE BLESSINGS OF PERSONAL STORYTELLING

Let's get more down to earth. Aside from increasing the chances that we'll give and receive pleasant feelings, are there more substantive reasons to improve our storytelling abilities? If we already talk about ourselves frequently and comfortably when we're with our relatives and friends, why bother crafting more and better stories? If we already tell folk and fairy tales, why extend our repertoire to include personal tales? If we're already good at telling stories about ourselves in speeches or concerts, why should we challenge ourselves to be even more successful?

These questions are easily answered because the benefits that anyone can gain from more effective personal storytelling, regardless of his or her present skill level or situation, are numerous and compelling:

- Storytelling invests our lives with more meaning.

- It connects us more vitally with others.

- It develops our creativity.

- It strengthens our humor.

- It increases our courage and confidence.

- It renders our lives more memorable.

Let's consider each of these blessings individually, so that you can relate them more specifically to your own experience.

PERSONAL STORYTELLING INVESTS OUR LIVES WITH MORE MEANING

Every personal story expresses a point—or at least a point of view. It also creates wholeness out of disparate parts: a beginning, a middle, and an end; characters, settings, and times; causes and their corresponding effects. Thus, on the most basic level, composing a personal story in our mind is the act of making order— or "sense"—out of a chaos of memories, thoughts, and emotions. Actually telling the story to others is the act of breaking out of an inscrutable silence into intelligible, meaningful language.

Here's an illustration from my own life of how this kind of meaningfulness can evolve through personal storytelling. Every spring and fall I assign myself the task of developing a personal story to tell, a way I have of making the traditional planting and harvesting seasons more significant to me. Two springs ago, while still in the throes of picking a story subject, I woke up in the middle of the night with my heart pounding. I'd just been dreaming that I was chasing my Uncle Bill (my mother's younger brother) down a dark, snowy street, trying to warn him about something awful that I sensed was going to happen to him very soon. Now, wide awake and shaking with the impact of a big dream, I knew Uncle Bill would be my story subject.

Long before my dream, in 1979, Uncle Bill died suddenly of a heart attack at age forty-seven. The last time I saw him was eight years prior to his death, when he moved away from our common hometown, Columbus, Ohio, to Duluth, Minnesota; but during my childhood and adolescence he was a semiregular presence. He was a quiet, enigmatic man thirteen years older than I—too

If we hope to live not just from moment to moment but in true consciousness of our existence, then our greatest need and most difficult achievement is to find meaning in our lives.

BRUNO BETTELHEIM

young and solitary to be thought of as a father, too old and emotionally distant to be thought of as a brother.

Nevertheless, despite Uncle Bill's peripheral status in my life, he gradually assumed the character of an alter ego or "other self" in my imagination. Relatives often compared me to him in appearance and personal habits. Perhaps because of such comments, I remained more curious about him and more likely to be rattled by thoughts of him than our distant relationship warranted.

For a long time after his death, the character "Uncle Bill" in my mind was just a heap of ragtag images and ideas. They didn't fit together in any acceptable way. I had a hazy, early memory of the whole family waiting excitedly at my grandparents' house for Uncle Bill to return from Japan after the Korean War. Superimposed vaguely on top of that memory was a rumor I heard—or fantasy I brewed—about a Japanese woman he wanted to bring home to marry but left behind because of my grandmother's objections. Dimly associated with the mood of that rumor or fantasy was the memory of an afternoon years later when I was rummaging in my grandparents' attic and discovered a dusty box labeled "BILL." It was filled with memorabilia of the popular singer Al Jolson: sheet music for "Swanee," "April Showers," "Sonny Boy," and many of Jolson's other hits; several old book-style record albums containing 78 rpm disks in slipcover pages; and yellowing newspaper reports of Jolson's movie deals, concerts, and death in 1950.

Aside from these recollections all I had was a handful of photographs showing Uncle Bill at different ages, plus my equally random memories of actually being with him. Among the latter was a time when I was just beginning to learn (or, rather, to care about) table manners and, looking from relative to relative during a Thanksgiving meal, decided to model the way I chewed and handled silverware after him. There was also a time when he scolded me for bullying a friend, and the time when he slyly slipped me a copy of *Playboy* magazine as I boarded the train to go off to college.

After my big dream about Uncle Bill, which I do believe was

A life becomes meaningful when one sees himself or herself as an actor within the context of a story.

GEORGE HOWARD

15

What is true is what I can't help believing.

Oliver Wendell Holmes, Jr.

subconsciously triggered by my search for a story subject, I finally took it upon myself to create a meaningful narrative out of all these pieces of him I'd been carrying around. To give it a framework, I was instinctively drawn toward using the heart image that had so recently impressed itself upon my thoughts about Uncle Bill. I decided to talk at first about how my heart thumped so violently after that dream, and the ways we tend to think of the heart as a different kind of mind—with its own logic, urgings, and secrets. I then decided to use that image recurrently during the story to help weave connections among things that were, or might have been, dear to his heart, or dear to mine, or dear to both. I ended with his literal heart attack, and the resulting small, ever-sore wound that this event caused, much to my surprise, in my own "heart."

Throughout the process of developing my tale, I felt obliged to exercise creativity in plotting and describing certain events so they would make appropriate sense to a listener, command the attention they deserved, and reflect the actual quality of what I'd experienced. For example, I did not remember the exact circumstances of the bullying episode when Uncle Bill reprimanded me, so I found it necessary to invent actions and dialogues that were true to the characters involved, so that my listeners—and I— could relive that episode more effectively.

However, despite the creative choices that the story occasionally demand of me in order to come alive, the most important elements of Uncle Bill's life, and of our relationship, remained entirely true to my memory as well as true to history. And these elements would not have sorted themselves out, interresonated, and spoken to me, or others, if I had not cast them into story form. In this instance, the story-developing process *created* meaning for me out of a messy pile of memories that I'm certain would otherwise have remained obscure, detached, and only rarely reviewed.

I used to think I didn't have many personal stories to tell because I didn't have many clear memories. Now I know it was the other way around: I didn't have many clear memories because I didn't tell many personal stories.

On a deeper level, engaging in personal storytelling can be one of the most comprehensive, healing, and useful ways of validating experiences that we tend to reject. Through transforming our negative, painful, or chaotic experiences into stories, we take responsibility for them, and we bring them to bear more constructively on our lives. Psychotherapists give their clients time, space, and encouragement to articulate what has happened in their lives because this activity in itself does a great deal to raise their self-respect and sense of integrity. A client transforms him- or herself quite literally into the *hero* of stories—someone whose life has newly perceptible and impressive patterns, logic, and heft.

Outside the realm of psychotherapy, a similar kind of self-redemption emerges when we develop and share stories of difficult, embarrassing, or guilt-ridden experiences—like going through a divorce, growing up overweight, or behaving badly when first encountering a person of another race. The significant difference between cathartic outpourings in therapy and effective personal stories based on the same material is that the stories can, and should, be more thoughtfully crafted and communicated *with an audience in mind*. And the stories can, and should, aim toward acceptance, resolution, and self-transcendence.

Through examining awkward or painful experiences from a number of different storymaking and storytelling angles, we can discover ways to talk directly or indirectly about them that are comfortable for everyone involved: the speaker, those who are spoken of (usually absent in body but always present in spirit), and those who are spoken to. In so doing, we eventually come to healthier terms with the experiences themselves.

If we've hitherto been unable or unwilling to talk about certain people, places, or events in our past, experimentation with personal storytelling can be truly liberating. The alternative is remaining, at least to some degree, reluctant strangers to our family members, friends, and society in general. Even more alarming, if we don't tell our own stories, it's almost certain that others will tell our stories for us. The result can be a disastrous self-diminishment. We may wind up empowering others not

All sorrows can be borne if you put them into a story or tell a story about them.

ISAK DINESEN

A human life is a declaration of identity, significance, role, place: all action is the living out of a story in a cosmos.

MICHAEL NOVAK

From my perspective as a depth psychologist, I see that those who have a connection with story are in better shape and have a better prognosis that those to whom story must be introduced.

JAMES HILLMAN

only to create the *public* perception of who we are and what we've experienced, but also—given time and the right circumstances—to shape our own *private* memories and sense of self.

Finally, getting involved in developing and telling personal stories keeps us from unfairly dismissing large portions of our lives as boring, routine, or unremarkable. It's a common type of self-denial, one that I sometimes commit (for example, in thinking, "I grew up in the suburbs—what can I possibly say about *that*?") and one that I hear repeatedly in my storytelling workshops:

- "I don't have a colorful background: I'm a Midwestern, middle-class, white, Anglo-Saxon Protestant."

- "No one wants to hear about my job. Trust me, it's really dull."

- "What can I tell you about high school? I was just a geeky kid."

- "Nothing much happens to me. I lead a pretty average, ordinary life."

Personal storytelling helps us go beyond these tired, easy, blind responses and see the full range of wondrous moments and meaningful themes that exist in our day-to-day lives. We revitalize our sense of the miraculous. Viewed with this kind of sensitivity, even the most apparently featureless, unexplored life can metamorphose into a story-rich odyssey.

PERSONAL STORYTELLING CONNECTS US MORE VITALLY WITH OTHERS

The process of storytelling requires special, ongoing consideration of the listener. As we develop, rehearse, and revise a story, the audience we try to accommodate is usually a hypothetical one, forcing us to imagine—and, in some cases, research—what back-

The real difference between telling what happened and telling a story about what happened is that instead of being a victim of our past, we become a master of it. . . . We can't change our past, but we can change where we stand when we look at it.

DONALD DAVIS

What is the source of our first suffering? It lies in the fact that we hesitated to speak. It was born in the moment when we accumulated silent things within us.

GASTON BACHELARD

Well-meaning people are often deceived by the fallacy of "plain vanilla." An aspiring storyteller might say to me, for instance, "You're lucky. You have those great Jewish stories to tell. . . . I wish I had your kind of culture." Please remember: vanilla is a flavor.

DOUG LIPMAN

ground and perspectives certain broad categories of people might have in common.

During the actual telling of a story, our sensitivity to our audience sharpens. If we're faced with a large crowd of people we've never met before, we can still pick up a lot of information about them by making eye contact, reading body language, and, in response to the cues we get, modulating the way we speak and listen throughout the story so that we maintain the greatest possible rapport with them. If we're conversing with just one person whom we know intimately, we can go much further in tailoring our story and style to fit our listener. The more we share stories with people, and the more different kinds of audiences we find or create for this purpose, the more skilled we become at relating to others, both during the tellings themselves and during other kinds of encounters.

The primary purpose of personal storytelling is not to entertain listeners, or to educate them, but to *engage* them in one's own experience. This goal distinguishes personal storytelling from stand-up comedy, which is hell-bent for laughs; from psychodrama, which seeks to heal the performer; from teaching, which aims to transmit information; and from acting, which is geared to impersonating a scripted role.

Because we seek in our personal storytelling to entice others into our world, both our tale and its telling have to strike some sort of balance between our own interests and our audience's interests. Striving to achieve this dynamic equilibrium yields some of the most profound insights and greatest joys of being a storyteller.

Think, for a moment, about all the different ways in which you talk with people. How much of this talk is mechanical, back-and-forth conversation or idle chatter? How much of it is asking or answering questions? How much of it is "power-playing" with words: that is, ordering, accusing, complaining, persuading, apologizing, negotiating, letting off steam, or crying for help?

Storytelling offers a wonderfully humane alternative and antidote to all these other, less congenial ways of talking. Because it

If there is a sin against life, it consists perhaps not so much in despairing of life as in hoping for another life and in eluding the implacable grandeur of this life.

ALBERT CAMUS

The storyteller takes what he tells from experience—his own or that reported by others. And he in turn makes it the experience of those who are listening to his tale.

WALTER BENJAMIN

Storytelling reveals meaning without committing the error of defining it.

HANNAH ARENDT

To believe your own thought, to believe that what is true for you in your private heart is true for all men — that is genius.

RALPH WALDO EMERSON

Self-expression must pass into communication for its fulfillment.

PEARL BUCK

is serious in intention, it doesn't have the slightly shameful superficiality of gossiping or reciting what we've been up to lately. It's not targeted toward accomplishing anything specific, and it doesn't ask for, or require, any particular response. It's not even linked to the same kind of crude, workaday reality testing that other kinds of talk are. As children tend to appreciate even more than adults, storytelling is an exceptional "time-out" activity from the world of true or false, right or wrong, and need-to know or don't-need-to-know. It refreshes individuals and relationships in a very spiritual way.

Many of us have been socialized into the notion that it is somehow intrinsically impolite to talk about ourselves in any direct or extended fashion. We can't help but flinch a bit when we're given permission, or opportunity, to do so. Storytelling can indeed become overly self-centered or self-indulgent when it's done carelessly, with little regard for the listeners. However, when it's done well, it's an act of reaching outside ourselves to commune with others, not going inside ourselves to separate from them.

The truly selfish course in life is to withhold experiences and insights that we personally consider valuable and to do so for no good reason at all. Many people unwittingly render themselves increasingly self-absorbed and self-promoting through refusing to share their stories directly with others and, consequently, resorting to more indirect and manipulative ways of making their points or getting the attention they need.

In fact, personal storytelling can be a powerful means of liberating ourselves from potentially crippling self-involvement. Like King Arthur's Merlin, who ultimately became a prisoner of his own magical spells, we all to some degree risk stranding ourselves in our own subconscious world, where images of people, places, events, feelings, and thoughts from our past continuously enthrall or bedevil us. The only way to break out of such a self-enervating mental and emotional paralysis is to translate those images into stories that have some sort of practical meaning to us—and, ultimately, to others—in the real world.

By "breaking out" into stories, we inspire others to break out into stories as well. As a result, life-enhancing storytelling exchanges are set in motion among whole networks of people. Once asked to define what "sacred" means, the New York–based storyteller Laura Simms recalled a time when she unexpectedly found herself swapping life stories with an otherwise taciturn, tough, six-foot-two, thirteen-year-old she met at a junior high school. "I told my story, and she told me hers," Simms said. "It's really quite simple. It's just being human together. Maybe that's what 'sacred' is."

Another way in which personal storytelling can help connect us more vitally and spiritually with others involves the actual conception of a tale, long before it is ever told. When we reconstruct an incident from our past, we inevitably rebreathe the atmosphere that we shared with other people, retrace the ties that linked us one with the other, and remind ourselves of our "fit" in the human community.

Dr. Daniel Taylor, in his 1996 book *The Healing Power of Stories*, calls attention to this activity:

> "Finding myself" is less a matter of uncovering some supposedly pristine and genuine self within, one uncorrupted by outside influences, than it is discovering my role in various stories in which I am only one of many characters. Being one character out of many in a larger story does not diminish me; it enlarges me and my possible significance. I am not an isolated individual desperately searching for an illusory self and plaintively insisting on my needs and rights; rather I am a character in a story with other characters, making choices together that give our lives meaning.

PERSONAL STORYTELLING DEVELOPS OUR CREATIVITY

The art of putting together a personal tale requires us not only to recall certain details from our past but also to revive them in our minds: to see them once again with our mind's eye, hear

A treasure-trove of imaginative powers lies within us all. These powers often lie stunned and dormant, yet to awaken the pictures that live in our story-imagination is to become more fully and radiantly alive.

NANCY MELLON

Those who do not have power over the story that dominates their lives, power to retell it, rethink it, deconstruct it, joke about it, and change it as times change, truly are powerless, because they cannot think new thoughts.

SALMAN RUSHDIE

them with our mind's ear, smell them with our mind's nose, taste them with our mind's tongue, and feel them with our mind's skin. We must then endow the tale with a body, heart, and soul of its own and bring all these attributes to life in our telling, so that our listeners can adopt and relive the tale.

To follow the path of a personal storyteller, therefore, is to become an ever more vigorous and forceful imaginator. Story by story, and telling by telling, we expand our capacity to savor our experience, to realize its myriad possibilities, to transform some of these possibilities into realities, and to imbue these realities with the power to influence others in new and positive ways.

This capacity can go far beyond just enriching our storytelling endeavors. It can give us insight and inventiveness in everything we do, because it's nothing less than an outlet for our own, instinctive genius. Modern civilization tends to keep us from recognizing, valuing, and developing this fundamental aspect of ourselves, but the process of cultivating our innate storytelling abilities helps to restore it to a more conscious, operative level. The adventurer, writer, and filmmaker Laurens van der Post once warned:

> Man's spirit has lost contact with the storymaking pattern in himself, which is largely his instinctive side. He's pursuing an increasingly arid, rational, and materialistic approach where there is no story. . . . I think we have to return to the instinctive values of life, and automatically the storymaking pattern will be there. (*Common Boundary*, November/December 1993.)

By engaging in personal storytelling, we unlearn a lifetime of subtle social conditioning *not* to think or act creatively. In my many years of conducting storytelling workshops, I've discovered that the single biggest obstacle faced by would-be tellers of personal tales is not lack of memories, low self-esteem, or stage fright. Rather, it's a culturally induced fear of being inaccurate, of misrepresenting things, of failing to be objective, or of committing a lie. We can easily take this fear to extremes and refuse to grant ourselves the right to say *anything* that can't be completely substantiated by some source outside ourselves.

As we go on to explore the benefits of overcoming this fear through creating stories, it's important to consider one central question: Does all this talk of creativity and instinct mean that a personal storyteller has a license to stray from the literal truth, changing the details of what "really" happened to fit the needs of the tale, the teller, or the listener, or making up details when "real" ones can't be remembered?

The quick answer to this question is yes. There is a certain degree of license allowable in any kind of storytelling to go over, under, around, or beyond the facts of everyday life. As I mentioned before, storytelling offers a blessed timeout from a world that's bound up in literal definitions of yes-no, black-white, true-false, right-wrong, reality-fantasy. A story is a story, regardless of whether it's a personal story or a folktale. A story is *not* a newspaper account, historical record, investigative report, or sworn affidavit.

A more thoughtful and helpful answer involves rephrasing the question: What does "truth" mean in regard to a personal story? Assuming we accept that a personal story is, to some degree, a creative act, how much freedom should we have to change or make up details that go into the story?

Here's my own basic position on the subject—one that's been corroborated by every other personal storyteller I've consulted. Tellers of personal stories *do* need to be true to themselves and to their experience in order to tell an authentic and effective tale. However, this truth is immutably based on the teller's own perception and interpretation of that experience, not on its objective, "factual" reality—if, indeed, that kind of absolute reality can even be determined.

Earlier, when I discussed fabricating dialogue in my story of Uncle Bill, I alluded to my need to make specific creative choices in order to help events translate more effectively from my mind to my listeners' minds. I know the conversations I invented are true to the characters, true to the situations, and, perhaps most

True does not mean factual (though it may be factual); true means accurately reflecting human experience. . . . In the presence of a true story, we say, "Yes, this is how it feels; this is how it would happen; this is what one might think."

DANIEL TAYLOR

You don't have to be right. All you have to do is be candid.

ALLEN GINSBERG

important, true to my own overall sense of what happened. The actual dialogues that took place years ago are no longer obtainable. Even if they were somehow on record, I know from analogous cases that they might not have the same impact if reproduced word for word in my story that they did when they occurred in my real life. And they might not resonate at all with the memory that I've lived with, and that's helped to shape my life, for several decades.

More to the point, without that invented dialogue, I wouldn't have much of a story to tell. Sometimes our literal memories of a person, place, or event are just too sketchy, painful, or confusing to be made into a story. At such times, we need to do the best we can with our imagination, or the story will never be told, and our memory fragments will become all the dimmer.

My favorite statement on this issue of creativity and truth in personal storytelling comes from the North Carolina–based storyteller Donald Davis: "Think of storytelling as painting a picture instead of taking a photograph." In painting a picture that reflects accurately our experience of its subject and that deals effectively with the peculiarities of the painting medium, we may feel called upon to alter the precise shape of some features or leave some out or add new ones. Also, just as every painter has a unique style—some apparently more "realistic," or representational, than others—so every personal storyteller has his or her own style. This book can help you find one that suits your particular level of comfort with the "truth."

Of course, even a photograph does not necessarily reflect objective reality. I'm reminded of a story about Pablo Picasso being confronted by an amateur critic of his abstract act. The critic said, "You ought to try to make pictures of things the way they truly are—objective pictures." Picasso answered, "I'm not quite sure what that would be." The critic opened his wallet and pointed to a photograph of his wife. "There, you see," he said. "That's a picture of how she really is." Picasso looked at it and replied, "She's rather small, isn't she? And flat!"

PERSONAL STORYTELLING STRENGTHENS OUR HUMOR

Our "humor" is our general elasticity of mood, our resiliency, our give-and-take, our play, our flow. I might have said, "Personal storytelling stengthens our *sense* of humor," except that I don't necessarily mean our ability to be funny or to see yuk-yuk potential in the world around us, which is how the phrase "sense of humor" is commonly interpreted. Instead, what I refer to as humor is a broader, more soulful, more metaphysical quality. It may or may not include outright chortles, giggles, or guffaws. It's not strictly our ability to poke fun at people or at ourselves, which can often turn vicious, cynical, or world-weary. Rather, humor is our ability to delight, smile, and laugh at the wonder of life, as a child does.

Humor is comedy in slow motion.

GARRISON KEILLOR

Creating and telling personal stories trains us to see through the vagaries and trials of day-to-day existence to what T. S. Eliot called "the laughter at the heart of things," and what Dante referred to as "the divine comedy." We feel, appreciate, and share with others the life force that throbs at the core of everything human, regardless of whether the surface situation is light, heavy, tragic, or funny.

This connotation of humor is, in part, a carryover from the common belief during the Middle Ages and Renaissance that a healthy disposition was dependent on the well-coordinated functioning of four distinct "humors" within the body: the sanguine (hopeful or cheerful, present in blood), the phelgmatic (placid or apathetic, present in mucus), the choleric (passionate or agitated, present in yellow bile), and the melancholic (sad or pensive, present in black bile). The theory was that the four humors needed to operate in harmony, with no one humor becoming too far out of balance with the others, for the human spirit to be properly buoyant and energetic.

The word *humor* is derived from the Latin word *umor*, or *fluid*. I wish the words humor, human, and humility had the same etymological root, instead of three separate ones, because they seem to me so intimately interconnected with each other in meaning. By calling attention to the many different ways that people relate to each other—be they foolish or wise, amazing or commonplace, deliberate or accidental, hilarious or horrible— personal storytelling helps restore our equanimity, our sensitivity to the right proportion of things, our "humor," so that we can be more humane. And it tempers our feelings of self-importance, superiority, self-righteousness, and smugness, so that we can be more humanely humble.

As personal storytellers, we come to realize that it's not we ourselves who are noteworthy but our stories. Inevitably, these stories involve other human beings, and they work toward putting things in their proper, human perspective.

A coherent life experience is not simply given, or a track laid down in the living. . . . The thing must be made, a story-like production.

STEPHEN CRITES

PERSONAL STORYTELLING INCREASES OUR COURAGE AND CONFIDENCE

Putting together personal stories, possessing them for our own gratification, and, from time to time, telling them to others, are all trust-building activities. We come to respect the fact that our life, like any human life, does, in fact, contain stories worth preserving and perpetuating. We learn to depend on our own memory, judgment, and creativity to cast our stories into good narrative formats. And we learn to rely on our own communication skills to express our stories effectively. Time and again, we prove ourselves in these activities. We emerge from darkness into light, just as a photographic negative "proofs" itself in its own developing process.

Simply monitoring our life with the mind of a storyteller can help us to live with greater self-assurance and bravery. We've all undergone painful, stressful, or crisis-ridden periods when we've tried to comfort ourselves by thinking, "Someday this will all be over" or "Someday I'll look back at this and laugh" or maybe even "Someday this will make a good story." To bring to our lives a more conscious, storytelling point of view is to recognize the more objective, anxiety-controlling story elements of a challenging personal experience *as it is happening*. While we're trying to cope with a maddening work project, for example, or a rebellious child, or a seemingly endless streak of loneliness, we can maintain our sanity and empower our survival by keeping track of the story we're living through.

How, more specifically, can we do it? General approaches you can take toward *any* particular crisis in your life are:

1. Keep a journal of events relating to this overall experience *as they unfold*, writing in a narrative mode, as if you were composing a letter to a dear friend or an ongoing story about these events.

2. Every few days, sit alone with a cup of coffee, go for a solitary stroll, or lounge by yourself on the couch and return mentally to the following storybuilding questions, answering them with more and more specific details from your own observation or imagination:

   • How did it all begin? What sources can I see in the near past? In the distant past?

   • What are the significant moments, milestones, or "chapters" in this story so far? The high and low points? The shifts in tone and pace? The changes in my own personal fortune or identity?

   • Who are the major and minor characters at this point? How do things appear from each character's perspective? What other stories is each character living simultaneously with this story?

   • What other stories am I living simultaneously with this one? What's going on simultaneously in the outside world?

   • What are some possible endings or consequences of this story for me? For the other characters?

As you practice this kind of storytelling mindfulness during a particular crisis, eventually one or more explicit, fairly substantial stories will begin to coalesce that will give you a clearer sense of direction. When this happens, you'll feel more powerfully, purposefully, and creatively involved in the experience that previously was oppressing you.

We can apply the same sort of multidimensional storyweaving to tame or resolve an episode in the past that still bothers us. We can also use it to help bring about a richer, better-storied future. In her 1992 book *Storytelling and the Imagination*, Nancy Mellon alludes to the positive spin that this activity can give to our own life and to the lives of our listeners:

> Above all, storytelling gives us love and courage for life: in the process of making up a wonderful story, new spirit is born for facing the great adventures of our lives and for giving wise encouragement to others, of any age, along their own pathways. Every storyteller collects and arranges vital inner pictures; behind these live universal ordering principles.

As we share stories with others and learn to trust our own storytelling voice, we find ourselves using it more confidentally and courageously in all sorts of other ways. We discover that it shines forth not only in telling stories but also in speaking to groups, conversing with our friends, lecturing to our students, consulting with our clients, advising our colleagues, comforting our children, leveling with our mates, or confiding in our parents.

PERSONAL STORYTELLING RENDERS OUR LIVES MORE MEMORABLE

On a literal level, being a personal storyteller gives us a more "memorable" life because we continually nurture and enhance our powers of memory. The exercise that our memory gets in recalling, developing, learning, and telling our stories makes it much stronger and more servicable in every aspect of our living.

Stories knit together the realities of past and future, of dreamed and intended moments. They teach us how we perceive and why we wonder.

JOAN HALIFAX

We listen to other people's stories with more curiosity and atten-tiveness, and we find that we remember these stories, and the events surrounding them, much more vividly. We also discover that we take greater note of meaningful moments in our own lives that we may, in the future, want to communicate in stories.

On a symbolic level, personal storytelling makes our lives more memorable because it ennobles them in ceremonial words, images, and gestures that can then be used to create special occa-sions, such as a neighborhood storyswapping night, and to achieve remarkable purposes, like passing down family history from one generation to another. Personal storytelling not only celebrates individual lives but also gives them greater significance and power within the human community.

A human life is a story told by God and in the best of stories told by humans, we come closer to God.

HANS CHRISTIAN ANDERSEN

The commemorative nature of personal storytelling holds particular value for today's Americans, who, among all human beings throughout history, are uniquely lacking in self-defining, self-regenerating, and self-reminding cultural rituals. At the 1995 United Nations Conference on Women, held in Beijing, China, an African delegate stunned a United States–dominated assembly by declaring her countrypeople's essential distrust of "blank and mysterious" Americans: "How can we know who you are, or understand you, much less cooperate with you? What are your community stories, songs, and dances? What customs do you have for welcoming strangers? For marking the important passages of your life? For letting others know what has happened to you, and what you believe in?"

Storytelling has been called the oldest and the newest of arts. Human beings seem to have an inbuilt need to structure their world and to communicate their feelings and experiences through storying.

ELLIN GREENE AND
GEORGE SHANNON

If our culture doesn't provide us with many distinctive ways to express who we are, to celebrate our insights and achieve-ments, and to make strangers into friends, then we can give our-selves the means to do so through developing and telling our own stories. The storyteller and author Garrison Keillor, famous for his national public radio program *A Prairie Home Companion*, once noted:

Each person has a large secret life, dreams, stuff we don't know how to tell yet, and if we are in a family or community whom we can't tell our stories to, then we're not really related, we're just polite strangers sitting down to dinner. We are all more complicated than we appear to be, even the ones whom everyone makes fun of or pities, and all we ask—all we need—is the chance to say our piece and tell who we are. (*Sesame Street Parents*, July/August 1994).

Man is the storytelling animal par excellence. We live for, and die for, our stories.

GEORGE GERBNER

As individuals, we have both a personal and a social obligation to bear witness to our own experience, rather than letting it sink into oblivion. If we respect the people we've loved, the places we've lived, the issues we've championed, the lessons we've learned, the jobs we've performed, and the feats we've accomplished, then it's up to us to preserve them in stories and to share those stories with others who might benefit from knowing them, or, in many cases, from knowing us better than they do already.

The Baal Shem Tov, founder of Jewish Chasidism and a much revered storyteller, was once asked by a disciple why he always answered a question with a story. He replied, "I answer your questions with stories because salvation lies in remembrance." This notion that stories communicate information in a more memorable manner has inspired me throughout my professional storytelling career. A major shift in that career occured several years ago, when I realized I didn't have to limit myself to telling fictional tales that I'd researched or made up. I finally awakened to the fact that my life could give me personal stories to tell. Since then, I've progressed to the point where I see the situation from the opposite perspective: It's my personal stories that give me a life. And the same miracle can happen for you.

ACTIVITY
Benefiting from Personal Storytelling

How can you realize—or better enjoy—the blessings of personal storytelling in your own life? The process begins by looking inward and asking yourself key questions relating to each individual benefit that's been discussed in this chapter. These questions will steer you toward promising story ideas and telling ventures to pursue, as well as toward a better understanding of what you specifically have to gain from learning to tell personal stories more effectively.

You'll find some questions more interesting, or easier to answer, than others, and the complete list is fairly extensive, but I encourage you to respond to each question in each category as best you can. However slight an individual response may be, it will start you thinking about that particular issue— and your thinking may end in a story that blesses not just you, but everyone who hears it.

A. A Meaningful Life

The answers to the following questions will trigger the process of using personal storytelling to *make your life more meaningful*:

1. Think of a relative or friend in your past who remains a bit of a mystery to you—someone who was not a major figure in your life yet continues to haunt your imagination. Ask yourself:

   - Why am I curious about this person? What importance does he or she have for me?

   - What specific memories do I have of this person?

   - What rumors or fantasies do I associate with this person?

   - What might be important or interesting for other people to know about this person?

2. Recall a major experience in your life that you don't like to talk about. Ask yourself:

   - Why don't I talk about this experience?

When one is a stranger to oneself then one is estranged from others too. If one is out of touch with oneself, then one cannot touch others.

ANNE MORROW LINDBERGH

31

- What parts of it are the least difficult to talk about?

- Besides myself, who might benefit from hearing me talk about it?

B. Connecting with Others

The answers to the following questions will trigger the process of using storytelling to *connect yourself more vitally with others*:

1. Identify two people—or two groups of people—with whom you would like to share personal stories. For each person or group, ask yourself: What subject matter would I like to cover in my stories?

2. Recall a recent, significant event in your life. Ask yourself:

- Who were two other people somehow involved in this event?

- What different perspective does (or might) each of these people have of the event?

- What role(s) did each of these people play in the event from my own perspective?

C. Creativity

The answers to the following questions will trigger the process of using storytelling to *develop your creativity*:

1. Identify a meaningful period or event in your own past, or in your family's past, that you'd like to talk about but that you don't feel you remember clearly enough, or know enough about, to do so. Ask yourself:

- What information is lacking in order for me to make a story out of this period or event?

- In the absence of this information, what can I imagine as a close-enough or possible "truth," based on my own instincts and intelligence?

2. Identify a work of fiction or fantasy (such as a story, legend, book, TV program, or movie) that has had a significant—that is, "real"—

influence on your life. Ask yourself: What actual events in my life were affected by this influence? How?

D. Humor

The answers to the following questions will trigger the process of using storytelling to *develop your humor*:

1. Think of a time (one you haven't yet explored for this book) when you heard a personal story, in any context, that not only made you laugh but also caused you to feel more mellow about people or life in general. Ask yourself:

   • What was the subject matter of the story?

   • Why did the story affect me the way it did?

2. Recall an event in your own life that had the same effect: making you laugh and feel good about people or life in general. Ask yourself:

   • What, specifically, happened?

   • Why did it affect me the way it did?

E. Courage and Confidence

The answers to the following questions will trigger the process of using storytelling to *increase your courage and confidence*:

1. Recall a recent event or period in your life that was difficult for you to go through. Ask yourself:

   • What is one general thing that I learned from this event or period that was positive?

   • What details (sights, sounds, etc.) of this event or period can I specifically associate with this positive teaching?

2. Recall a recent time when you wanted to share an incident from your personal experience with another person or a group of people, but, to your regret, you didn't do so because you were afraid.

   • What, specifically, did you want to talk about?

When we are really honest with ourselves, we must admit our lives are all that really belong to us. So it is how we use our lives that determines the kind of men we are.

CESAR CHAVEZ

- What, specifically, were you afraid of?

- Taking the most positive attitude toward the matter, how might things have gone if you had *not* been afraid, or if you had been able to overcome your fear?

F. My Memorable Life

The answers to the following questions will trigger the process of using story-telling to *render your life more memorable*:

1. Ask yourself: What particular stories about myself do I most often tell new acquaintances I like so that they can get to know me better?

2. Identify a period in your life (no earlier than five years old) that you want to remember more clearly. Ask yourself:

   - Aside from simply "learning more about myself," why do I want to know more about this period? What, specifically, are my questions about this period?

   - What resources do I have—or could I tap—to get more information about this period, or to answer my questions?

PART II

RECLAIMING YOUR STORYLOVING SELF

I am of old and young, of the foolish as much as the wise,
Regardless of others, ever regardful of others,
Maternal as well as paternal, a child as well as a man . . .
WALT WHITMAN

YOUR INNER
STORYTELLER

We all are made of stories. They are as fundamental to our soul, intellect, imagination, and way of life as flesh, bone, and blood are to our bodies.

As we might expect, wisdom tales from every culture point to this truth. The philosopher, writer, and storyteller Elie Wiesel once recounted this famous Jewish legend. When the great rabbi, the Baal Shem Tov, was alive and sensed disaster coming to his people, he would retreat to a certain part of the forest, make a special fire, chant a specific prayer, and thereby invoke a miracle from God to avert the calamity. In the next generation, his disciple, compelled to perform the same ritual, didn't know how to make the fire, but the act of going to the forest and say-ing the prayer was sufficient for God to cause the miracle. A generation later, the succeeding rabbi, intent on rescuing his people, didn't know the the ritual for the fire or the prayer, but he could find the special place in the forest, and that was suffi-cient for God to bring about the miracle. In the following generation, the next rabbi in line, faced with yet another catas-trophe, moaned to God: "I don't know how to make the fire, say the prayer, or find the place! All I can do is tell the story about it!" And that was sufficient for God because it is said that

To be a person is to have a story to tell.

ISAK DINESEN

37

people live through stories, and God made people because he loves stories.

In essence, this tale teaches us that beneath all our intellectual means of knowing is a core "story-knowing" that is God-given or, if you prefer, innate. Intellectual-knowing is based on information and processes that we try, studiously, to memorize: sometimes successfully, sometimes not. Story-knowing represents our naturally evolving memories—our instinctive recording, in our own language, of the most impressive life experiences we've lived through or heard about.

Recollecting these memories is not just a mental act but a spiritual act because it enables us to relive experiences—in other words, to live anew. Imbued with such new life, we can even inspire miracles for others. To extend the message of the tale, if God made people because he loves stories, then people love stories because they are children of God. Or, from a nonbeliever's perspective, if we love stories, it's because we are made that way.

An ancient Teutonic myth featuring the creator god Odin uses different but equally distinctive imagery to convey the same theme, proving that it transcends any particular cultural or religious context. Odin dwells far above Earth in the branches of the World Tree with two pet ravens, Memory, who perches on his right shoulder, and Thought, who perches on his left shoulder. Every sunrise, Odin sends his ravens down to Earth for observational purposes. After they fly back to his shoulders at sunset, they take turns reporting all night long on what they've observed. First Memory recounts stories; then Thought extrapolates, speculates, and evaluates. One morning, as his ravens fly off, Odin is troubled by doubt. "What if one of my ravens fails to return?" he wonders. "What would I do? How could I live?" After mulling over the possibilities for most of the day, he concludes that he can live without Thought, but he can't live without Memory.

The myth of Odin and the two ravens depicts storytelling as the essential creative force that gives us not just an existence but a life. Commenting on this myth in her essay "Drawing Your Own Story," the Roman Catholic artist Meinrad Craighead indirectly links it to the first sentence of the Gospel of John: "In the beginning was the word." She states,

> Remembering binds us together. Indeed, one of the meanings of *religion* is to bind back to the origin. At this point of origin in God's being, we are all bound together at the same source. Stories begin in silence waiting for a word. In stories we rely on remembering, and remembering implies celebrating the word you have heard, that you must now speak, that is the visitation of the Spirit in your life. (*Sacred Stories*, edited by Charles and Anne Simpkinson).

And so we hear the message echoed and re-echoed in Judaism, Teutonic mythology, and Christianity: As human beings, we have a fundamental affinity for storytelling, and it represents a divine energy burning within us. We can trace the same message in countless other religions as well. Indeed, regardless of what religious beliefs we hold, or whether we consider ourselves religious at all, our own internal storytelling is the mysteriously spellbinding and definitely spirit-stirring medium through which we each give meaningful shape to the things we witness. At its deepest level, it's a generative, self-nurturing, and, therefore, loving enterprise that starts soon after we're born and continues for as long as we live.

And our stories are sacred to us. They become even more spiritually potent when we take special care of them and craft them into more conscious and complete—or, if you will, wholistic—form. Simply *embodying* these products of our own genius, without communicating them directly to others, gives us greater personal integrity and power. We can draw on them privately for solace, centering, grounding, and decisionmaking. If and when we do tell them to others, we transmit to our listeners a refreshing form of living energy that is undeliverable, and unobtainable, in any other fashion.

Lately science has joined folk wisdom and religion in supporting the truth that we are all story-built creatures. Cognitive

[A]ll men and women are religious. The completed lives of each trace out a story, whose implications reveal what they took the world in which they lived to be, who they thought they were, what in their actions they actually cared about.

MICHAEL NOVAK

What got people out of the trees was something besides thumbs and gadgets. What did it, I am convinced, was a warp in the simian brain that made us insatiable for patterns—patterns of sequence, of behavior, of feeling—connections, reasons, causes: stories.

KATHRYN MORTON

God gives us songs in our sleep.

JOB 35:10

scientists now say that the left hemisphere of the brain's cerebrum tends to specialize in logical thought, computation, and judgment, while the right hemisphere tends to function in an imaginative, narrative mode—recognizing faces, reconstructing melodies, and visualizing scenarios and other nonlinear patterns to make random bits of data more memorable.

This "new" discovery is, in fact, little more than the scientific correlative of Odin's right-shoulder and left-shoulder ravens! One can trace similar correspondences again and again in relating modern scientific breakthroughs to ancient, story-shaped beliefs. These correspondences suggest that the evolution of each individual human life follows the same pattern as the historical evolution of human consciousness: We first know by instinct and communicate through story what we later verify by intellect and communicate through logic.

Some brain researchers attribute dreaming during sleep to right hemisphere activity that's relatively unfettered by wide-awake, left hemisphere censorship. This shift in balance toward dreaming may occasionally occur during our waking life, resulting in daydreams and possibly even creative flashes, psychic experiences, or *déjà vu* sensations, but it's generally associated with our sleeping life. Whatever causes the latter kind of dreaming, we all dream wondrously rich personal stories four or five times during every full night's sleep, in roughly ninety-minute cycles. During these periods, we also move our closed eyes in distinctly rapid patterns, as if we were visually following our story images, which is how sleep researchers can tell their subjects are dreaming.

Many of us don't recall these dreams on awakening because they defy rational retention and, sadly, because modern culture now socializes us into devaluing not only our dream life but so-called fictional stories in general. When we were less than one year old—long before our formal schooling began—we may have been much smarter in this regard. At that age, we dreamed during a whopping forty percent of our average fourteen sleeping hours per day. Many scientists attribute this high percentage to a baby's innate drive to make story sense of the surrounding new world and to build a mental and emotional basis for survival.

Computer scientists also corroborate the notion that we are natural-born creatures of story. Roger C. Shank, an expert in artificial intelligence and author of the book *Tell Me a Story*, describes the human memory as "story-based." He points out, "Not every experience makes a good story, but if it does, the experience will be easier to remember." Portraying the human experience as a "world of stories," he writes, "We know them, find them, reconsider them, manipulate them, use them to understand the world, adapt them to new purposes, tell them in new ways, and we invent them. . . . Our ability to utilize these stories in novel ways is a hallmark of what we consider to be intelligence." Gregory Bateson, in his book *Mind in Nature*, describes a recent breakthrough effort in creating a computer program to function more like the human mind. The programmers typed in the question, "How does the human mind work?" It replied, "Let me tell you a story. . . ."

Psychotherapy is based on the premise that we each create our own life story from the time we are born. It's a natural, inevitable process in our maturation. It's also one in which we can more consciously and creatively engage in order to redeem our past and restore our psychological health. First, however, we need to reclaim that core part of ourselves that is the teller of our story. A recently emerging practice called narrative therapy assists people to do this, and to revise or replace their negative stories with new ones that are more positive and practical.

For example, a woman suffering from memories of having been pushed around all her life might be led by a narrative therapist to reorient her concept of her past around the times when she did, in any way, feel strong, confident, or in command. She could accomplish this conceptual shift by consciously developing richer, more vivid stories of the positive occasions to compete with, and eventually outshine, the negative stories she had long been repeating obsessively to herself and others. In doing so, she'd be tapping the same, innate storytelling genius that orchestrated the original, problematic events into self-punishing stories. She'd be authentically reconstructing her personal identity, making a new, more sustainable form out of old, shoddy materials.

Stories heal because we become whole through them. In the process of . . . discovering our story, we restore those parts of ourselves that have been scattered, hidden, suppressed, denied, distorted, forbidden.

DEENA METZGER

Paradoxically, the human soul must see itself in many ways to understand its single grand adventure.

STEPHEN LARSEN

41

Even a lie is a psychic fact.

CARL JUNG

Or so narrative therapists claim. Critics of the practice contend that it distorts an individual's personal truth and, in so doing, risks denying his or her entrenched psychical needs. Responding to this criticism, Michael White, an Australian counselor and early advocate of narrative therapy in the 1980s, argues that neither "the truth" nor "the psyche" is a fixed phenomenon. Instead, each is a field of supple stories that can justifiably be adapted.

The core of the human mind, White insists, is a storyteller. It cannot take in the full range of sensory, mental, and emotional experience that it encounters without some sort of artificial frame of reference, so it collapses this experience into stories. These stories are certain to change on their own, to some degree, as time goes by: not only in details and structure but also in tone, significance, and relative rank of dominance within the story possessor's mind.

If our personal stories can change on their own, says White, then why can't we deliberately change them, especially if it does us—and the people we encounter—more good? Personal storytellers must ask themselves the same question about "the truth," story by story, and come to their own, appropriately personal, decisions. They do this by recommuning with that deep, inner part of themselves that is the true teller of their tale.

The writer Anna Quindlen tells a personal story about the time she ran out into the street and got hit by an automobile when she was five years old. In a *New York Times* column on October 7, 1988, she recounted the ending she usually gives to her story: "My mother, pregnant—when was she not?—runs to the scene and promptly passes out. After all is said and done, I have nothing more to show for it than a black-and-blue mark on my backside that is shaped like the continent of Africa." Then Quindlen comments on the realities (or, rather, probable realities) behind the story. She's not sure her mother was pregnant. She's pretty certain her mother didn't really faint. And she's almost positive the "bruise like Africa" is a fabrication: "I could swear that I looked at my back view in the mirror on my closet door and that I had a bruise that was shaped like Africa. Except that I am fairly sure I didn't know how Africa was shaped until fourth grade, when I took geography."

Defending the value and beauty of "embellished truth" in family stories (although I believe her statements apply just as well to personal stories in general), Quindlen writes:

> It is difficult to explain that there are some things more important than—or perhaps just different from—the literal truth, and that one of these is creating the life of the family in hindsight. We need not necessarily aggrandize ourselves with these stories, although sometimes we do. . . . Perhaps we need to add something that was there, but not fully realized, whether it is texture, or drama, or hearts and flowers, or eccentricity.
>
> It's the telling details that make the tale, but sometimes we cannot tell precisely what the details were. Hence the stories in which Grandpa becomes, with a little of this and a little of that, larger than life. After all, everyone's Grandpa *is*, at least in their mind's eye.

When I was younger, I could remember anything, whether it happened or not.

MARK TWAIN

Individuals and families are not the only beneficiaries of storytelling "from the mind's eye," whether or not the stories themselves occasionally stray from the literal truth. Sociology, anthropology, and criminology inform us that storytelling also plays a critical sustaining and healing role for entire societies.

Never before in its history has Western civilization so sorely needed this particular form of inspired, highly personal nurturing. Richard Stone, a consultant in life-review processes for therapists, social workers, and chaplains calls one of our culture's greatest maladies "destorification":

> Just as clear-cutting an old-growth forest leads to a phenomenon called deforestation—the stripping of the landscape of more than just trees—our culture has been devastated by the loss of storytelling as a tool for communicating, passing on values, learning, and, most important, healing. . . . When you cut down the trees, you also destroy the multitude of microenvironments in which a host of other living creatures make their

home. . . . So it is with destorification. (Stone, *The Healing Art of Storytelling*)

Over the past 150 years, rapid advances in technology, education, and social mobility have brought people around the world increasingly closer together. In many ways, this closeness holds a great deal of promise. Each of us can now see more deeply into the lives of a greater variety of people than individual human beings could ever see before; and, for the first time in history, we have the power to contact almost anyone we want, at any time, fairly easily.

But how do we understand and absorb what we see? And what do we say to the ever-growing numbers of people we can reach? We teach ourselves the answers by listening more attentively to our storytelling self.

Paradoxically, the same modern advances that have brought us closer together in some ways have wrenched us farther apart in others. Thanks to the greater independence and mobility that most of us in Western culture now exploit, we don't have anything like the same comforting intimacy with our families, friends, and neighbors that our ancestors thrived on, nor do we feel the same sense of common destiny with the other people who live in our home, community, state, or nation.

How do we recapture this intimacy? How do we relate our private vision more constructively and compassionately to the visions of others? We do these things by giving our storytelling self a greater role in our lives.

Personal storytelling offers us a wonderful vehicle for capitalizing on the new opportunities that our increasingly dynamic culture opens up for us, and for overcoming the new problems that accompany these opportunities. It works to merge our inner ecology more compatibly with the outer ecology. It enables us to communicate more resourcefully with a wider variety of individuals and groups, and to listen more sensitively to what they say to us. And it helps to bind us all back to our common, story-based origin.

The analytical psychologist James Hillman, who often writes about the prevalence and psyche-building power of personal

I can't promise that your stories will give you certainty or objective truth any more than the ancient myths gave the Hebrews or Greeks accurate maps of the world. They will, however, fill you with the stuff from which romance, tragedy, and comedy are made. . . . They will hollow you out so you can listen to the stories of others, as common and unique as your own. And that remains the best way we storytelling animals have found to overcome our loneliness, develop compassion, and create community.

SAM KEEN

storytelling among children, praises personal storytelling *after* childhood as the act of "re-storying the adult." By telling personal stories when we're adults, we can reinvest our grownup persona—a highly conditioned, well-behaved product of human culture—with some of the same story-loving energy that brought us to life in the first place.

In discussing Hillman's concept, P. L. Travers, philosopher, essayist, and author of the much beloved "Mary Poppins" series of children's books, once remarked:

> "We love only what is our own," said AE, the Irish sage, "and what is our own we cannot lose." But as we grow older, what is our own is not so easily perceived. It becomes silted over with what is not the true story, like a penny lost in the puddle. For the adult to restory himself, a certain process has to be set in motion, a process in which he himself must relive intentionally what was organically lived by the blood. He must take an active and enquiring part; no one can do it for him. (Travers, *What the Bee Knows*)

The activity I am recommending to set this process in motion is reconnecting with your inner storyteller. It's a matter of realizing your truest, most creative self so that you can start bringing it out into the world around you.

I began the chapter with a Jewish teaching tale. I'd like to end it with another Jewish story that serves as an excellent introduction to the act of meeting your inner storyteller.

Once the ancient Rabbi Zusia appeared before his disciples crying and wringing his hands. Alarmed, they asked him, "Why are you so upset, Zusia?"

Zusia replied, "I have just had a vision telling me the one, all-important question the angels will ask me about my life after I die!"

"But Zusia," his disciples exclaimed, "you have had led such a noble and exemplary life! What question could possibly scare you so?"

Zusia heaved a great sigh. "I have learned that the angels will

Adults are obsolete children.

THEODORE GEISEL
(DR. SEUSS)

Childhood is the world of miracle and wonder; as if creation rose, bathed in light, out of the darkness, utterly fresh and astonishing. The end of childhood is when things cease to astonish us. When the world seems familiar, when one has got used to existence, one has become an adult.

EUGENE IONESCO

not, after all, ask me, 'Why weren't you a Moses, delivering your people from bondage?' "

"Very well," said his disciples, "so what *will* they ask you?"

Zusia, still lost in his grief, cried out, "And I have learned that I will not, after all, be asked, 'Why weren't you a Joshua, bringing your people into the promised land?' "

Frustrated, the leading disciple stepped forward and, grasping Zusia's shoulders to calm him, spoke more sternly, "Tell us, I beg you! What exactly is it that the angels will ask you?"

Zusia answered in a chastened voice, "The angels will say to me, 'Zusia, there was one great being that you could have been, and that no power in Heaven or on Earth could have kept you from being but yourself.' Then they will ask me, 'Why weren't you Zusia?' "

Everywoman has a leading role in her own unfolding life story.

JEAN SHINODA BOLEN

A man is always a teller of tales, he lives surrounded by his stories and the stories of others, he sees everything that happens to him through them, and he tries to live his own life as if he were telling a story.

JEAN-PAUL SARTRE

ACTIVITY
Meeting Your Inner Storyteller

The goal of this activity is to gain a clearer, more dynamic image of yourself as a storyteller. You can then use this image throughout the book and the rest of your storytelling life as a talisman, guide, and motivator. Appropriately, it's an instinctual image that you realize by going deep within yourself to make contact with what's already there, and has been there since you were a child: your essential, story-loving genius. By translating this abstract quality of yourself into a more specific, envisionable form, you are, in effect, turning your inner genius into a more easily invoked "genie."

The method that I offer for summoning this genie is a visualization, which involves first relaxing your body and mind and then deliberately picturing in detail the images that are suggested. Visualization in itself is a beneficial activity for storytellers because it exercises the mind's eye, which storytellers must rely upon to show them their story while they are telling it.

This particular visionary quest, "Meeting Your Inner Storyteller," is somewhat like the trancelike journeys that shamans take, often by way of a monotonous drumbeat, to discover or reconnect with their power animals. If you're interested in pursuing a more shamanic version of this activity, I recommend consulting Robin Moore's cogent, practical, and enthusiastic guide-book, *Awakening the Hidden Storyteller.*

If you are uncomfortable following the full process of visualization that I outline here, it can be helpful simply to read the directions and engage in whatever comparable type of interior meditation or creative brooding best suits you, as long as you come through it with some specific, helpful images to associate with the concept of your inner storyteller.

To perform the full visualization, first read the directions several times, until you feel you know them well enough to recall, on your own, the gist of each step in sequence. Certain key words are italicized to help you do this. Also, dots are used to indicate when it's appropriate to pause for a few moments.

Then, assume a relaxed position somewhere that's quiet, dimly lit, and free from distractions or interruptions. Once you've settled down, repeat the guidelines silently and slowly in your mind as well as you can remember them. Take a minute or two after each guideline to visualize as fully as you can whatever is suggested; once you've done this, savor for a few moments the vision that you've created. Note that in certain steps, "visualizing" means going beyond imagining that you are just *seeing* something, to imagining that you are also hearing, smelling, tasting, or feeling something.

1. Close your eyes and take *three deep breaths* to relax.... Release any tension you feel in your body.... Let the thoughts and cares of the day drift away, leaving your mind empty and open....

2. Imagine that you are taking a *pleasant walk through the woods* in the fall.... See shafts of sunlight streaming through the trees, and brightly colored leaves.... Hear fallen leaves crunch under your feet.... Smell the scents of pine and earth.... Feel the warmth of the sunshine and a hint of chill in the air....

3. As you continue walking, come to a trail winding up and around a gentle hill.... Follow this trail at a leisurely pace.... Come to a sharp bend in the trail, and, as you round this bend, see that the *trail leads to a temple....*

4. Go up to the temple and enter it.... See a comfortable armchair facing a big curtain.... Settle into that armchair.... Hear a voice

saying, "*In a moment the curtain will open*, and you'll be face-to-face with your inner storyteller. . . ."

5. See the curtain open and reveal *your inner storyteller*. Observe your storyteller's face . . . hands . . . clothes. . . .

6. Ask your inner storyteller, "*What will help me the most to become the storyteller of my dreams?*" . . . Hear your inner storyteller's answer. . . .

7. See your inner storyteller *give you a gift*. . . . See this gift in your hand. . . .

8. *Make a vow* to your inner storyteller. . . . Hear *your inner storyteller repeat* this vow. . . .

9. See the *curtain slowly close*. . . . When you are ready, *open your eyes*.

READING YOUR
OWN MIND

In 1913, the American writer Willa
Cather, who had just turned forty and published her widely ac-
claimed novel *O Pioneers!*, told a lecture audience, "For the most
part, artists work out of the first ten years of their memory." Re-
stating her claim at age fifty, she drolly extended the span to twenty
years, but the essential point remains the same: Our earliest memories, the ones that have steeped within our minds for the longest
time, have exerted the most influence on our perceptions of life
and can provide us with the richest material for our creative endeavors.

Childhood memories are especially valuable in helping us
choose, compose, and enliven the stories we tell to others. As
tellers, we seek not only to invest our stories with a flavor that's
uniquely and profoundly ours but also to elicit a childlike openness, attentiveness, and awe from our listeners. Our earliest
memories offer us the best hope of achieving both of these goals.

In addition, our childhood memories can inspire stories
whose subject matter has the best chance of appealing to listeners of every age, temperament, and cultural background. Childhood is the grand common denominator among human beings.
It's an era of innocence, wonder, and flexibility for all of us,

*Anybody who has survived his
childhood has enough
information about life to last
him the rest of his days.*

FLANNERY O'CONNOR

Childhood is the small town everyone came from.

GARRISON KEILLOR

Every child begins the world again.

HENRY DAVID THOREAU

Wise men hear and see as little children do.

LAO-TSE

before we begin to crystallize into separate, more restricted, and more rigid identities. A repertoire of childhood-related stories is invaluable to parents or those who work with children, but it's also beneficial to *any* member of a large, multigenerational family or *any* professional teller of personal tales because it applies to the widest possible range of telling opportunities.

In some cases, we may decide to incorporate our earliest memories quite literally into our stories, whether these narratives are entirely autobiographical or only partly so. For example, we may devote a whole tale to the time we helped our grandmother look for her lost teeth, the first crush we had on a teacher, or the friend's home that once seemed like paradise to us but somehow lost its special charm as we grew older. Or, alternatively, in the course of spinning a fabulous yarn about Davy Crockett, Heidi, Crusader Rabbit, or a wily leprechaun, we may talk a little bit about why we liked this character during our childhood and perhaps about how we first encountered him or her. Real-life and fictional stories that are reinvoked from our own childhood are especially compelling for us to tell, and for our listeners to hear, because they issue directly from our longest-preserved and most heartfelt sense of what a story experience is.

In other cases, we may just allude briefly to a long-ago memory in order to dramatize or expand a narrative about more recent events. Suppose we're recounting an apartment-hunting or house-building ordeal we went through last year. During the course of this saga, we might cite an analogous time in our youth when we scoured the neighborhood for a secret hideaway, or built a backyard retreat with boards, sheets, rope, and mud. An alternative would be to fashion a running subtext for that same apartment-hunting or house-building story out of a bit of fiction that was dear to our past and, possibly, to our listener's past as well. For example, we might compare specific incidents in *Robinson Crusoe* to our own ingenious attempts at creating a home out of limited materials or adjusting to a strange neighborhood. We might draw parallels between "Goldilocks and the Three Bears" and our own intrusions into other people's "for sale" or "for rent" homes to see how they suited us. These kinds of allusions enhance our stories with both a personal and a cultural resonance.

We can also draw private, storytelling inspiration from our earliest memories even if we don't mention them explicitly in the true or fictional tales we tell. Assuming our story is about an immigrant in our family history, we can reproduce within it the same fluctuating moods of hope and despair that we ourselves went though as kids when we had to transfer to a different elementary school. In our made-up description of a fantasy forest, we can surreptitiously add the most alluring charms of an actual woodland we roamed during our childhood. Either way, our early memories indirectly add a special depth of feeling and authority to our telling.

Bill Harley, a Massachusetts-based storyteller and regular commentator on National Public Radio's *All Things Considered*, likes to define the process of becoming a storyteller as childhood work. Perhaps because of his many popular recordings of original children's tales, his remark has sometimes been taken out of context to mean that storytelling is essentially for young people. In a workshop at the 1996 "Sharing the Fire" conference in Boston, sponsored by the League for Advancement of New England Storytelling, he dismissed the perception that storytelling is just for kids and clarified what he means by the expression "childhood work":

> To evolve into better storytellers to any type of audience, no matter what age range, we must dig as far back as we can into our own life's history. In effect, we must each become what I call an "emotional archeologist." There is so much to gain from developing stronger connections with our most formative years, the ones when our feelings were the strongest, our senses the most wide-awake, and our minds the most impressionable.

Resurrecting memories from our childhood gives us a bigger, bolder, and more important life. We literally re-collect who we are, and become storylovers anew. We bring more noteworthy

[T]he dreams of our childhood can inform our lives—our real, creative lives—as adults.

RAFE MARTIN

The child must teach the man.

JOHN GREENLEAF WHITTIER

moments to consciousness, and, as they accumulate and interact with each other, a wondrous synergy occurs: We perceive each moment more vividly, play with it more creatively, and care about it more passionately. As a result, everything that we communicate in our tales, speeches, and conversations is enriched by our broader, deeper, and more committed involvement in human experience.

So how do we perform this all-important "childhood work"? How do we go about reviving memories of our early years?

Many of us have trouble recalling details from last week, let alone from a year ago, our sixteenth year, or second grade. This difficulty is especially common among people who didn't have a long-term, stable, or comfortable home base during childhood. If you moved frequently as a child, it's possible that your memories didn't accrue long enough in any one place to build the kind of associative links that make whole periods of life easier to recall. If your parents divorced when you were young, afterward you probably heard less, talked less, and thought less about family life *before* the divorce (a period that included your earliest years) than you otherwise would have. If you were unhappy, traumatized, or abused during your childhood, you might have subsequently resisted going back to this period in your memory, despite the fact that it also contained moments of joy, accomplishment, and pride. If your adult life has been especially eventful, it may now be preoccupying your mind to the extent that you seldom give yourself time or space to dwell in the more distant past.

Another major stumbling block in our attempts to recall our earliest years can be a self-imposed insistence that we remember things *accurately*. Our schooling trains us to come up with right answers as quickly as possible, and most of us tend to apply the same standard to our reminiscences of childhood. If, for example, we can't immediately summon a clear, mental picture of our favorite childhood toys—one that we intellectually recognize as correct—we lose patience. We don't just give up trying to develop that clear picture, we give up the whole activity of remembering childhood toys.

In chapter I, I examined several basic distinctions in life—

Whatever else the child may suffer from, it does not suffer from remoteness of life, normally . . . it is fully alive, and that is why people, thinking back to their own childhood, long to have that naive vitality which they have lost in becoming grown-up. The child is an inner possibility, the possibility of renewal.

MARIE-LOUISE VON FRANZ

Artists don't seek reasons. They are all by definition children, and vice versa.

NED ROREM

The truth is more important than the facts.

FRANK LLOYD WRIGHT

and in storytelling—between "truth" and "accuracy." I discussed how a story is a transmission of *meaning or impression*, rather than of *fact or certainty*, and how, in this sense, it needs to be understood as a *painting* of a person, place, thing, or event rather than a *photograph*. Right now, before we've actually begun the process of developing a specific story, our proper goal is to set the memory free of any inhibitions and allow it to move, play, realize, and reveal as it will.

Fortunately, a great many of our earliest memories are still recoverable. If you have difficulty reconnecting with significant moments in your past, you can be reasonably certain that it's not due to a loss of memories, but to situational or attitudinal barriers that keep memories at bay. These barriers are not insurmountable: You learned them into existing, and you're fully capable of unlearning them, a piece at a time.

Based on what I've discovered from my own creative work, from witnessing the experiments of participants in my workshops, and from my research into cognitive science, I recommend one basic strategy for overcoming these barriers—or any other mental or emotional blocks—so that you can reclaim your earliest memories. I call it "loafing and inviting your soul."

The goal of this approach is to let go of having a goal. Just lie back and muse, brood, ponder, and ruminate over your early years. Allow images—true or false, clear or fuzzy—to arise as they will, and be content just to enjoy them. Wallow in any memory that relaxes or enchants you. Play any mind game that occurs to you for gathering more memories, and feel free to drop that game when something better comes along. Pursue any fleeting glimpse of the past that beckons you, and if you lose your way, let your imagination take over and offer you one.

It sounds simple, and it is. But that doesn't mean it's easy. We all lounge from time to time, but usually in the context of doing something else: watching TV, reading a book, listening to music, or doodling in the sand. Perhaps this additional activity helps ease our guilt that we're not doing something else altogether that's more practical and goal oriented. Just to lie back and relax goes against all our conditioning *not* to lie back and relax.

To hear the voice of your own genius you must learn to silence the competing voices.

TOM COWAN

The crisis is in our consciousness, not in the world.

J. KRISHNAMURTI

The phrase "loafing and inviting the soul" is borrowed from Walt Whitman's poem, "Song of Myself." Writing in the 1830s and '40s, when America's industrial revolution was just beginning, Whitman could already see that the tempo of people's lives was being artificially accelerated by a rapid growth in technology and commerce, to the point where people were losing touch with their own inner rhythms, the natural pulse of their thoughts and emotions. Simultaneously, they were learning to devalue idleness and aimlessness. The words *idleness* and *aimlessness* themselves, etymologically neutral in meaning, were starting to acquire negative connotations, as a freshly minted and much admired word, *productivity* ("product" + "activity"), cast an ever-darker shadow over them.

Whitman insisted that we need to appreciate and occasionally cultivate idleness and aimlessness, to spend more time loafing and inviting the soul, in order to become more receptive to the human part of us. Idleness and aimlessness are the very states of mind that free us to see once again the narrative shape of our lives, and to listen once again to the stories that speak most eloquently to our story-loving soul.

Since the days of Whitman it has become more and more difficult for human beings to value or cultivate these life-enhancing states of mind. In his 1987 book *Time Wars*, Jeremy Rifkin warns: "We have quickened the pace of life only to become less patient. We have become more organized but less spontaneous, less joyful. We are better prepared to act on the future but less able to enjoy the present and reflect on the past. . . . Humanity has created an artificial time environment punctuated by mechanical contrivances and electronic impulses."

In a recent issue of the *Utne Reader* devoted to the subject (April 1997), editor Jay Walljasper referred to this modern dilemma as a "speed trap" and called for a "conscientious slowdown" to get out of it:

Revving up, in fact, is often heralded as the answer to the problems caused by our overly busy lives. Swamped by the accelerating pace of work? Get a computer that's faster. Feel like your life is spinning out of control? Increase your efficiency by learning to read and write faster. No time to enjoy life? Purchase one of those handy products advertised to help you to cook faster, exercise faster, and even make money faster.

Yet it seems that the faster we go, the farther we fall behind. Not only in the literal sense of not getting done what we set out to do, but at a deeper level too. I feel this keenly in my own life. . . . It has gotten to the point where my days, crammed with all sorts of activities, feel like an Olympic endurance event: the everydayathon.

The process of becoming a storyteller involves trying out a conscientious slowdown in our minds, traveling at our own leisurely pace, not only to get where we want to go, but also to make the getting there better. It's a skill that we can initially apply toward coming up with a good story idea, and later utilize in the telling itself, helping our listeners to relax and enjoy the ride.

Like storytelling, loafing and inviting the soul may well be simple-minded—in the best possible sense of the phrase. To cultivate this mental facility is to recapture the wondrously simple and fully alive wakefulness of a child. In Zen Buddhism, this state of consciousness is called beginner's mind, and Zen students are urged to maintain it throughout their practice, regardless of how far along the Buddha path they progress. Beginner's mind gives itself completely to the activity at hand, without worrying about why or wherefore, without having any fixed expectations, and without giving side thoughts to what just happened or what's going to happen next. It's a mind that can tolerate ambiguities, resist making judgments, entertain possibilities, attract inspiration.

We spend most of our time and energy in a kind of horizontal thinking. We move along the surface of things going from one quick base to another, often with a frenzy that wears us out. We collect data, things, people, ideas, "profound experiences," never penetrating any of them. . . . But there are other times. There are times when we stop. We sit still. We lose ourselves in a pile of leaves or its memory. We listen and breezes from a whole other world begin to whisper. Then we begin our "going down."

JAMES CARROLL

Don't just do something! Stand there!

CONTEMPORARY BUDDHIST
SAYING

ACTIVITY
Loafing and Inviting the Soul

The act of loafing and inviting the soul helps restimulate the kinds of personal memories that make for good stories to tell. It also helps you entertain and understand these memories more creatively.

To perform the activity right now, read through all the following material. Then, after you've assumed a comfortable loafing posture in a quiet environment, devote at least a few minutes — ideally, twenty or more — to going through the numbered directions.

To perform the activity in the future, whenever you want to revisit your past, follow these guidelines:

The first step . . . shall be to lose the way.

GALWAY KINNELL

- Select a time of day when you have a least twenty minutes free and don't feel overly tense or tired. An ideal time is when you're already accustomed to settling down, such as before or after a meal or any other daily event that's pleasurable or routine.

Turn aside from highways and walk by footpaths.

PYTHAGORAS

- To keep from the clock-watching to see if your loafing time is up, you may want to set an alarm, or use a sand-timer, or light a short stick of incense (the average five-inch stick burns for about thirty minutes).

- Choose a pleasant, dimly lit room where you can rest without being disturbed or distracted. It should be as quiet as you can make it: no soft music or telephone ringer. Hang a "do not disturb" sign on the doorknob. When you're ready to loaf, sit or lie in a posture that will be comfortable for an extended period of time. In nice weather, you can go to a secluded place outdoors.

- Before actually loafing, you may want to perform some kind of simple ritual that sets the activity apart from the rest of the day and helps your mind to shift gears to a slower pace. Among possible rituals are: lighting a candle and letting it burn until you've finished loafing; writing a few lines in your storytelling notebook about the subject that you want to loaf on (see step 1 below); or doing a set of stretching exercises to help your body relax.

Here are the directions for this activity (which, to some especially speed-stressed people, may be more properly considered a nonactivity):

1. Once you've relaxed into your loafing posture, bid your mind to ponder your childhood in general. You can leave the timespan vague or you can pick a particular age range. If you prefer a tighter focus, at least as a starting point, then choose one general subject that you can relate to this period, such as holidays, playmates, food, or "my room."

2. Turn your mind loose to wander freely within the parameters you've set, recalling specific people, places, events, sounds, smells, and stories that were significant. If your mind roams too far away from the general subject, or if it gets distracted by outside noise, gently lead it back. Many people find that it's better to loaf with their eyes open and slightly unfocused, since closed eyes can easily cause either sleep or overly chaotic imagery.

3. Don't take notes, or do anything else, during your loafing time. Give yourself a few minutes *afterward* to jot down on paper or in your storytelling notebook any significant images, thoughts, feelings, or ideas that came to you.

Try to loaf at least once a week—more often if you're intent on developing a particular story or body of story material. Loafing is a good way to overcome "creator's block," when you're stuck without images or ideas. It can also be rewarding right after you've had a major creative breakthrough, because it helps you absorb, expand, and play with what you've learned.

5

THE QUEST FOR THE PAST

A child's spirit is like a child, you can never catch it by running after it; you must stand still and, for love, it will soon itself come back.

ARTHUR MILLER

What can you expect to gain as a story-teller from loafing and inviting your soul to speak to you? Inevitably, familiar memories will take on surprising new life, buried memories will resurface, and you will find yourself instinctively weaving all these memories together with storythreads.

Sometimes, you won't get a finished product from your loafing, such as a tellable anecdote, but you will still benefit from having exercised your creative powers and having increased your store of memory material. Other times, applying this process to your memories will be like adding hot water to the best imaginable freeze-dried food. Tiny, almost invisible memory fragments will expand and blend with other memories to produce something unexpectedly wholesome and delicious—a full-fledged story meal.

After participating in one of my storytelling workshops, Curtis, a fitness club owner and yoga instructor, wrote me this account of a story meal that his loafing mind cooked up:

I decided to go back in my head to my grade school playground. I couldn't get a clear picture, so I just put together what it was *probably* like. I imagined my eight-year-old self seeing the type of gym structures that I know were there, even though I can't remember for sure how they were shaped or

58

laid out. As I did this, I suddenly remembered, in exact detail, the ladder bars [two upright ladders, facing each other at some distance, and supporting a "top ladder" parallel to the ground]. It came to me in a flash how I had struggled with that top ladder, trying and always failing to swing myself, hand by hand, all the way across. I remembered that one day I overheard a kid call this apparatus "monkey bars," and somehow I finally got it. Just by pretending I was a monkey, I made it all the way across. It was a big lesson I'd forgotten about: perspiration-plus-inspiration.

I went on to connect that epsiode with an earlier grade school memory of making animal movements to music, such as imitating an elephant by trudging with my arms clasped in front of me for a trunk. I could even see the room where I'd been an elephant, an auditorium with a middle aisle that made a great elephant pathway, something I can't ever recall thinking about as an adult. That, in turn, reminded me of the animal mimicry that I now do in kung-fu, arching my arms like a mantis, or that I teach in yoga, like the cobra posture.

Children, like animals, use all their senses to discover the world. Then artists come along and discover it the same way, all over again.

EUDORA WELTY

Curtis can now apply these interrelated memories to many storytelling purposes. He can use the entire network of memories as the framework for a enlightening personal story: one that will probably evoke comparable memories and similar revelations among his listeners. He can transform any part of that network into a teaching tale, either with or without the explicitly personal dimension. Or he can recount one particular memory, when appropriate, to enrich a conversation.

But what can we do if, after loafing and inviting the soul, we don't recall any significant memories regarding a certain era in our past? What if we come away disconcerted by the blurriness and randomness of our impressions, despite our intention not to be bothered by the outcome? What if we can't afterward trace actual story threads through the mazy meanderings we otherwise enjoyed?

On the spur of the moment, or even during a loafing exercise, we may not be able to recall vividly or meaningfully many of

Childhood is not only the childhood we really had but also the impressions we formed of it in our adolescence and maturity. That is why childhood seems so long. Probably every period of life is multiplied by our reflections upon it in the next. The shortest is old age because we shall never be able to think back on it.

CESARE PAVESE

Time is a good storyteller.

IRISH SAYING

the feelings, images, and experiences that shaped the first ten or even twenty years of our life. These memories, however, still persist in our minds as important reference points around which many of our later feelings, images, and experiences oriented themselves. Therefore, if we take the time to work more methodically backward through what we *do* remember from more recent times, we can come, eventually, to those older, less distinct memories and see them in a much clearer light. Furthermore, in the process of performing this more methodical kind of memory work, we track a course back through our past that links together many different memories by association and, thus, leaves us with some story threads that we can then start spinning into whole cloth.

The process of focusing our attention more systematically on our earliest memories can take two different forms: *thinking* backward or *feeling* backward. Thinking backward involves mentally pursuing a certain, prechosen image or subject, step by step, year by year, era by era, into our personal past: for example, "dating experiences," "automobiles," "hiding places," "math." Feeling backward entails digging down, layer by layer, into a particular aspect of our emotional history, becoming what Bill Harley calls an emotional archeologist. The area of concentration might be "peak experiences," "jealousy," "my feelings about my mother," "times when I was torn by conflict," "people I've had crushes on," "fear," "physical pain."

Naturally, any single act of backward contemplation is certain to involve both thinking and feeling. I distinguish between the two modes here because I believe it serves a creative purpose. To focus *primarily* on thinking helps our memory to work around barriers relating to our feelings, and vice versa.

Because we're culturally conditioned to suppress our emotions, and because they are intrinscially less associated with language than thoughts are, many people find it much more difficult to feel than to think backward. On a psychological level, the inability to recognize or process feelings is called "alexithymia," and it's especially prevalent among men. Psychologist

Dr. Ronald Levant of Harvard Medical School attributes this fact to the way they are typically socialized:

> Not only were boys not encouraged to identify and express their emotions, but more pointedly they were told not to. They might have been told that "big boys don't cry," and admonished to learn to "play with pain." These exhortations trained them to be out of touch with their feelings, particularly those feelings on the vulnerable end of the spectrum. As a result of such socialization experiences, men are often genuinely unaware of their emotions. Lacking this emotional awareness, they tend to rely on cognition and try to logically deduce how they should feel. They cannot do what is automatic for most women—simply sense inward, feel the feeling, and let the verbal description come to mind. (Wainrib and Haber, *Prostate Cancer*)

Our feelings are our most genuine path to knowledge.

AUDRE LORDE

Because men are especially liable to be estranged from their feelings and, therefore, from many of their early memories, I generally encourage them to try feeling backward a bit more often than thinking backward. Even though it may be more challenging for them to feel backward, doing so may also, in the long run, be more revealing and helpful.

Using primarily either a thinking or feeling process is an effective way to give structure and momentum to a single act of backward questing; but for backward questing in general, it's important for anyone—male or female—to experiment with *both* processes. Regardless of whether you favor one approach over the other, you can keep yourself from getting caught in memory ruts (where the same few images come up again and again) if you occasionally switch approaches. A certain percentage of your life experiences are bound to yield more readily to a thinking search, and another percentage to a feeling search. You can even conduct both kinds of searches on the same general body of experiences—one time, concentrating on the facts, images, and thoughts; and the other time, paying greater attention to the emotional and physical feelings.

Whatever you do, an individual quest is ultimately going to stimulate both thoughts *and* feelings to a certain degree. Choosing one mode or the other is merely a matter of emphasizing one point of view over the other, not totally controlling your perspective.

You're never too old to become younger.

MAE WEST

ACTIVITY
Thinking or Feeling Backward

The best way to begin building up a story is to start digging below the surface through an activity called thinking or feeling backward. First, read through all the directions that follow until you feel you can recall them fairly well. Then choose either a thinking or feeling quest and devote at least a few minutes—ideally, twenty or more—to going through it.

Whatever their nature, stories begin, and have always begun, quite simply: with a moment, an experience, a feeling.

JIMMY NEIL SMITH

1. Choose the object and mode (thinking or feeling) of your backward memory search.

    As the object of a backward-*thinking* quest, you could select a specific person, place, or thing that has been in your life for a long time, going way back to a period that you can't remember clearly; for example: your Aunt Jenny, the neighborhood where you grew up, the rocking chair that you've loved for twenty years. Alternatively, you could think backward in terms of a more general subject or category of images: neighborhoods you've lived in, sports, TV, clothes, birthdays.

    As the catalyst for a backward-*feeling* quest, you could choose a general feeling common to every life—such as pride or envy. Or you could choose a particular feeling that has been, or once was, very prominent in your life for a long time; for example: your shyness with the opposite gender, your love of nature, your rebelliousness against your parents, your fascination with the supernatural. Or you could choose a subject category that's based on feelings: people who have made you laugh; times when you felt very bold; places where you've been scared; stories that have offered you solace. This can be especially helpful to people who have difficulty identifying or understanding their feelings because it ties a feeling to something more concrete.

2. When you have chosen a quest topic, determine an appropriate *time scale* for going backward.

   Given the particular topic you've chosen, your mood, and the time you have available, you may want to think or feel backward in one-year, two-year, five-year, or ten-year increments from your present age. If, for instance, you are now thirty-five years old and you choose five-year increments, you would first go back mentally to when you were thirty and linger there for a few moments, then go back to when you were twenty-five and do the same, and so on, through twenty, fifteen, and ten, until age five.

   Another option is to choose several progressively younger milestone periods to dwell on, like "when I first came to this town," "when I graduated from college," or "when I was in elementary school."

   For the purpose of examining your most potent, early childhood memories, I recommend paying particular attention to age sixteen (a compromise between Willa Cather's ten or twenty years) and then to each one- or two-year increment going back from that age. You can actually *begin* the process at age sixteen; but if you don't remember much about that time—beyond, say, getting your driver's license—start at a more recent, memorable age and work back to age sixteen and then to the years before.

3. Assume a loafing position in a quiet environment and begin the process of thinking or feeling backward.

4. After you inwardly announce a particular age or period on your time scale (don't worry about being exact),
spend a while loafing and inviting your soul to speak about the object of your quest at that particular point in your life.

Everyone is the child of his past.
EDNA G. ROSTOW

GOING BACK IN TIME, WHEN HAVE I FELT ESPECIALLY....?		
proud	confident	resentful
envious	disgusted	adventurous
crazy	grateful	ignored
benevolent	confused	accepted
humiliated	brave	defeated
hateful	annoyed	enlightened
loving	relieved	lonely
angry	cowardly	blessed
sorry	victorious	competitive
amazed	foolish	terrified
sad	reverent	caring
loyal	disappointed	rejected
obsessed	hopeful	honored
guilty	desperate	embarrassed
joyful	incompetent	masterful
alienated	peaceful	shocked
impressed	rebellious	misunderstood
ashamed	shy	privileged

Despite the overall mode of your quest—thinking or feeling—your soul will probably speak to you in a variety of ways: with pictures, words, and thoughts as well as physical sensations and emotions. Enter into that discussion, and direct it as you will. Ask any questions that occur to you, regardless of whether they specifically involve either thinking or feeling, like:

- Why am I seeing this image?

- What did I feel about it back then?

- What else does it remind me of?

- What was going on during this period in the outside world, or with other people I knew, that might have had something to do with this memory?

5. When you've finished your journey back in time, you may want to take a few moments to jot down what you've learned on a sheet of paper or in your storytelling notebook. You can also experiment with writing brief notes *while* you journey, to capture more details.

Your Hero, Your Self

Lee Pennington—storyteller, poet laureate of Kentucky, and founder of the International Order of Ears, a storytelling guild that's mysterious even to its members—can testify to the benefits of guiding our memory backward, period by period, in a deliberate but leisurely fashion. It brought him one of his favorite and most popular personal stories, "The Color Green."

Pennington recovered this buried treasure as he dug backward, year by year, into his memories of childhood on the family farm, in particular, into his memories of cutting wood each year for the heating and cooking stoves. He came to a summer afternoon in the year he first began to enjoy the task instead of hating it. That turnaround had to do with a strange, wandering woodchopper named Jim, who helped him cut wood and also taught him a wonderful lesson.

Jim was, in Pennington's words, "so ugly that when he walked by, women wept." His face resembled a big bull sheep's; he had hair like wool; and instead of talking through his mouth, he seemed to bleat through his nose. The more Pennington thought about this face, the clearer, more grotesque, and more endearing it became. He remembered that he had loved Jim for his patience and skill in teaching him the best kind of wood to look for in the woods—dead, straight, hardwood limbs that didn't bounce much

I have found my hero and he is me.

GEORGE SHERIDAN

65

As a storyteller, as a human being, each of us is one of a kind. And until we learn to celebrate our own unique style, culture, and gifts, we cannot appreciate the wealth of diversity around us.

DOUG LIPMAN

The present is only a moment and the past is one long story. Those who don't tell stories and don't hear stories live only for the moment, and that isn't enough.

I. B. SINGER

when you dropped them—and then he recalled the unusual challenge Jim had made that summer as they were working together in the woodyard: "You go up on that hillside, and you go to every different kind of tree you can find, and every different kind of plant you can find, and you pick one leaf from each different one, and you bring 'em back to the woodyard, and if you find any two—*any two*—the same color green, I'll give you ten dollars!"

Pennington relived how he had combed the surrounding woods for the next few hours, plucking a single green leaf from every different kind of plant or tree he could find. "Even poison ivy leaves didn't bother me," he claims, "with a whole ten dollars at stake!" He overlapped all the leaves on the packed earth floor of the woodlot, the better to compare their hues, and it was obvious that no two leaves were close enough in color to make a match. As he pondered and polished that memory, it dawned on him that Jim may not have extended this challenge simply to get him out of the way. Jim might have also meant to teach him something, because, looking back, Pennington "felt" that this leaf-comparing exercise was one of his first recognitions that every living thing—leaf, plant, tree, or person—has its own unique and equally valid hue.

The process of thinking or feeling backward is something that we no doubt go through subconsciously far more often than we realize, both during the day, while our conscious minds are taking care of business, and during the night, as we dream. Sometimes we make a more deliberate effort to go back in time, reviewing previous events in our life in a rapid, investigative manner, but our primary focus still remains on the present and how it might advance into the future. Most of us assume that time marches forward and, therefore, that our minds should do the same.

But we're only partially right. Albert Einstein, author of today's most widely-held scientific theory about time, described it as "a continuum, without any beginning or end." And countless generations of storytellers, representing the humanist tradition in our culture, have expressed the same point of view by bidding their listeners to travel in their minds to "once upon a time," whether it be past, present, or future. Because time unfolds in many dimensions and directions, according to how we perceive it, we can uncover an astonishing amount of otherwise lost memories and misplaced memory-meanings just by periodically changing the course of our conscious thinking and feeling.

Why should we make the effort? Why is it important?

There are several good reasons. If we don't make the effort, we remain haunted by shadowy images from our past that never quite deliver any clear information or inspiration but nonetheless refuse to go away. Meanwhile, we're subtly compelled to repeat the same patterns over and over again in our lives simply to relearn or re-experience what we've overlooked or forgotten. If we don't make the effort, we lose our sense of our life story as a whole, and of all the stories within that story that only we can speak for. If we don't make the effort, we lose sight of ourselves as the heroes of our own lives.

Both of the activities we've already explored in part II— "loafing and inviting the soul" and "thinking or feeling backwards"—are valuable components of *any* memory search. The former activity frees us from the insistent demands of the present so that we can dwell more wholeheartedly in the past. The latter gives us a rudimentary trail to follow so that we can start connecting one memory more effectively with another. To generate and develop a bona fide story idea, however, it may be necessary to incorporate these two general processes into a more tightly circumscribed search: one more likely to provoke that type of intensive, multidimensional memory work that psychologists call deep remembering.

The method most commonly prescribed by experts for conducting this kind of intensive search is to work with a preset memory trigger or catalyst: the more specific the trigger, the more focused the search. For example, "elementary school playground" was a trigger my workshop participant Curtis used while loafing and inviting his soul, and "TV," "sports," and "birthdays" are triggers that I suggested earlier as thinking backward topics.

I first became aware of how potent memory triggers can be

during a week-long workshop, "Life Stories," conducted by Donald Davis. The first day of the workshop, he dumped a pile of folded slips of paper onto the floor in the middle of our circle of chairs. One by one, as the spirit moved us, we were to walk over to the pile, pick a slip at random, and tell a story based, however loosely, on what was written on the slip. He called these slips story prompts; here are a few that his workshop participants drew over the course of the week (others can be found in his book, *Telling Your Own Stories*):

Telling someone about your experience breathes new life into it, moving it out of the inchoate swirl of unconsciousness into reality. It takes on form, and allows us to examine it from all sides.

MANDY AFTEL

- A store you loved to visit as a child

- An unforgettable boss

- Something you once wanted very much, only to be disappointed when you finally got it

- A place that very few people but you know about

- A memorable time when you had—or were—a house guest

- How you met a former boyfriend or girlfriend

I picked a prompt that read, "a time when you did something you weren't expected to do." At first my mind was a complete blank, but the workshop rule was clear: I had to come up with a personal story that somehow related to this prompt, and the rest of the class had to wait patiently until I did. Each silent nanosecond that went by seemed like an eternity as my mind rummaged fruitlessly through my past. Then my thoughts for some reason turned to my younger brother, Paul, and the tip of a story line appeared out of nowhere. I grabbed it, and a story unfolded *as* I told it, a very strange and exhilarating sensation.

I started telling the other participants about the first year that Paul and I were both in he same school in Columbus, Ohio. I was in fifth grade, Paul in first. As I was talking, it occurred to me that this was a time when I felt a new responsibility for my brother—

and a new interest in showing him things. To my own wonderment, and perhaps that of everyone else in the family, I voluntarily took him downtown to help him pick out Christmas presents to give. I described in my story my newly mature, substitute-parent perception of Santa Claus Land in Lazarus Department Store; some of the strange gift options my brother and I jointly considered; my occasionally brutish supervisory tactics; and the celebratory trip that we took afterward, on the spur of the moment, to the observation room atop the tallest building in town.

Were it not for the pressure I felt in the workshop to perform right away, these memories might never have popped into my conscious mind, or blossomed into such storymaking detail, or assumed such a personally satisfying story shape. Other people who were there—and participants in my own, similar workshops—have admitted the same thing. For this reason, I recommend that trigger users, after pondering a trigger for a few moments, try telling aloud a reasonably full story *right away*, either to someone else, to an imaginary listener, or to a tape recorder. This kind of forced delivery can be amazingly productive and confidence building.

One of the most effective triggers I use in my own workshops is "recall a childhood hero." Our childhood heroes—some, fictional characters; others, real people—starred in the first important stories we ever took to heart. Recommuning with one of these heroes can bring his or her stories back to compelling life in our imagination, enabling us to tell them in ways that are all the more likely to enchant and inspire others.

By "hero" I mean someone with whom we identified as a child in a positive manner: someone we admired, emulated, valued, or imagined we'd like to be. Our hero may not have been someone exceptionally virtuous, talented, or larger than life. He or she may have been someone who was simply special to us for personal reasons. When I ask my friends or workshop participants to name their heroes when they were kids (the younger, the better) they respond with a wide variety of hero types: Luke Skywalker, Roy

69

Rogers, Helen Keller, Grandma, King Arthur, Lassie, Dorothy Hamill, Charlie Chaplin, the older girl next door, Big Bird, Pippi Longstocking, Dumbo, Muhammad Ali, Snow White.

Sometimes, in addition to naming a hero, I ask people to explain *why* this person or character was a hero to them as a child, and then to identify aspects of their current life that can be related in any way to this hero. For example, when a man I'll call Barry did this exercise, he claimed Spiderman as a hero. As an adult he spends five days a week sitting in front of a computer designing software. This is hardly a Spiderman-like existence, but on weekends and holidays, he's a rock climber! Before the workshop, he hadn't thought to associate his hobby with Spiderman. Now that he does, he can regard it—and himself—more heroically, as the stuff of stories.

My friend Rachel Pollack, a fantasy novelist and author of numerous books on the Tarot, gave one of the most unusual "hero" responses I've ever heard. She confessed that her childhood heroes were the comic strip characters Huey, Dewey, and Louie, the school-age nephews of Donald Duck. She envied them because they always knew how to resolve any emergency by consulting their *Junior Woodchuck Handbook*, a parody of the kind of encyclopedic handbooks used by Boy Scouts and Girl Scouts. She can now trace a connection between her early attraction to possessing such a handbook and her current fascination with the Tarot, a mystical source of all-encompassing information.

Another surprising answer came from my friend John Perkins. His childhood hero was Quasimodo, the main character in Victor Hugo's novel, *The Hunchback of Notre Dame*. "I was attracted to Quasimodo right away because he was so misjudged and yet so very sensitive," Perkins told me. "He also led a life of service to others—he rang the bell—but he wasn't very good socially. As a child, I could really relate to that!"

Perkins first encountered Quasimodo in a television broadcast of the film *The Hunchback of Notre Dame* starring Anthony Quinn. Later, he made a point of catching the two preceding movie Quasimodos: Lon Chaney (in a silent version) and Charles

I used to be Snow White, but I drifted.

MAE WEST

The three stages of a man's life:
1. *He believes in Santa Claus.*
2. *He doesn't believe in Santa Claus.*
3. *He is Santa Claus.*

ANONYMOUS

Laughton. Perkins recalled, "I was especially moved when Laughton, sick at heart, turned toward a stone gargoyle on the roof of the cathedral and sighed, 'How come I'm not made of stone, like you?'" Perkins remained faithful to his childhood hero well into his twenties, when he dressed up as Quasimodo for the annual Halloween parade through New York's Greenwich Village. Since then, he's been a bell-ringer in his own right, as a peace activist, conflict mediator, and self-esteem workshop leader.

A childhood hero of mine was Johnny Appleseed. I grew up in central Ohio, major planting turf for the early-nineteenth-century wanderer John Chapman, whose life and nickname inspired the legend, so I heard, saw, read, and thought a great deal about him. My adult self realizes that I admired him back then as a noble outlaw who was half-man, half-child. He lived defiantly apart from the mainstream, refusing as much as he politely could to grow up, wear shoes, or sleep indoors, and consorting on equal terms with so-called wild creatures—including Native Americans as well as native animals. Yet he had a keen sense of purpose, worked hard, and made a vital contribution to society. He spread orchards throughout the frontier in advance of home-steading pioneers. He assumed the role of a local peacemaker among the various central Ohio factions embroiled in the War of 1812: French, British, new American, and Native Americans. He spread the Christian gospel, Swedenborg-style, from settlement to settlement in a unassuming manner, and, best of all, he told stories to anyone who would listen.

Other reasons that I adopted Johnny Appleseed as a hero—not necessarily a role model but a character of particular interest to me—may strike you as either more mystical or more pedestrian, depending on your point of view. His first name was the same as my father's and a variant of mine, and all three of us looked somewhat alike, at least as Johnny Appleseed looked in the eyes of Walt Disney!

For years after I became a professional storyteller, I kept trying to create interesting stories about Johnny Appleseed, but nothing seemed to gel. Much as the man appealed to my imagination, the stories I tried to carve from his life were too passive,

The purpose of the stories is to put an adult mind in a child's heart and a child's eye in an adult head.

ROBERT D. PELTON

Unless [artists] can remember what is was to be a little boy, they are only half complete as artist and as man.

JAMES THURBER

71

tame, or goody-goody. To my chagrin, I had much more success with the blustery tree destroyer, Paul Bunyan, than with the gentle tree creator, Johnny Appleseed. Bunyan's mythic saga is rich with dramatic hyperboles and outrageous conflicts. Appleseed's more homey legend is not.

Then, about ten years ago, I shifted my thinking away from Johnny Appleseed's life and toward aspects of my own life at the time that could somehow be related to him. I was struggling to give up smoking—quitting and starting up again month after month, week after week, day after day. Finally, I began following a ritual that I thought, sooner or later, might enchant or shame me into quitting for good. Whenever I felt I was ready to smoke my last cigarette, I would buy a new pack of Camels at the corner deli, walk about a half-hour to Prospect Park in Brooklyn, sit at the foot of a big maple tree overlooking the Long Meadow, smoke one fragrant Camel from the freshly opened pack, and then surreptitiously bury the rest of the pack in the soft dirt around the trunk of the tree.

I performed this ritual countless times before the autumn afternoon when it succeeded—that is, when I finally quit smoking. Meanwhile, I'd become aware that my act of burying something in the "wilderness," as part of an esoteric quest for better health, was symbolically analogous to Johnny Appleseed's messianic planting of apple seeds. Perhaps, I thought, the Johnny in me not only concocted the ritual, but also decided that autumn afternoon to stop any further poisoning of the maple tree with nicotine!

After this episode, I realized that the stories—or story fragments—I could best develop and tell about Johnny Appleseed might concern not his life in itself but rather his life in terms of its subtle influence on my life. Some of the story fragments I've since created are mock-heroic fantasies based on the truth: for example, a tale in which Johnny Appleseed does help me as a kind of secret conscience in the effort to quit smoking. Other story fragments communicate more literal memories of Johnny Appleseed's influence on my life: for example, my dressing like him, complete with a pot as my hat, for a pageant when I was ten years old.

As you conduct your own memory experiments regarding childhood heroes, you may recall whole stories that you can simply adapt and tell. For example, if one of your heroes was Bugs Bunny, you may remember specific Bugs Bunny stories that you can enthusiastically pass along to others with very little editing of your own. You may have the same luck with revived memories of real-life heroes, like your sister, your fourth grade teacher, or the mail carrier who came to your childhood home. Even if you don't recall complete stories, you may easily be able to track them down or reimagine them later on. Conversely, you may wind up with small but usable story fragments instead of full-blown stories, or an interweaving mix of fictional and real-life storytelling materials, as I did in thinking about Johnny Appleseed.

Genius is childhood recaptured at will.

CHARLES BAUDELAIRE

ACTIVITY
Your Childhood Hero

Specific memory triggers help reveal more specific story material that we can then shape, refine, or expand as we wish. This activity is based on the especially evocative trigger, "Your Childhood Hero." A list of other triggers can be found in the appendix.

Read all the directions that follow *before* doing the activity. When you have finished reading, it can be valuable to go through the whole activity quickly, so that you're forced to blurt out your automatic and therefore probably most authentic responses. However, take whatever amount of time you feel is most comfortable and productive for you. In the hours, days, and weeks that follow, more memories and ideas will inevitably occur to you as you think back to this activity or repeat it with another hero.

1. Identify *one* hero—either fictional or real-life—that you had as a child. Starting at age sixteen, go as far back into your childhood as you can remember. When you've thought of a hero, write the hero's name on a sheet of paper or in your storytelling notebook.

Every child is an artist. The problem is how to remain an artist once she grows up.

PABLO PICASSO

2. Distinguish several qualities of this hero—or aspects of this hero's story—that you believe made him or her your childhood hero. List these qualities and/or aspects next to the hero's name.

3. Establish points of comparison between you and/or your life now and the hero and/or the hero's life. Use the list you've just made (step 2) to get started, but be open to other points of comparison that may come to you as you ponder the subject. Record each point of comparison in writing.

4. Review what you've written about your hero and identify several different ways that you might be able to use him or her in your storytelling. Consider the following options:

- Retelling the hero's story either as is, summarized, or adapted

- Creating a new story starring the hero

- Creating a story about a person or character who is similar to this hero, or who is in a comparable situation, without even mentioning the hero

- Creating a story about your relationship with this hero, or this hero's potential or actual influence on your life

Jot down several viable possibilities.

PART III

GETTING
STORY IDEAS

In oneself lies the whole world and if you know how to look and learn,
then the door is there and the key is in your hand. Nobody on earth can give
you either the key or the door to open, except yourself.

J. KRISHNAMURTI

LIFELINES AND
STORYLINES

The blues singer Bo Diddley used to boast, "Everything I know I taught myself." In terms of personal storytelling, I would apply a paraphrase of this statement to all of us: The most valuable things we know are the stories we teach ourselves.

In part two, you reconnected with one of your childhood heroes. Like a constellation emerging from the night sky, this image began to shine forth more recognizably from the darkness of your memory. Now it's time to start constellating other parts of your past, so that eventually they can inspire personal tales that illuminate your own life and the lives of your listeners.

What you'll be looking for in this part are story *ideas*. You might be lucky and discover entire stories lying in wait, virtually ready to share as is. At the very least, you'll spot a number of images and image clusters that you'll instinctively recognize as good material. The rest of the storymaking process then comes much like tending a seed through the stages of germinating, sprouting, flowering, and fruiting. You do a certain amount of mental gardening work to help move things along, but basically you can depend on the story seed to evolve a life of its own: marvelous to witness and, ultimately, nourishing to all who partake of it.

The questions which one asks oneself begin, at last, to illuminate the world, and become one's key to the experience of others.

JAMES BALDWIN

The artist "lies" in order to reach another kind of truth.

PABLO PICASSO

True places are not found on maps.

HERMAN MELVILLE

For just a moment, to gain a clearer perspective on the full range of possibilities that lie ahead, let's consider the fulfilment of the story seed's potential: it's "restoryation" of a part of our life. In many respects, this kind of restoryation is comparable to more conventional restoration projects that involve buildings or neighborhoods. In most such operations, the goal is not—and often cannot be—an exact duplicate of the original. Key plans, photos, or eyewitness accounts from the original time period may be missing. Modern construction materials, lifestyles, and legalities may make certain adaptations highly desirable, if not mandatory. And the need to convey the historical significance of a place, or to accommodate modern mindsets and sensitivities, may require omitting some features and adding or modifying others. Thus, many building and neighborhood restorations have such a palpable life of their own apart from the original model that they are more properly viewed as history-friendly *translations* rather than historically accurate *reproductions*.

On Philadelphia's Independence Mall, for example, Benjamin Franklin's house is reinvoked on its former site by a full-scale, three-dimensional wooden outline of the original building. In keeping with Franklin's spirit, it's an imaginative and intellectually stirring work of open-air art. Looking at the wooden beams, we can visualize Franklin's era with our mind's eye. Looking *through* them, we can admire a living legacy of Franklin's work: modern Philadelphia, USA.

Auschwitz, the Nazi concentration camp in Poland, has been reinterpreted as an austere pilgrimage site. It preserves haunting details from the past, like the railway lines and the crematoria chimneys, in an otherwise almost parklike setting stripped of clutter and devoid of replicated buildings. The revised Auschwitz still testifies to the horrors that once occurred there, but in a manner that suitably memorializes its victims instead of representing more faithfully its makers' original intentions.

When we undertake the restoryation of our lives, we inevitably find that certain story ideas require analogous translations on the path to becoming full-fledged personal tales. Some memories are too fuzzy, painful, complicated, or private to express directly, and so we need to figure out ways to communicate them indirectly. The challenge and joy is to enliven these memories with our creativity and, at the same time, respect their essential truth, our own sense of rightness, and our listener's sensitivities and comprehension needs.

Suppose, for example, we recall a ghastly but noteworthy incident relating to a blind date we once had. We can't remember the name of the other person or anything else specific about the date, but we still think the incident is worth sharing in a story. We then have several story-translation options:

Every creative act involves . . . a new innocence of perception, liberated from the cataract of accepted belief.

ARTHUR KOESTLER

- We can embroider on whatever we do remember, making up an appropriate name for our date and embellishing each and every step of that one incident with drama and detail until it becomes an epic all on its own.

- We can turn that incident into the centerpiece of a larger, imaginatively re-created story about the entire date or about that particular time in our life, adding details that are authentic to the period and to our personal experience back then.

- We can work on recalling other memories of blind dates— or dating in general—until we have a string of related images and scenes we can incorporate into a larger story: "My Dating Life," or something to that effect.

- We can think about times when we behaved similarly in altogether different contexts, such as during our family, school, or job life. The original blind date incident would then become only one, broadly sketched episode in a story more pointedly about self-realization or self-development that features episodes from the other contexts as well.

Suppose we do, in fact, recall the name of our blind date and many other details involved in the incident. We may still want to translate matters as far as our story version is concerned, so that

79

What really happens is that the story-maker proves a successful "sub-creator." He makes a Secondary World which your mind can enter. Inside it, what he relates is "true," it accords with the laws of that world. You therefore believe it, while you are, as it were, inside.

J. R. R. TOLKIEN

So stories are a history — of a sort. . . . This does not mean that stories lie but rather that they look at humanity's history obliquely, through slotted eyes. Emily Dickinson once wrote something to that effect: "Tell all the Truth but tell it slant."

JANE YOLEN

we don't violate the rights of the other individual, or display too nakedly the shabbiness of our own behavior, or inadvertently depress, anger, or confuse a listener whose frame of reference may be radically different from ours. To avoid any of these potential pitfalls, we can certainly make minor fictional adjustments in details without disturbing the real-life heart of what we have to say.

If the blind date incident had some horribly painful aspects that we can't bring ourselves to discuss, we can shift our story's standpoint slightly to put that material into the background, or completely out of sight, while we focus on elements that are easier or more fitting to share with others.

For example, we can imagine out loud how an embarrassing blind date situation that mortified us might have amused our friends, our family members, or an outside observer. Or we can simply inform our listeners that, as the story's narrator, we want to talk not about the heavier issues involved in that experience but instead about what was heartening, curious, funny, or revealing.

At all times, we must remember that we're developing a *story* to tell, not a formal deposition. We want to be as factually accurate as we can be; but if we're not sure of the facts, or if we feel that the facts we know won't effectively convey the truths we believe, then we need to grant ourselves the freedom—and our listeners the benefit—of a more skillful approach toward reconstructing the past. Crafting stories that reflect not only factual memory but also personal meaning and consideration for others (our listeners as well as the people we talk about) can be a wonderful exercise in judgment, kindness, integrity, and creativity.

First, however, we must come up with the initial story idea! Once we have that idea, we can go about restorying it in ways that the idea itself suggests.

Let's try another analogy for this developmental process: making a movie. The story idea is our original movie "concept": something from our own life experience that we can express in a few, simple words—such as "my worst enemy," "the summer I learned to swim," or "motherhood deserves a medal"—and yet something that we instinctively know is rich in story possibilities.

As we brood on this idea, we start producing a rough "film" in our minds that we periodically review and refine. We lop off boring or murky scenes and augment others to fill in critical narration or information gaps. We sharpen key visuals. We polish dialogue for clarity, humor, or dramatic effect. We give the overall flow of sights, sounds, and sensations an appropriate and compelling rhythm. And we strive, frame by frame, to maintain as much authenticity as possible.

Memory is a complicated thing, a relative to truth, but not its twin.

BARBARA KINGSOLVER

This mental moviemaking is basically the same process that we instinctively go through with *any* memory we're in the habit of revisiting. For storymaking purposes, we just engage in the process more consciously and creatively. We make this greater effort so that later, when we're actually telling our story, we can "replay" it easily in our minds, edit it efficiently as we go along to fit the situation, and project its beauty clearly into the minds of our listeners. And our constant touchstone throughout this process—the single image that serves as our best guide and governor—remains our original story idea and all its implications, whatever final form the story takes in any individual telling.

Creative minds have always been known to survive any kind of bad training.

ANNA FREUD

It's important and inspiring to remind ourselves, throughout this beginning, idea-searching stage, that restorying ourselves is a *healing* activity, not simply a rehashing of the past. We do it to rescue meaningful personal experiences from oblivion, render them whole again, and give them—and ourselves—new, more vigorous life. Because of the relentlessly increasing complexity, speed, and regimentation of contemporary society, we are each sorely in need of this kind of healing on a regular basis.

Chinua Achebe, a Nigerian novelist who grew up in a storytelling family, draws a significant distinction between the self-debilitating world of pragmatic routines and the self-renewing world of story: "There are so many things we have to do all at once today, because the world is changing so fast around us, and a lot of it we are not in control of, but what we do control I think we should think about seriously. This is especially true with story, because that's really the basis of our existence."

Ellen Dooling Draper, coeditor of *Parabola* magazine, strikes the same chord in her introduction to the August 1992 issue, "The Oral Tradition":

> We remain comfortable in our ignorance and isolation and satisfied with an everyday spoken language of inexact words verbalizing incomplete thoughts. Most of what we express is conveyed by means of a similarly undeveloped vocabulary of tone and body language. But there comes a time in most of our lives when for one reason or another we face an impossible and inescapable choice. Our sense of comfort disappears and we begin to suffer our aloneness. Why are we here? How do we go on?

To answer these questions, we need a new and better language, and storytelling can give it to us. What kinds of stories might we ultimately develop? The possibilities are unlimited and entirely up to us, depending on our own personal ingenuity and our repertoire of life experiences and telling styles—combined, of course, with the situation at hand, the listeners before us, and the mood of the moment. Stories worth telling can be long or short, light or heavy, candid or subtle, sad or funny, weird or wise, gentle or wild, plain or fancy. You name it!

You'll come to appreciate different possible types of stories—and give them your own descriptive labels—as you pursue the activities in this chapter and in the rest of the book. That's how it should be: *your* own sense of story and story structures evolving from *your* own personal experience. However, to start you thinking about story types, I'd like to make a critical distinction between two very broad story categories—what I call big stories and little stories.

In this context, the words *big* and *little* do not have pejorative meanings. They do not refer to the length, complexity, quality, or value of a story. Instead, they describe a story's psychic potency: how large it looms in the teller's personal history, how strongly it's charged with emotional significance, how much it exposes the teller, and how great a risk he or she takes in telling it.

The big stories in your personal repertoire are the ones that

[Memory] is the mythologist in us that turns certain events into symbols or representative metaphors for our lives.

PENNINAH SCHRAM

Our lives are at once ordinary and mythical. We live and die, age beautifully or full of wrinkles. We wake in the morning, buy yellow cheese, and hope we have enough money to pay for it. At the same instant we have these magnificent hearts that pump through all sorrow and all winters we are alive on the earth.

NATALIE GOLDBERG

say the most to you—and, presumably, to your listeners—about who you are. They feature you as the main character and, as a rule, they reveal one or more of the major people, places, or events in your personal history. Possible subjects could be the severe economic hardships you faced as a child, the love of your life, a horrendous car wreck you survived, your biggest accomplishment as a teacher, your wartime ordeals, the birth of your child, the death of your parent.

In my workshops, big stories are generally the first ones that participants bring up when I ask them to talk about real-life experiences. Because big stories have great personal significance, they can usually be recalled more vividly—and, therefore, shaped and developed more easily—than other, less life-defining stories. Our big stories are the ones we fantasize as the splashiest scenes in the movie version of our life or the meatiest chapters in our memoirs. Whether or not they translate into our best stories to *tell* is another matter altogether.

Sharing a big story with others can be a uniquely profound experience for you and for them. However, big stories are not necessarily easy to relate or appropriate for a wide variety of telling circumstances. Certain big stories may be too poignant for you to communicate comfortably to more than one person or a few people at a time, or to people whom you don't know very well, or in a situation where you don't have complete control over the time, setting, and atmosphere. And they may be too intense or intimate for certain listeners to handle.

In comparison, little stories are tales in which your own personal identity is less significantly involved. You may still be the main character, or you may be a costar, minor player, bystander, or nonwitnessing narrator. The tale itself concerns a person, place, or event from your own history—or that of someone you know—that may have been remarkable in many respects, but that is still relatively minor in terms of its overall impact on your life.

Little stories tend to have a broader appeal to listeners precisely because they aren't so deeply personal. Rather than spotlighting an intense and unique *individual* experience, their main point is to illuminate a gentler, more common aspect of *human* experience: for example, struggling through the first day of a new job, being charmed by the playfulness of a wild animal, getting lost on a vacation, dealing with obnoxious neighbors, receiving an unexpected gift from a stranger.

In many cases, little stories are about the teller when he or she was, literally, little. Viewed with adult detachment, even our own childhood can seem like another life lived by another person: a very dramatic existence, to be sure, but still a giant step removed from the more pressing drama of our present world.

And our childhood has so many, great little stories to offer. As children, we could become completely caught up in whomever we met, wherever we were, and whatever we were doing, no matter how objectively "important" the particular person, place, or event was. If we can recreate that special enthrallment in a personal story, it can magically captivate our listeners.

Many stories don't fall neatly into either the big or the little category but are overlaps or hybrids. For example, we may invoke our torturous puberty (typical big story material) only to focus on one humorous aspect of it: our misconceptions about the opposite sex, say, or our colorfully fearsome basketball coach (both typical little story subjects). We may start a story by describing an unusual shop we like to patronize (little story stuff) and wind up depicting how our visits to the shop once helped us cope with a serious illness (big story stuff).

These mixed-breed stories are often our most effective ones. We can provide safe, meaningful glimpses of a very upsetting but important event in our lives by confining it to the background of a smaller, less disturbing drama; or we can give a relatively minor but special experience even greater resonance by linking it to a more significant episode in our lives.

A simple but very powerful way to generate personal story ideas of all kinds—big, little, or hybrid—is to use a "lifeline" for inspiration. A lifeline is a handmade tool commonly used for life review work in psychotherapy, counseling, or self-help endeavors. On a blank sheet of paper, you draw a straight vertical line representing your life. Then you note significant things that happened at appropriate points along that line.

The moment one gives close attention to anything, even a blade of grass, it becomes a mysterious, awesome, indescribably magnificent world in itself.

HENRY MILLER

I am the poet of the Body and I am the poet of the Soul,/ The pleasures of heaven are with me and the pains of hell are with me,/ The first I graft and increase upon myself, the latter I translate into a new tongue.

WALT WHITMAN

In the following activity, you'll learn how to make an expansive lifeline that is especially useful for stimulating story ideas. But first, to prepare yourself, consider the following Zen Buddhist koan, or teaching tale, which I first learned from John Daido Loori Roshi, the abbot of Zen Mountain Monastery in Mt. Tremper, New York. It's called "Senjo and her Soul."

There was once a man in China who had two daughters. The elder daughter died very young, and so he poured all of his attention into the younger daughter, Senjo. During that time, marriages were often arranged by the parents, usually the father. Senjo had many suitors, and her father chose the man that he thought was the best of them.

But Senjo had a secret lover. He had been her playmate since they were children. Back then, their parents had often kidded them, saying, "Oh what a wonderful couple you'll make when you get married!" The children grew up believing that this would actually happen, so Senjo was shocked when her father announced that she was expected to marry a stranger. Her lover was also stunned. He couldn't bear the thought of staying in the same village where Senjo lived as the wife of another man, so he decided to leave.

On a moonlit night, he slipped a boat into the river and began paddling downstream. When he was about an hour away from the village, he noticed a shadowy figure flitting along the shoreline, following the boat. He went ashore to see who it was. To his great joy, it was Senjo! She was running away from home to avoid the arranged marriage. So Senjo and her lover continued the journey by boat and settled in a remote country, where they married.

Five years passed. Senjo was then the mother of two children, and she and her husband were very happy together, but they both missed their parents and yearned to visit their home village. Finally they decided to make the journey and risk the consequences. When their boat neared the

Truth is a river that is always splitting up into arms that reunite. Islanded between the arms, the inhabitants argue for a lifetime as to which is the main river.

CYRIL CONNOLLY

ELIZABETH ELLIS' STORY TYPES

Texas-based storyteller Elizabeth Ellis divides stories into these categories:

HA-HA!
(stories that are funny)

AHA!
(stories that surprise or delight the mind)

AHHH...
(stories that touch deep emotions)

AMEN
(stories that move the spirit)

landing of their old village, the husband said to Senjo, "Let me go ahead, to see how it is for us. You wait here with the children."

So the husband went to Senjo's old house and knocked at the door. Her father came out. Right away, the husband burst out apologizing for how he and Senjo had run away together, but the father looked at him strangely and then finally interrupted, saying, "What are you talking about? Senjo is here! She has always been here! For five years now, she has been sick in bed, sunk in sadness, not talking or responding to anyone." Now it was the husband's turn to look strange. "No!" he cried. "Senjo is with me! We have two children. You are a grandfather now."

The husband ran to get Senjo for proof. In the meantime, her father went back into the house to Senjo's bedroom, and there she lay, as listless as ever. He told her the husband's story. Senjo sat up and smiled for the first time in five years. She got out of bed and walked outside. And as the two Senjos came toward each other, they merged into one.

Believe in the holy contour of life.

JACK KEROUAC

ACTIVITY
Crossroads

If you were a Zen student being tested with this story as a koan, you'd be asked, "Senjo and her soul are separated: Which is the true one?" Without any further explanation of "soul" or "true one," you might also be advised, "The answer is not one, or the other, or both, or neither."

Luckily for you, the challenge I'm presenting in this activity is not nearly as mind-busting. Instead of answering the question directly, you will be responding to it indirectly with a new, more story-minded consideration of memorable turning points in your own experience: times when you made a decision that altered your fate, or when something—or someone—made the decision for you. Using this material, you can create stories that engage your listeners delightfully and constructively in the mysteries of life as you have encountered them.

Here are the instructions:

1. On a blank sheet of paper at least 8½ inches high wide by 11 inches long, draw a straight vertical line that divides the paper in half. Start-

ing at the bottom of the line with "O," representing your birth, go up the line dividing it with short crosslines into five-year segments, ending with your present age at the top of the line.

2. Mark at least three significant turning points along that lifeline: times when you chose between two basic alternatives, or when the choice was made for you. Remember that a turning point can be thought of as something positive, negative, neither, or both.

   Indicate the two basic alternatives involved as follows:

   • An arrow pointing to a word or phrase on the *right side* of the line that describes what you *did do*

   • An arrow pointing to a word or phrase on the *left side* of the line that describes what you *did not do*

3. Consider the decisionmaking environment surrounding each turning point, and ask yourself:

   • What various factors were involved in the decision?

   • What other people were around at the time, and what influence did each of them have?

   • What was the main or "final" reason for the decision?

   • How did I feel about the decision at the time?

   • What thoughts and feelings have I had about the decision since?

4. Focus on what you *did not do* in each situation, and ask yourself:

   • What might my life have been like if it had taken that turn instead?

He led a double life. Did that make him a liar? He did not feel a liar. He was a man of two truths.

IRIS MURDOCH

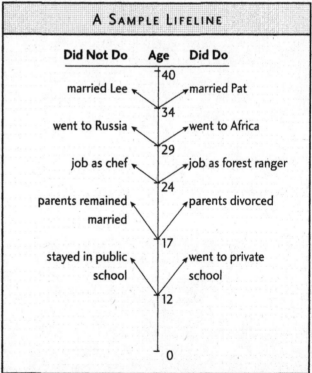

A SAMPLE LIFELINE

Did Not Do	Age	Did Do
	40	
married Lee		married Pat
	34	
went to Russia		went to Africa
	29	
job as chef		job as forest ranger
	24	
parents remained married		parents divorced
	17	
stayed in public school		went to private school
	12	
	0	

- In the time since the decision was made, in what ways have I lived that other life to some degree, either in my imagination, or in certain aspects of my real-life experience? In what other subtle ways has my life been affected by the choice not taken?

What a wonderful life I've had! I only wish I'd realized it sooner.

COLETTE

5. Consider both options at each turning point, and ask yourself, "At what times in my life have I faced a similar crossroads?" Define "similar" however you see fit.

MEMORY LEGWORK

8

The road taken and the road not taken: Therein lies the story. Concentrating on the decisionmaking episodes in our lives can yield exceptionally rich personal story ideas. All the essential elements of drama are there: surprise, challenge, conflict, suspense, resolution, and consequence. Typically, such times also bring into new and illuminating play many different, contrasting components of our lives, including logic and emotions; freedom and responsibility; past, present, and future; family members, friends, lovers, and strangers.

For us as tellers, the process of composing and then living with a better-defined narrative of a personal turning point results in much greater self-understanding and self-confidence. Our story constantly reminds us that we can and do make creative choices, not only in how we conduct our lives but also in how we regard them and talk about them.

For our listeners, hearing and then living with our story can provide vital encouragement and guidance. At the very least, they gain insight into how a particular individual faced the complex personal and interpersonal dimensions of coming to a crossroads in life. Whether or not we handled the situation well, our listeners can be enormously reassured by the simple fact that we not only survived it but also cast it into a coherent story worth telling. And sometimes they derive an even greater benefit from

All of us … have been formed by experiences that still inhabit us. Memory is not only a trip but also a structure. Recollections are not only stories retold but also aspects of present feeling. Our hopes at any given moment are fashioned by our previous disappointment. Our need to share pain is as strong as our quest for pleasure. Every pain that is not purely physical is also retrospective. Our need to make sense of our lives has continually to take account of all this.

JOHN BERGER

There comes a time in every man's life and I've had many of them.

CASEY STENGEL

I was going through the hardest thing, also the greatest thing, for any human being to do; to accept that which is already within you, and around you.

MALCOLM X

our tale: They can directly or indirectly apply what they've experienced as listeners toward coping with their own crises. This kind of help in information processing and decisionmaking is especially meaningful to children, adolescents, mature adults going through what is euphemistically known as "change of life," and elders facing retirement and death.

The point of the crossroads activity you just completed is that it gets you to look at your past history in an unfamiliar, oblique, two-sided way that gives it new texture, dimension, and depth. As a result, you can spot possible story ideas that you may not otherwise see. After all, stories, like life itself, endlessly interweave the real with the possible.

In a workshop featuring the crossroads activity, a participant I'll call Clay, a self-proclaimed Generation X–er from Manhattan, marked on his lifeline the point when he was eleven years old and his family moved from a farm in Iowa to New York City. Back then, Clay perceived the change as a miraculous opening up of his world. He so quickly and eagerly adapted to his new, urban, multicultural environment that his parents kidded him about being a traitor to his roots. Back then, he didn't pay much attention to their teasing, but he now realizes that at some level it must have stuck.

During Clay's college years at Duke University, a friend talked him into taking a retreat at a communal farm in western Tennessee. Clay couldn't believe how much he enjoyed it. Ever since then, he has periodically escaped from his urban homes to nearby rural settings to hike, camp, or work the land. Even at the time of the crossroads workshop, when he resided in an apartment on Manhattan's Upper West Side, he was raising his own crops on the roof of the six-story building: oregano, lettuce, and a lone tomato plant, all in a single wooden whiskey tub. In a tale he told for the first time at the workshop, he connected this tub farming with "keeping my roots."

Another participant in that same workshop, Sherry, was fifty-six years old and had recently celebrated her silver wedding anniversary. On her crossroads lifeline, she marked a date four years prior to her wedding when she ended her engagement to another man. Her decision to break off from that first fiancé grew from a painful awareness that she was far more in love with him than he was with her. They soon lost all contact with each other. Then, two years prior to the workshop, she stumbled across his name in an e-mail directory and reconnected with him via the Internet. They agreed to get together face-to-face for dinner in Chicago, where he lived and she was coming on business.

As the dinner progressed, Sherry was stunned to realize that the man who had popped up so vividly in so many unsettling thoughts and dreams throughout her married life didn't really exist anymore, except in her imagination. It was a bittersweet but liberating moment. It somehow rendered her long-ago memories of him all the more valuable, and it freed her to relive that part of her past in ways that could relate more harmoniously—and more meaningfully—with her present.

A situation that you consider to be a significant personal turning point may not involve what others would call a major life event. My friend Lou, a forty-five-year-old family man, tells a personal story of this kind about the last few months before he and his wife had their first child. During that time, he yearned to purchase a jazzy red sportscar—a final act of craziness before taking on the serious obligations of fatherhood—but he gradually talked himself into buying a sensible station wagon instead. For years afterward, he kept confronting the same sort of decision in other contexts, and always wound up choosing the safe, rational option instead of the risky, more glamorous one. Recently, at age forty-five, he inherited some money from his father, and he immediately spent it all on a Piper Cub airplane. Now he's taking lessons to learn how to fly!

Certainly we can derive good story ideas from turning points in our personal history that did *not* have any remarkable aftermath. However, the fact that one of our past experiences does strike us as a significant personal crossroads means that we have probably relived it numerous times in our thoughts and feelings ever since, and, therefore, that it has somehow imprinted our life over and over again. If we can trace and articulate this later imprinting phenomenon, no matter how subtle it may be, our story

The life you have led doesn't need to be the only life you have.
ANNA QUINDLEN

of that turning point can be all the more multidimensional and vibrant.

In addition to the crossroads activity, there are many other ways we can use lifelines to survey our past experiences for story material. We can mark periods along a lifeline according to who was our best friend, lover, or major influence at the time. We can devote separate lifelines to noting important emotional events, learning experiences, or spiritual awakenings.

Tales are created from the world around us, given life by everything we know and understand, taken in through our senses, and gleaned from our memories. All we must do is pay close attention and when the image comes that promises a story, be willing to follow wherever it might lead.

JIMMY NEIL SMITH

Next to any or all of these lifelines, we can draw parallel life-lines for individual family members and other special people. Then we can look for interesting comparisons and contrasts between what was happening to us at a given time and what was going on concurrently in the lives of the people around us.

We can take a similar approach with a parallel timeline of historical events, especially ones that were personally meaningful to us or, perhaps, to our listeners: the date of Martin Luther King, Jr.'s "I Have a Dream" speech, President Kennedy's assassination, the first Woodstock music festival, the national bicentennial, the last episode of the TV show *MASH*, the *Challenger* shuttle explosion, the Hale-Bopp comet, Princess Diana's death, the biggest snowstorm in fifty years. Our memories of what we were doing when a particular historical event occurred may serve as the nucleus for a good story that ultimately doesn't even allude to the event itself!

Working with parallel lifelines and timelines is a wonderful way to enlarge and enliven the process of getting ideas and developing them into stories. Many people become obsessed with the beginning-to-ending plot of a story. Their creative thinking goes relentlessly upward along a *vertical* line. Their one overriding question is, "How do I start my storyline from the ground zero moment and dramatically build it up, over time, to a good conclusion?" They assume that the key to a good story lies solely in answering this question.

In fact, we can realize many of our most engaging and impressive story ideas through *horizontal* thinking: that is, through cross-referencing the same moment in time among different, parallel lifelines or timelines. Listeners enjoy the richness of scope that such an expanded moment in time offers. They're motivated to imagine it in more detail, and, if it's specifically identified by year or era, to add to it their own fanciful, real-life, or historical associations.

Creating parallel lifelines and timelines to get story ideas may require some outside research, which in itself can be entertaining and thought provoking. To find out more about family members and other special people, you may need to question them—or people who knew them—in person or by phone, e-mail, or letter. Establishing personal contact in this manner gives you an opportunity not only to gather the information you seek, but also to discover new story ideas, to hear tales you've never heard before, and maybe even to tell some tales of your own. For more details about historical events, you may need to consult year-review books and magazines or other kinds of chronological reference works in the library, a project which can also inspire yet more memories and story ideas.

Doing research to fill in lifelines is one example of a general strategy for getting story ideas that I call doing memory legwork. It's a type of venture that can enrich us personally whether or not we're seeking answers to a particular set of questions. Among other things, it involves lingering over old photograph albums and scrapbooks, rereading journals and letters we've saved, and revisiting places that once figured prominently in our life, like our childhood neighborhood, our high school, a resort where we vacationed, or the site of a former job.

Here's an example of memory legwork from my own recent experience. Regrettably, my mother and I have lived a considerable distance apart from each other ever since she raised me, so there hasn't been much in-person, back-and-forth memory reinforcement between us. During a visit last winter, she mentioned in passing that whenever I was sick as a preschooler, I insisted on playing Walt Disney's recording of Sergei Prokofiev's musical tale "Peter and the Wolf"—not just once but over and over and over until I eventually wore the record out.

The test of a civilized person is first self-awareness, and then depth after depth of sincerity in self-confrontation.

CLARENCE DAY

Having no memory of this ritual myself, and rarely having heard anything about my early childhood, I was eager to explore this "news" in more depth. As a storyteller, I wanted to feel a reconnection with that child who apparently managed to derive so much comfort and healing (at least emotionally) from a particular story. I also thought that this piece of evidence might help me reconstruct the larger history of that forgotten period in my life.

First, I tried to track down a copy of the actual Disney recording, circa 1948–50. I couldn't locate one right away, so I bought a more recent version. Although, like most of us, I'd probably half-heard fragments of the highly popular "Peter and the Wolf" music many times in my life since childhood, especially in supermarkets and elevators during the Christmas season, I couldn't recall ever having listened to the whole work with my full attention. When I finally did so with my newly purchased tape, the impact of the music *and* the story, separately and together, was remarkable. Even my adult self identified strongly with Peter's part-adventurous, part-timorous personality. Each of the animal descriptions—the bird (flute), the duck (oboe), the cat (clarinet), and the wolf (horns)—fit exactly my own current sense of that animal. And the basic structure of the plot—cooperation among human beings and animals to overcome trouble—was one that I'd used in many of the stories I'd created as an adult storyteller: stories not just for children but also for adults.

Later, while browsing for the Disney recording in a store that specializes in rare books, prints, and photographs, I came across something I hadn't anticipated: an illustrated book that had accompanied the original recording. As I paged through it, I did, indeed, recall the illustrations and found them unusually stirring.

As time went on and I did more memory legwork, I also recollected more images from that period in my life to go with the "Peter and the Wolf" ones. In other secondhand bookstores, I came across several other books that I had loved as a child in the same editions I'd known back then, among them a lavishly illustrated, oversized version of Robert Louis Stevenson's *Water Babies* and a well-worn volume of Hugh Lofting's *Dr. Doolittle*, bound in nubbly red cloth, with a sketch of the doctor himself on a rectangular white pasteboard patch inlaid in the center the front cover. Through conversations with other relatives, I revived more childhood illness memories, possibly forgotten because I haven't been sick many times in my life and, therefore, haven't gone through many same-state occasions to revive them. I recollected a time when my mother served me a swordfish cut from a piece of toast because I'd grumpily requested swordfish as a sickbed treat, and the early mornings of school days when I tried to create fake vomit out of milk, flour, Thousand Island dressing, and mushed bananas to fool my parents into letting me stay home from school.

After putting together these images and others acquired by memory legwork, I now have a much better sense of what I was like as a young child and, therefore, what that period can be like for children in general. This kind of understanding has greatly enhanced my storytelling overall, no doubt because of the strong correspondences among childhood, the creative process, and the storytelling self. As a bonus, I also have plenty of material to start developing a good illness-related personal story!

Like this example, the following activity deals with family memories, an abundant source of personal story ideas. I believe that along with life itself, we inherit from our ancestors a responsibility to translate family memories into our own stories, and then to tell those stories not just to other family members but also to other people in the family of humankind. As Elizabeth Stone says in her seminal book on the subject of family stories, *Black Sheep and Kissing Cousins*, "The particular spirit of a family is newly imagined every generation, with old family stories disappearing or coming to mean something different, and new ones being coined."

ACTIVITY
A Photo Opportunity

When I was a boy, my family took great care with our snapshots. We really planned them. We made compositions. We posed in front of expensive cars, homes that weren't ours. We borrowed dogs. Almost every family picture taken of us when I was young had a different borrowed dog in it.

RICHARD AVEDON

Old photographs of people, places, or events that have helped to shape our lives are powerful tools for storymaking. They appeal directly to our visually-oriented right brain, the suspected fount of our creativity, avoiding the possibly complicating interference of the written word.

To do this activity, you need a photograph of yourself and one or more family members that's at least five years old, preferably older (other people can also be in the photograph). If you can't easily obtain this kind of photograph right now, read through the instructions and think about photographs you have or could get that you'd especially like to use for this activity later on. Here are the guidelines:

1. Place the photograph in front of you so that you can comfortably study it as you go through this activity.

2. Take a few moments to ponder the photograph, noting the following things:

   • The expressions on the faces

   • The postures and other body language messages

   • The clothes

   • The surrounding environment in general

   • Specific objects within that environment

   Try to identify more precisely when and where the photograph was taken, and who or what is in it, but don't let this effort be your *main* concern. Instead, focus on the picture primarily as you would on *any* photographic composition, regardless of whether you've ever seen it before or know anything about it, and try to read its elements accordingly.

3. Ask yourself the following questions about the photograph (if you don't know a particular answer, make up a close-as-possible guess, based on your powers of observation, background knowledge, and imagination):

- If I didn't know the individuals in the photograph, including myself, what kind of people would I take them to be?

- If I didn't know the occasion for the photograph, what would I assume it to be?

- Who actually took the photograph, and why?

- How do I seem to be feeling in the photograph?

- How does each other family member seem to be feeling?

- Confining my interpretation strictly to the photograph at hand, what kinds of relationships seem to be suggested among the figures?

- What was happening in my life at the time of the photograph? Shortly before? Soon after?

- What was happening around this time in the lives of other people in the photograph?

- If this photograph were the central image in a personal story, what would that story be?

Your responses to these questions can start you on the path to many good personal stories. As a follow-up, do your own memory legwork to answer any lingering questions. Contact individuals who are in the photograph, and who know (or knew) people in the photograph, to get their input. Check out other photographs that somehow relate to this one (same time period, same people, same environment, and/or same type of event). Investigate other materials — personal journals, old letters, historical records, or physical sites — that can tell you more about the photograph, its contents, or its context.

9

ROVING REPORTER FOR THE FAMILY NEWS

The images, inspirations, dreams, nightmares, intuitions, hunches, understandings that arise from the inner world are the prima materia from which everything, including ourselves, is constructed. To be willing to live within the imagination is to commit oneself to the gathering together of the pieces that might begin to form a self. To avoid this territory is to avoid the encounters that might validate, inform, or enhance one's experience.

DEENA METZGER

To uncover and develop story ideas, we must each become a roving reporter—exploring not only outside sources but also, over and over, our own internal memories from long ago, not so long ago, and yesterday. By taking this more curious and active approach to our life, we teach ourselves to value it more. We can then share its wealth with others more confidently and successfully.

Among the most instructive and entertaining subjects to investigate are the family tales we grew up hearing again and again: how our ancestors came to America, the practical joke Mom played on Dad, rumors about a long-lost cousin, the day our sister was born, our grandparents' hilarious business venture, why Aunt Jenny is afraid of cows, the vacation when the hotel caught on fire, the meaning behind Uncle Harry's expression, "I'll wait till my pants fall down." These tales are also *our* personal stories, whether or not we appear in them or were even alive at the time they happened. Because they originated within our own kinship tribe, we are their most appropriate recipients and stewards.

In some respects, these often-repeated stories from our childhood qualify as our most deeply personal tales. We may not remember them clearly now; however, we once listened to them with a very special interest—one that's rarely been duplicated since—and, as a consequence, they had a profound, early impact on our sense of identity.

In *Black Sheep and Kissing Cousins*, Elizabeth Stone claims that many of the family stories we heard as we were growing up have more meaning as myths of belief than facts of history. She says:

> What the family tells us has a force and power that we never quite leave behind. What they tell us is our first syntax, our first grammar, the foundation onto which we later add our own preceptions and modifications. We are not entirely free to challenge the family's beliefs as we might challenge any other system of belief. And even when we do challenge, we half disbelieve ourselves.

Built on this foundation, and deriving strength from it, are all the family stories that accumulated later, during our own waning childhood and afterward: the summer we went camping with our father, the day our sister went off to college, our Uncle Henry's lottery windfall, the time we reunited with our grandmother in a nursing home.

To track down or recollect family stories—or any kind of personal story—our most useful piece of equipment is a good list of questions. First, we must review our own starting-point knowledge to identify gaps that we'd like to fill. In the case of family stories, we might begin by drawing a rough family tree and then identifying which people and branches are the most interesting or mysterious to us, or which figured most or least prominently in family stories. We might even be moved to create what family therapists call a genogram: a more elaborate family tree diagram in which each member's entry includes not only birth, death, and marriage information but also references to educational background, divorces, major illnesses, and any other significant life events deemed noteworthy.

From this kind of research, you might come up with an intriguing question cluster. For example, "What were my grandmothers' three brothers really like? What prompted her brother Robin to move to California? Why did her brother Martin get divorced? How did her brother Jay amass his fortune? Why were they each named after a bird?" You could then ask your grandmother or other relatives for more details. You could also prowl through family records. You might come up with something that makes a great story all on its own or, instead, good secondary material for a larger story about your grandmother, your family in general, or yourself in particular.

Another, less formal way to generate questions about family history or lore is to loaf and invite the soul, as you learned how to do in chapter 4. Our loafing subject could be very broad, like "special family stories." We might come out of the activity remembering only fragments of various stories, tellers, or occasions, but these fragments could be all that we need to construct a list of tasks or questions for memory legwork. We might get better results—sharper images and, therefore, more pointed questions—loafing on a more specific topic: for example, "my father," even "my father's habits," "things my father said," or "my father's favorite possessions."

After you've come up with topics to explore based on your own personal memory review, consider any other questions that are appropriate to the subject in general, or that you'd like to ask the particular people you plan to interview. I've found that the following questions posed to individual family members work well to stimulate storytelling:

What was your childhood like? Your home, neighborhood, school, parents, siblings, pets, chores, meals? Your favorite things to do? The ways you celebrated good times, coped with bad ones, conducted daily or weekly business?

What stories or legends did you hear as a child about the family background? Ancestors, migrations, name origins? Heroes, villains, victims, oddballs? Triumphs, catastrophes, courtships, marriages, feuds, alliances?

What goals or dreams did you have as a young person? What people, events, and things influenced you the most? What major learning experiences did you have?

I am a Harp, that is my history, Irish and Catholic, from steerage to suburbia in three generations.

JOHN GREGORY DUNNE

We never talked, my family. We communicated by putting Ann Landers articles on the refrigerator.

JUDY GOLD

I have an elbow that bends the wrong way, and [when I was a teenager] I'd do things like stand in an elevator and the doors would close, and I'd pretend that my arm had caught caught in it, and then I'd scream, "Ow, ow, put it back!"

GEENA DAVIS

I went straight from shenanigans to crimes against nature.

GEORGE CARLIN

How did you first meet . . . ? Your mate, your mother-in-law, Aunt Mary, me (the questioner)?

What difficult/successful/unusual experiences stand out? In your job history? In your friendships? In your marriage? In raising a family?

What memories do you especially associate with significant people, places, or events? For example, grandfather's funeral? The cabin on Tucker Lake? The Vietnam War protests? Me (the questioner) as a child?

Here are guidelines for making story-related interviews of family members—and other people—easier and more productive:

- If possible, try to meet alone—that is, on a one-to-one basis—with the other person. Keep in mind that interviewing two people separately about the same event can be very informative, especially in regard to the relativity of "truth."

- Choose a time, place, and situation that is comfortable for both you and your interviewer and free from disturbances or distractions. Stay focused on the interview. Don't divide your attention by simultaneoulsy eating a meal, playing cards, or taking a walk.

- Start out the interview on common, familiar ground, so that both of you can relax into the spirit of things. Bring an old photograph, object, or document that you believe the other person might know something about. Or ask the other person to recount a story that you remember him or her telling before. You're almost certain to hear something new now, when you're paying closer attention.

- As much as possible, keep the interview flowing in a conversational manner, even though the other person will be doing most of the talking. To encourage lengthy discussion, ask open-ended questions that can't simply be answered with yes or no. This kind of question tends to begin

I was the seventh of nine children. When you come from that far down you have to struggle to survive.

ROBERT KENNEDY

Courtship stories, whatever else they do, are instructive. To the generation still at home and listening, such stories offer at least one possible way to enter into this intricate human dance; they suggest what to feel about love, how to recognize it, what to do with it. When a courtship story goes sour or when it dies, a resource is lost.

ELIZABETH STONE

with one of a roving reporter's six favorite words: *who*, *what*, *why*, *when*, *where*, and *how*. Listen with your full attention when the other person is speaking, respond to what you hear, and don't make too many abrupt breaks or transitions.

- Although you want to concentrate on what the other person has to say, be prepared to offer a story or two of your own if you're asked, or if you feel it would help to give the other person an example of the type of response you're seeking.

- Come prepared with a list of questions in your head (conceal any written version), but don't expect to cover all of them in the course of the interview. The very first question you ask may tap an unexpected wealth of good material.

- The point is to give the other person a certain amount of freedom to take things where he or she wants to go. In that direction may lie the best story ideas, perhaps even the best answers to questions you never actually get to pose. You can always set up another interview to pursue any remaining questions.

- Remember that you are collecting *stories* and *story ideas* from the other person, not documenting family history (which, perhaps, can be done at another time). In true storyteller/storylistener fashion, rely on your memory to retain what you hear. Put off taking written notes until after the interview. Only use a tape-recorder during the interview if it's unobtrusive and you're both thoroughly comfortable with it.

- Typically, people begin to tire of this kind of probing discussion after about an hour (sometimes earlier). You may want to plan not to conduct this interview for longer than an hour so that you don't wear out the other person and your own memory. However, if, after an hour, you're both still raring to go, talk on, and listen on!

In part VI, we'll examine more aspects of storytelling within the family and in other contexts where you want to inspire story-sharing. Now it's time for you to plan on getting story ideas by assigning yourself specific roving reporter tasks.

ACTIVITY
The Family Beat

Gathering the personal recollections of individual family members can not only give you good story material but also bring you and your interviewees closer together.

First, identify at least one person in your family whom you feel reasonably comfortable about contacting for this purpose. Ideally, the two of you should be able to meet face to face for an hour to engage in the type of discussion just described. If it's impossible, impractical, or undesirable to meet with an actual relative, then identify someone who knows (or knew) your family or who has long been a part of your chosen "family" of intimate friends.

Once you've identified this person, ask yourself the following questions:

1. What people, places, or events in my own past might this person know more about? (State at least two.)

2. For each major person, place, or event that I've identified, what specific, open-ended questions could I pose to this person? (State at least three questions for each item.)

3. Apart from his or her connection to, or insights about, the people, places, and events in my past, what things most interest me about this person's life? (State at least two items.)

4. For each subject of interest that I've identified, what open-ended questions could I pose to this person? (State at least three questions for each item.)

5. How, specifically, should I approach this person and describe the meeting's purpose?

6. What are three different options I could propose to this person for meeting with me? (Include date, time, place in each option.)

Daily our grandfathers are moving out of our lives. . . . When they're gone . . . the eloquent and haunting stories of suffering and sharing and building and healing and planting and harvesting—all these go with them, and what a loss. If this information is to be saved at all, for whatever reason, it must be saved now; and the logical researchers are the grandchildren.

ELIOT WIGGINGTON

What makes the recent reevaluation of reminiscence so culturally significant is that nothing less than our attitude toward old people is at stake.

MARC KAMINSKY

10

FROM ABSTRACTION
TO REALITY

*For the duration of a story,
children may sense how it is to be
old, and the elderly may recall
how it is to be young; men may
try on the experiences of women,
and women those of men.
Through stories, we reach across
the rifts not only of gender and
age but also of race and creed,
geography and class, even the
rifts between species or between
enemies.*

SCOTT RUSSELL SANDERS

It's a stock joke in TV sitcoms: One of the characters, typically the doofus in the cast, launches into a long, rambling reminiscence while the rest of the characters roll their eyes, squirm, and swear under their breaths, waiting for the self-enraptured speaker to shut up. What's the problem? The reminiscence is so specific to the person speaking, and so inscrutable to its listeners, that the latter can't help crying out internally, "What on earth is the point of this story?" Or, more selfishly, "What does this have to do with *me*?"

Like life itself, a good story mediates between two different worlds. One is the concrete world of details—sights, sounds, smells, tastes, textures, and physical actions that an *individual* experiences. The other is the abstract world of concepts—subjects, themes, thoughts, and theories that relate to *common* experience. A good story combines the timebound (specific moments) with the timeless (general meanings). It connects the teller (a specific person) with the outside world (listeners in general).

Most of us can appreciate that an effective story is one that offers distinctive images to appeal to the senses. Most of us can also understand how a talespinner goes about achieving this effectiveness: by refining certain important, concrete details until they're palpable to listeners, giving them "virtual reality" experiences of their own. We're less certain about the story value of stimulating the mind with general concepts, or about how a talespinner accomplishes this feat.

We know how Aesop did it. He would craft his story to fit a definite moral. A thirsty crow finds a pitcher with some water in it but can't reach the water with her beak. She winds up dropping pebbles in the water to raise most of it to beak level. The moral: Necessity is the mother of invention. Many of the family stories I grew up hearing—and enjoying—had similarly strong morals. For every form of bad behavior, from jaywalking to eating raw hot dogs to lying, there seemed to be a tale about a relative who suffered misfortune, injury, illness, or even death, because of it.

Not every story needs a moral. In fact, moralizing is often inappropriate in storytelling. Except when the tale itself conveys a stark and inequivocable message, a moral can mar the beauty of a story's mystery, complexity, or subtlety, and it can rob listeners of the opportunity to extract their own personal meanings from what they've heard.

Nevertheless, every story does need a larger, more idea-based frame of reference than simply its details. Otherwise, it's not so much a story as it is a mere recitation of events. Novelist E. M. Forster once offered a very succinct but instructive illustration of the difference: "To say 'The king died, and then the queen died' is not a story. To say, 'The king died, and then the queen died *of grief*'—now *that* is a story." As listeners to such a story, we may not be royal, and we're certainly not dead, but we have each known grief of some kind, and the concept of grieving to death stirs all sorts of thoughts and speculations in our minds.

In most cases, the more abstract meaning of a story, commonly called its point or points, will emerge naturally and subtly from the way its details are brought out, arranged, and described by the teller. Speaking purely as a narrator, the teller might also make comments from time to time that gently allude

Whether a person counts a theory as true, or relevant, or useful depends upon his or her own autobiography; only through autobiography do theories touch ground.

MICHAEL NOVAK

to larger issues, thus avoiding more explicit thematic statements that might turn the story into a speech or sermon.

For example, suppose you're telling a story about a month-long camp you attended for several summers when you were a child and then later revisited as an adult. Instead of simply recalling what happened during each stay, you could regularly focus on the changes you noted from stay to stay. In doing so, you would be commenting on the universal theme of change—perhaps by referring to certain objects or sites looking safer, scarier, more imposing, or more precious at one age than another. The beginning and ending of your story could also be tailored to support this theme. Assuming your adult trip took place during the fall, when the leaves were turning, you could open the story by referring first to the changing leaves and then to your inner sense of having changed a lot since you were last at the camp. At the close of your story, you could allude to having the same sad or "filled-up" feeling you used to have leaving camp as a kid (hence, some things *don't* change), or you could refer to a new sign you saw on the way out—"Rough Road Ahead"—that immediately had a double meaning for you (namely, the difficult changes to be anticipated in the future).

No matter how a story's meaning is communicated, it needs to be there, at the very heart of the tale, from its inception to its telling, because the meaning of a story is what shapes it for us *and* our listeners, and what gives life to its details. In our own minds, we're subconsciously predisposed to mold almost every experience we have into crude story form to give it a logical structure— a framework for remembering it and investing it with meaning. Thus, actually crafting an experience into a tale to tell others may be just a matter of recognizing and refining the form that's already there in our mind.

In *Ascent of the Mountain, Flight of the Dove*, Michael Novak describes "story" as a category in an individual's worldview that is more concrete than general principles and, at the same time, has greater meaning than day-to-day situations. Thus, an individual's truths are most apparent in his or her stories, since general principles can be the same from person to person despite great differences in the actual lives they lead. Novak states:

> The category "story" . . . helps one to understand why other people misunderstand one's own favorite words, or at least react differently to words or actions than one expects. Often they share the same general principles (liberty, justice, equality, honesty, etc.) and the same goals (peace on earth, domestic tranquility, racial justice, etc.). But the meaning of those principles and goals is different in their story from their bearing in one's own story. The struggle each person is living out is so different from the struggle another person imagines himself to be living out that all such principles and aims have a different meaning in each different story in which they occur.

What all persons have in common is their uniqueness.
SAM KEEN

Emphasizing the value of sharing our personal stories with each other, Novak goes on to say, "If we listen for one another's stories, there is more of a chance that we will understand our differences than if we listen for one another's principles."

How do we apply these insights about "understanding" and "meaning" to developing our story ideas? So far in this book, you've explored your life history according to particular people, places, feelings, or events. Now it's time to consider the opposite approach. It's important to keep in mind that stories can be not only *induced* from specific details (for example, pumping up your precise memories of a solemn pact with your brother into a story about trust) but also *deduced* from abstract concepts (for example, illustrating what community service means to you by telling about your best friend's response to Hurricane Hugo, or your own experience helping out at the town library).

An exercise in this kind of deductive creativity that I use frequently in storytelling workshops features a list of five, arbitrarily chosen abstractions: for example, freedom, love, childhood, February, achievement. For each item, you (as participant) are asked to list specific images in five sensory categories—sight, sound, touch, smell, and taste—that you personally associate with it. By doing so, you practice reaching through a familiar concept to grasp the details that lie behind it in your memory and imagination. In other words, you reconnect with your "story" understanding of ideas.

The real voyage of discovery lies not in seeking new landscapes but in having new eyes.

MARCEL PROUST

For example, the abstract term *freedom* might make you think of a perfectly clear blue sky, without a trace of anything earthbound or humanmade. It's not easy to get this view anymore. Even lying on your back in a huge empty field, you might still see tree limbs, planes, or utility wires. Thinking about this precious sight might bring back memories of a time you climbed to the top of small mountain near your home—perhaps instead of going to school, or keeping a business appointment, or doing your housework—and stared gratefully up at the blue heavens.

Further associating freedom with the scent of salty sea air and the taste of coffee, you might recall a vacation morning on the coast when you spontaneously rowed out to small island and made breakfast over a wood fire. Thinking about the sound of children singing freely from the heart, you may be led to recall a snowy evening when you took kids caroling in the neighborhood. In any event, you're on your way to some freedom tales!

Now it's your turn to experiment with a similar activity. It will help you make stories that have points. Or, if you have no trouble doing that, it will help you make the points in your stories more real.

ACTIVITY
Showing What It Means

This activity is modeled on the one I've just described (using freedom as a concept) but is geared more toward prompting story ideas. In it, you'll be exercising your powers to see through common, abstract terms to the specific story triggers in your own life that you most closely associate with them.

For each numbered abstract word or expression, imagine specific people, places, objects, and events in your own life that somehow relate to it. If you want, you can write down your answers. Then, reviewing your responses, briefly consider possible stories you can develop that might link one or more of the specific images to the abstraction. Again, make notes if you'd like.

1. creativity	2. environmental conservation	3. Don't jump to conclusions	4. resolution
a. specific images: people? places? objects? events?	a. specific images: people? places? objects? events?	a. specific images: people? places? objects? events?	a. specific images: people? places? objects? events?
b. possible stories to develop?	b. possible stories to develop?	b. possible stories to develop?	b. possible stories to develop?

GETTING THE PICTURE

Over the years, I've heard several storytellers recount the same real-life story: After they've finished telling their tales to a group of listeners, a child has come up and said, "Thank you for the movies!"

In each case, the child was absolutely correct. What he or she experienced during the storytelling session, thanks to the skill of the teller, was a dreamlike succession of pictures. To kids of the modern era, that's a movie. A few generations back, children after a good telling might have said, "Thank you for the photographs!" or "Thank you for the paintings!" and they would have been just as accurate.

More than anything else, storytellers trigger visual images in the listener's mind. Thus, it helps enormously if storytellers have a strong visual sense of what they want to communicate.

A wonderfully playful way to come up with story ideas is literally to draw them out. Creating pictures, patterns, or diagrams based on our memories can often key us into whole episodes from our past that are much more difficult to access intellectually.

A possible explanation is that visual images appeal strongly to our brain's right hemisphere, which also gives us our narrative sense of things. Or maybe the mere act of planning and producing a small work of art—even if it's little more than a doodle—indirectly sets in motion a larger, more imaginative memory retrieval process, just as the wave of a baton can stir up a symphony.

Some tellers like to organize or vivify their story thoughts by making sketches of relevant people, animals, buildings, or objects. New York–based storyteller Rafe Martin, for example, drew woolly mammoths to create his wondrously visionary story, "The Boy Who Loved Mammoths," inspired by an elephant-shaped Ice Age boulder he used to play on as a kid. He eventually collaborated with the illustrator Stephen Gammel to produce the award-winning picture book based on this story, *Will's Mammoth*. In his afterword to a third, literary version of the story (*The Boy Who Loved Mammoths*), Martin noted, "Part of the beauty of picture books is that they're very much like storytelling. Listening to a story told, we don't see words in our minds, but pictures."

Other tellers take a more schematic approach to their story-drawing: They draft floorplans of their most memorable rooms or buildings. Reproducing the layout of the house or apartment where we once lived can be a very evocative exercise, especially when we outline significant pieces of furniture, pinpoint spots where meaningful events occurred, and make whatever kind of notes we want about colors, sounds, smells, textures, styles, feelings, moods, changes, and associations.

Even if we can't be precise in our reconstructions, we can learn (or relearn) a surprising amount just by attempting to sketch things as closely as we can to our memories. For example, T.J., a workshop participant in his mid-forties, had difficulty recollecting the exact layout of the apartment where he first lived alone, at age twenty-one. He could roughly locate all the main rooms, but certain odd leftover spaces eluded him. He did recall painting certain newly plastered walls as soon as he moved in. He chose an exceptionally bright gold paint for one wall and a deep green paint for another. Much to his amazement at the time, his landlord, who lived downstairs, didn't raise any objection.

After T. J. finished drawing his floorplan in the workshop, he started storyguiding the other participants on a tour of the apartment, and suddenly he remembered what the leftover odd spaces were. His landlord had completely walled off certain

If you bring forth what is within you, what you bring forth will save you.

JESUS, IN *THE GOSPEL ACCORDING TO THOMAS*

sections of two existing rooms to create hideaways to store his paintings. He had access to these hideaways through cutouts in the ceiling downstairs!

T.J. told us he didn't realize this fact until the week before he moved out of the apartment. His landlord invited him over for a farewell dinner, and was prodded by his wife into showing his paintings to T.J. They'd been made as part of the landlord's psychotherapy. He hadn't wanted to display them openly or throw them out, and he'd had no suitable storage area for them, so he'd created the hideaways.

Describing for us a few of the bizarre images in the paintings (such as a man riding a giant crab into a church), T.J. remembered being simultaneously fascinated, embarrassed, and touched that his landlord had come to trust him so much. He also suddenly figured out why his landlord had been so understanding about the wild wall colors he'd chosen!

We can gain similar story-sparking benefits from drafting floorplans of the homes of close friends or relatives we've visited, schools we've attended, or offices where we've worked. I sketched the layout of my junior high school while developing a story I wanted to tell about my first real girlfriend. This memory tool enabled me to re-envision more vividly the doorway where I first encountered her and the gym where we used to dance.

We can also derive story ideas from reminiscently remapping trips we've taken or territories we've once claimed as our own. I frequently ask participants in my workshops to sketch a map of their childhood neighborhood. One woman came through this activity with a virtually complete story to tell, based on memories that she hadn't previously pieced together in any "storified" way. She began by explaining that her parents were poor when she was a child but the family lived in a wealthy neighborhood, renting an inexpensive apartment over another family's garage. One night, after everyone else was asleep, she sneaked out the front door of this apartment, crawled through some nearby bushes, and climbed over a fence into the yard of big mansion she admired. In an outbuilding in back of the mansion, she found a box of fresh, plump Campfire marshmallows, a delicious luxury

All the wonders you seek are within yourself.

SIR THOMAS BROWNE

112

to her. She couldn't resist stealing it. For the next several months, she slipped out of her garage apartment almost every week and performed the same ritual trek through the bushes and over the fence to filch the box of marshmallows.

Then came a period when, for some forgotten reason or, perhaps, for no reason at all, she ceased making these regular nighttime excursions. Months went by before she did it again; and when she opened the box of stolen marshmallows, she was shocked to find that they were all rock hard. So ended her final raid.

Years later, as an adult living far away from this neighborhood, she returned for a visit. On impulse, she decided to stop by the mansion and admit her childhood crime. The elderly woman who answered the door burst out laughing when she heard the confession and said, "Why, we left those marshmallows out for *you!*"

Gaining a better sense of the places that have shaped our lives doesn't just give us more and richer story ideas. It also helps ground us as individuals and tellers. For these reasons, I encourage you to revisit major sites in your past with renewed, storymaking sensitivity. Above all, I recommend re-experiencing territories from your childhood, when your perception of place was the strongest.

The poet and folklorist Gary Snyder, in his 1990 book of essays *The Practice of the Wild*, says, "The childhood landscape is learned on foot, and a map is inscribed in the mind—trails and pathways and groves—the mean dog, the cranky old man's house, the pasture with a bull in it—going out wider and farther. All of us carry within us a picture of the terrain that was learned roughly between the ages of six and nine." Whether or not we can *remember* the picture, much less translate it into a story to tell, is another matter altogether, and one we'd be wise to take up.

For the moment, however, don't worry about telling stories with your voice. It's now time to let your hands—and the rest of your body—do the talking!

And the end of all our exploring/ Will be to arrive where we started/ And know the place for the first time.

T. S. ELIOT

ACTIVITY
Body Language

This activity helps you take a creative approach to identifying stories that you literally embody. It requires minimal artistic skills, and is guaranteed to yield a wealth of storymaking details that relate to such important, real-life matters as health, physical expression, self-image, and aging.

1. Sketch an approximate outline of your body (frontal view, arms and legs slightly spread) on a blank sheet of paper at least eight and a half by eleven inches. The outlined figure should go from the top of the page to the bottom, with an inch to spare on either end and more space on either side. (Note: This activity becomes even more revealing if you lie down on a huge sheet of paper — for example, butcher's paper — and have someone else draw your actual outline.)

2. In whatever manner seems appropriate, mark and label different parts on the outline (that is, on your "body") that have been affected by any sort of illness, injury, dysfunction, procedure, program, or habit: places where you have scars, broke a bone, suffered an inflammation, made an improvement, and so on. Don't forget to consider, for example, your eyes if you wear glasses, your ever-widening bald spot, your exercise-pumped muscles, your smoke-damaged lungs, or your tattooed ankle.

3. For each place that you've marked, answer the following questions (interpreting them in whatever manner seems appropriate):

   - What events led up to this illness, injury, dysfunction, procedure, program, or habit?

   - What was it like to go through this illness, injury, dysfunction, procedure, program, or habit?

   - What events resulted from it?

4. Review your responses and identify possible story ideas.

12

STORIES WITHIN STORIES

Mention the word *storytelling*, and most people immediately think of folktales, fairy tales, myths, and legends. It is therefore entirely logical that personal stories so often imitate their more conventional counterparts in format, content, and style. It's also completely acceptable and, often, absolutely delightful.

The themes, structures, and devices of folktales, fairy tales, myths, and legends have passed the test of time in popularity. In the process, they have embedded certain story-related archetypes and expectations in the human psyche. These archetypes and expectations affect tellers and listeners alike, regardless of what kind of tale is being told.

Among the easiest and most compelling stories we can create are those that feature a direct interface between a traditional or literary tale and a personal one. When I first began composing stories from my own experience, I frequently adopted this strategy. For instance, after my father died, I wanted to devise a story to memorialize him, if only for my own benefit. He had succumbed to lung cancer after a long, painful ordeal of refusing treatment, denying his fate, and stubbornly relying on round-the-clock family care.

I flew in for the last two weeks of the deathwatch, and it was

Experience is connected to myth. Being immersed in self-experience is living one's own myth, one's own life story. . . . We are our own mythmakers, knowingly or unknowingly.

STANLEY KELEMAN

one of the most exhausting and impressive experiences of my life. For hours at a time, I took my shift sitting next to his bed, and what a strange world that was! The bedroom was awash in bright red: red-flocked wallpaper, sheered red curtains, red shag carpeting on the floor, and, on the bed, red satin sheets and a red satin comforter. In the middle of all this red lay my father, drifting in and out of consciousness as if he were floating up and down on the waves of a crimson sea. While I watched over him, I thought of all the other times I'd seen him navigate troubled waters in the same silent, inwardly defiant way, including the year he and my mother divorced; his subsequent hackabout bachelor phase; and the economically hard, early part of his marriage to my stepmother, when he started making his living selling costume jewelry in carnivals.

I incorporated some details from these periods in my story about my father, but others were too isolated, personal, or potentially upsetting to listeners for me to use. To give the story a more cohesive core, as well as more volume, I injected a homespun version of Hans Christian Andersen's tale "The Steadfast Tin Soldier" directly into the middle. It's a story my father often told me when I was a child. A one-legged tin soldier—there wasn't enough tin to finish him—nevertheless stands tall and proud at all times. He falls in love with a paper ballerina across the toy room who also stands tall and proud on one leg. He imagines she's just like him, but, in fact, she holds her other leg behind her, where he can't see it. The soldier accidentally gets knocked out the window. He goes through many misadventures before being swallowed by a fish, but he always remains steadfast, cherishing the image of the ballerina. The fish is caught and sliced open in a kitchen and, wonder of wonders, it's the same house! He's taken back to the toy room, where he's reunited with the ballerina. Then a mischievous child throws him into the fire. He starts to melt away, though still standing as steadfastly as possible, when suddenly the ballerina (by some trick of the wind?) spins through the air and lands beside him, where she bursts into flame as he dissolves into a pool of lead. I thought of the story numerous times as I watched my father dying, and it became enmeshed with my memories of his troubled past.

I therefore turned my personal story about my father into a story within a story: his life—and especially his death—being the outer, "frame" story, and his version of "The Steadfast Tin Soldier" being the inner story. The latter I pieced together from my own recollections (which were fragmentary) and various published translations, which helped to jog yet more memories of the idiosyncratic way my father had told it. In my father's version the maid comes the next morning and finds a tin heart in the ashes of the fire, and embedded in that heart is a shiny spangle the ballerina wore on her sash. Coincidentally or not, my father actually wound up making part of his living by engraving tin hearts that could be worn as necklaces, so combining the Andersen story with my memories of him seemed all the more appropriate.

There are other formatting alternatives I could have pursued for merging the two tales into one hybrid tale. I could have woven back and forth between them all the way through my story. I could have offered a quick summary of one story as the lead-in for the other. Or, instead of recounting the whole plot of "The Steadfast Tin Soldier" in the story of my father, I could have used it as a running metaphor, borrowing some of its tone, images, and plot twists.

At a recent potluck storytelling dinner, I heard James, a graduate student in environmental science, tell a hybrid story that utilized all three of these alternative formats. He interwove a Vietnamese legend that he'd always liked with memories surrounding his grandmother's death. The legend, which he began by recounting in full, depicts the first death there ever was: a caterpillar turning into what seems, to observing animals, like a gemstone (the gold-flecked chrysalis) and later re-emerging into life as a butterfly.

After recounting the legend, James described the way he worked through his grief over his grandmother's death. He went outside his Massachusetts home and watched a Monarch butterfly

The latest incarnation of Oedipus, the continued romance of Beauty and the Beast, stand this afternoon on the corner of Forty-second Street and Fifth Avenue, waiting for the light to change.

JOSEPH CAMPBELL

lay a single egg on a milkweed leaf. In memory of his grand-mother, he put this leaf in a bottle and kept it with him as he made a trip by car down South. Going through North Carolina, he spent most of one day searching everywhere for a milkweed patch so he could feed the newly hatched caterpillar.

Two thousand miles later, back in Massachusetts, James and his son watched the miraculous breakthrough of the butterfly from the crysalis, and then set the butterfly free in the same field where James found the egg. This coming July, they await the migration of the Monarchs back from Mexico to Massachusetts, including their own butterfly's great granddchildren: the cycle of life continually renewing itself.

At appropriate moments throughout James's reminiscence of that particular Monarch's evolution, he repeated the language—and recreated the wonder—of the Vietnamese legend. Thus, in a beautifully appropriate manner, he recycled the tale, and showed life restorying itself.

David Novak, a California-based storyteller, claims that Kenneth Grahame's classic children's book *The Wind in the Willows* "helped me to see the radiant possibilities of my own memories." In keeping with this experience, he often draws on folktales, myths, or literary works to inspire, shape, or reinforce his own personal tales. Sometimes the influence of the other story is quite subtle, but it still adds a magic touch. Describing his story "Smoke from the Everglades," set in his Florida hometown and tracing a family's disintegration, Novak says, "It begins with my memory of the Everglades burning. The Greeks used this framework. In *Oedipus* a plague covers the land because of the crime committed in the family."

This approach to grafting elements of a traditional or literary tale onto a personal tale is relatively sophisticated and indirect. A much more obvious way for us to combine the two kinds of stories, and thereby capitalize on the strengths of each one, is to create a personal story that's explicitly about our response to a traditional or literary tale.

During my childhood and adolescence, I was much more

We walk through ourselves, meeting robbers, ghosts, giants, old men, young men, wives, widows, brothers-in-love. But always meeting ourselves.

STEPHEN DEDALUS, IN JAMES JOYCE'S *ULYSSES*

rule-abiding than my free-spirited younger brother. As a result, I occasionally suffered what I considered to be unfair consequences, such as not being treated better than my brother, even though I behaved better. Feeling exceptionally self-righteous in these situations, I identified strongly with the New Testament parable of the prodigal son (Luke 15:11). A man gives his two sons their inheritance early, at the younger one's insistence. The younger son then goes off and wastes all his money partying, while the older son stays at home working with his father. When the prodigal younger son returns home destitute, the father throws him a big feast of welcome. The older son complains that he's never received such good treatment, despite his hard work. The father responds that it's right to celebrate so extravagantly because the son that was lost has now been found.

The most important question anyone can ask is: What myth am I living?

CARL JUNG

My personal story concerning this parable, tells about when, why, and how, specifically, I was bothered by it as I grew up—sympathizing with the older brother's complaint and disapproving of the father's answer—until I finally lived through certain incidents in my life that made me appreciate its wisdom. Many women who have heard my story confess to having had a similar life history in relation to the New Testament story of Martha and Mary (Luke 10:38). Jesus comes to visit the two sisters, and Martha does all the meal preparation while her sister Mary just sits listening to Jesus' message. When Martha complains about this, Jesus points out that Mary is doing the thing truly worth doing.

Instead of recounting your ambivalence toward a literary or traditional tale, you may want to talk about how much you've always loved a particular literary or traditional tale and recreate for your listeners those moments in your life when it's had a positive influence. On the other hand, you may relish the chance to lampoon a tale you've always hated by humorously evoking the complications its caused in your life (as I've heard a feminist do with "Cinderella"). Whichever route you take, it's yet another entertaining and enlightening way of telling a story within a story.

119

ACTIVITY
Tale-mates

In this activity, you'll be considering one of your own favorite traditional and literary tales, the impact it's had on your life, and the inspiration it can provide for your own personal stories.

Follow these directions:

1. Identify a story that particularly impressed you as a child, an adult, or both.

2. Thinking about that story, ask yourself the following questions:

    • Who are the main characters? (Briefly describe the personality of each character.)

    • Where does the story take place? (Briefly describe each main setting.)

    • What is the basic plot?

    • What are the story's major themes or subjects?

    • What particular details impress me in the story?

3. Consider separately your response to each of the questions in step 2; ask yourself, question by question, "How does this remind me of, or relate to, something from my own experience?" In each case, if nothing comes to mind immediately, think of the closest possible comparisons you can.

13

MAKING STORIES HAPPEN

We are not totally dependent on mining our long-ago past for anecdotal ore, however rich that soil may be. One of the main virtues of cultivating our inner, storyloving self is that we become more and more sensitive to the potential story material in our present and even our future.

If our curiosity about anything we're doing—or could be doing—in the present or future is strong enough, or if we find ourself suddenly caught up in an especially interesting experience, we can literally live through it with the conscious aim of developing a tale to tell about it. I call this extra-attentive engagement in life "storystalking."

Storystalking is much like the crisis management strategy that's described in chapter 2, in which you stabilize yourself by regularly considering the "story" you're suffering through and pondering its various elements and possibilities. The difference in storystalking is that you apply the same kind of reporterlike detachment and creativity not just to a crisis but also to a good time, a special project, or even a seemingly ordinary situation. And you do so with a much more specific intention to derive a personal story from it.

Different people I know have effectively stalked a story through a career change, a diet, an anniversary bash, a pregnancy, and a month growing a beard. My friend Michele Kinslow volunteered to build sets for a community theater production of

[C]reativity seems to be a combination of hard work and an openness to grace.

JAY O'CALLAHAN

121

The most beautiful music of all is the music of what happens.

IRISH PROVERB

the musical *Little Shop of Horrors* and decided midway through the first week to make her experience into a personal tale. She told that tale during a storytelling concert on the same stage the following year.

Inspired by the success of this venture, Kinslow started a monthly storytelling group with like-minded friends. The same thing happens every meeting: Members each tell a story about a "magic moment" that occurred in their lives during the past month. Kinslow said to me, "At first, because we knew we had to share a magic moment with the rest of the group, we were much more watchful for such moments than we used to be. As time went by, we started admitting to each other that we sometimes made those moments happen so we could talk about them later. I think that's great! I think it says something great about storytelling."

I have stalked stories several times to render vacations all the more meaningful. Once during a solo wilderness excursion in the Adirondacks, I closely monitored what happened as I set up a survivalist-style camp, studied trees with an armload of guidebooks, and nervously watched a huge thunderstorm develop—all because I wanted to have a tale to tell when I returned. Another time I made a premeditated, epic-generating journey through my home state of Ohio, visiting family members, friends, ancient mounds, camping grounds, and sites relating to Johnny Appleseed.

The storyteller Spaulding Gray, who refers to his theatrical monologues as works of "poetic journalism," has spun a career out of storystalking while (among other things) making a movie in Cambodia, writing a novel, and even suffering an eye ailment. He starts the latter monologue by saying, "I think it all began when I was doing a storytelling workshop in upstate New York." During a sensitivity exercise at this workshop, he was gazing into the eyes of a woman he calls Azaria Thornbird, when all of a sudden he saw her face start sliding off her skull. Only later, when something similar happened, did he start thinking the problem might be his vision, and not a quirk in the lighting, some kind of psychic tic, or work-related stress.

Gray continues his story by recounting in winceable detail the awkward consultations and tests he went through with various medical doctors. Afterward, while pondering a baffling array of treatment choices, he reconnected with Azaria Thornbird who, as a trainee in Native American healing, exposed him to a different world of therapy that struck him as equally bizarre. The entire, lengthy reminiscence, using his eye ailment as a continual reference point, meanders in mesmerizing and entertaining ways around the themes of health, sanity, sight, and insight as they threaded through his life during that period.

Occasionally we may want to give ourselves an assignment to do something expressly for the sake of the story we might get out of it. A Los Angeles—based storyteller Vicki Juditz, finding it harder and harder to ignore local headlines and editorials about gun-related violence and self-defense, finally decided for story-making purposes to put herself through the experience of shopping for a gun as if she were truly a prospective buyer, instead of an antigun pacifist.

Juditz returned from this adventure with an enthralling, double-barreled personal story. Beginning with a stark recitation of some of the violent headlines that prompted her decision, her story proceeds in chronological order to reflect her astonishment at the variety of weapons available to the person off the street; the complexity of issues involved in selecting the right gun; the dark, unintentional humor of her shooting trainer's suitably deadpan patter; and her simultaneous attraction and repulsion toward the power of the handgun she finally test-fired.

Being alert to the story prospects that currently exist or lie waiting in our life involves expanding our awareness of *everything* around us. A good way to do this is to practice what Zen teachers call beginner's mind, one that experiences things for the first time—even if it's not, in fact, the first time—to keep itself full of enthusiasm and wide open to all possibilities.

Do you want to weave a tale about the neighborhood you live in? Try walking around it with beginner's mind, as if you were a child, a tourist, or a brand-new resident. What strikes you as interesting? What story angles could you more attentively pursue over the next few weeks?

Do you want to tell a tale about your basset hound? Follow

her around for an hour, or an afternoon, or a day, or a week with a beginner's mind. Pretend you're just getting to know her, or even that you've never been around a dog before. What gets your attention? Amuses you? Makes you wonder?

ACTIVITY
Stories to Stalk

In this activity, you'll be contemplating specific ways that you can go about stalking stories now or in the near future. Here's hoping it helps you better appreciate, enhance, and actualize the story potential in your life!

Follow these directions:

1. Identify at least two personal experiences—adventures, dramas, stages, crises—that you are currently going through.

2. For each experience, ask yourself the following questions, applying creativity and your best guesswork whenever you're stumped for an answer:

   - How did the experience begin? What were its origins?

   - What have been the milestones so far?

   - What have I learned, or accomplished, so far?

   - What remains to be learned or accomplished?

   - Why and how might this experience make a good personal story?

3. Identify two possible occasions for storystalking in the future by answering the following questions:

   - What upcoming events in my life—such as vacations, special projects, or changes in lifestyle—might provide good story material? Why?

   - What contemporary issues, lifestyles, or subjects would I like to know more about? In what ways could I experience these issues, lifestyles, or subjects more directly? How might such an experience make a good personal story?

PART IV

BRINGING YOUR
STORIES TO LIFE

Our task is to say a holy yes to the real things of our life.
NATALIE GOLDBERG

OUT LOUD AND PROUD

Do you ever sing out loud to yourself? In the shower? The living room? Your car? On a beach, sidewalk, woodland trail, or mountaintop? You probably do, and I'll bet you find it wonderfully satisfying.

No doubt you also occasionally talk out loud to yourself, but chances are you feel much more ambivalent about it. In modern times, at least, talking to yourself is considered akin to madness—not as permissible, for some inscrutable reason, as singing out loud. Nevertheless, something deep within our nature does drive each of us to do it from time to time.

I believe that the "something deep within" is our inner story-teller, muttering through the muzzle we habitually make it wear. The ideal way to go about creating personal stories is to let our inner storyteller speak more audibly to us: in other words, to tell our stories out loud to ourselves, however and whenever we want, so that we can actually hear them—and feel them—taking shape. I know from personal experience that this kind of vocalization can be just as thrilling a release as singing to ourselves can be.

The concept seems clear enough, but it initially bewilders my workshop participants. Understandably, if ironically, they're shy about talking to themselves. Many even claim to be self-conscious about it, although, in a literal sense, what actually stands in their way is self-*unconsciousness*—a lack of familiarity with their inner storyteller.

[T]he sound of story is the dominant sound of our life.
REYNOLDS PRICE

Some people think we're made of flesh and blood and bones. Scientists say we're made of atoms. But I think we're made of stories. When we die, that's what people remember, the stories of our lives and the stories that we told.

RUTH STOTTER

Inside each of us is a natural-born storyteller, waiting to be released.

ROBIN MOORE

But the initial embarrassment or discomfort we may get from the sheer act of talking out loud to ourselves soon passes. A more lingering problem may be accepting the idea that we can create a good story simply by articulating it as we go along. This concept not only challenges our trained dependence on writing—rather than vocalizing—to develop stories but also flies in the face of our strongest preconceptions about the creative process.

We are culturally conditioned to believe that there are two basic and opposite modes of creativity. One I call the Newton mode. It involves being suddenly struck with inspiration, just as the famous physicist Sir Isaac Newton, sitting under an apple tree one autumn day in the 1700s, was allegedly hit on the head by a falling apple and simultaneously struck with the theory of gravity. For a would-be talespinner, the Newton experience would be a nearly complete story suddenly flashing into his or her mind, as if by divine intervention.

Once in a blue moon we might indeed be Newtonically blessed with a tale to tell. But if we hold out for this long chance, we cultivate an inner lifestyle of passivity and procrastination that may ultimately be fatal to our art. We can kid ourselves endlessly that the time, place, or situation at hand just isn't ripe for creative fruit. We can keep reassuring ourselves that a good story idea will sooner or later burst into flower all on its own. Meanwhile, most of the story seeds we've scattered here and there in our thoughts and our notebooks begin to rot from neglect.

The other, opposite mode of creativity that we're conditioned to enact is one I call the Sisyphus mode. In Greek mythology, Sisyphus, the king of Corinth, saw the god Zeus abducting a maiden and reported the act to her father. A vengeful Zeus then condemned Sisyphus to an eternally futile struggle in Hades: trying to a shove a heavy boulder over the top of a steep slope, only to have it roll back down, time after time, when he is just short of the summit.

In stark contrast to the Newton model of creativity, the Sisyphus model involves expending a great deal of energy, as if we were fighting against all the odds and the force of gravity itself to push a creative idea "over the top." When we're Sisyphusian, we convince ourselves that being creative means wresting ourselves away to our study day after day, week after week, regardless of our physical or emotional state or whatever else is going on in our lives, to pore over notes, files, books, and blank sheets of paper until we're too exhausted to go on.

In Sisyphus, we have a symbol for the tortured artist, as opposed to the inspired one. Picture your face clenched in concentration, your fist pounding your forehead, the folds of your brain wrinkling ever more deeply in the struggle to forge raw ideas into something tangible and wonderful. After hours of grunting and groaning, you may see a promising end product begin to emerge, only to fall apart moments later, so that you have to start the process all over again, and again, and again, as the clock chimes midnight, one, two, three, Wednesday, Thursday, Friday, June, July, August. It's a far cry from dozing under an apple tree on a lazy afternoon!

Sisyphusian determination may sometimes produce a story. However, it's much more likely to work story ideas to death than to give them life. It also intimidates beginners and, ultimately, wears down even the most committed practitioners. Certainly, it's a very difficult modus operandi to sustain over a lifetime, or in the context of maintaining a well-rounded, day-to-day schedule.

The strategy of developing a story by talking it out loud represents a middle, more feasible path between these two extremes of creativity. Like the Newton mode, it allows an easygoing reliance on what comes naturally. The difference is that we take it upon ourselves to *express* things (in this case, story parts and, eventually, the complete story) rather than just waiting around until they *impress* us. And like the Sisyphus mode, talking out loud involves a certain amount of effort to overcome hopelessness, inertia, or fatigue and get things rolling. The distinction is that we aren't obligated to take on a full load (the complete story) every time, nor do we have to follow a particular path toward a predetermined place. We can wander where we will, play along the way, and, as the poet Theodore Roethke says, "learn by going/ Where we have to go."

Become aware of what is in you. Announce it, pronounce it, produce it, and give birth to it.

MEISTER ECKHART

129

Here is how talking out loud works to help develop a story idea into a completed story:

- **Find a place where, for the time being, you can be comfortable talking out loud to yourself.** It can be any spot that's relatively free from distraction or interruption, and where you don't risk worrying about being overheard. It may be a place where you can move around or take a walk as you talk instead of just sitting still. Over time, you may discover several suitable locations, or you may become relaxed enough with the act of talking to yourself that you can do it wherever and whenever you find yourself alone.

- **Begin by pondering your story idea silently for a few moments.** Divide it into parts or scenes, visualize things you want to describe, imagine what listeners might like—or need—to know, ask yourself questions, or set parameters for playing around. In essence, you are minding and reminding yourself of your story idea's potential aspects and getting yourself prepared to vocalize them.

- **Start talking out loud, spinning out the story as you go along.** Precisely how you do this can vary according to your mood, the material you're working with, or the developmental stage of your idea (you may or may not have already worked out some parts of the story mentally or in writing).

  Some people go for the dramatic and inspiring challenge of talking out loud in a storytelling fashion, speaking as if they were recreating the final story from start to finish in front of a group of rapt listeners. Others like to adopt a more informal, conversational tone, talking as if they were reminiscing to a friend in a leisurely way, unconcerned about the overall sequence or shape of their remarks.

  Alternatively, you may want to imagine that you are answering an interviewer's questions about the life event at issue: You could even play the interviewer's part (literally asking the questions out loud) as well as your own. Or you may simply want to think out loud *about* the story, articulating what you'd like to include, framing questions that arise, practicing different options, and simultaneously listening for solutions.

Whatever form your talking takes, it should be at least roughly as audible and organized as it would be if you were talking to someone else. Avoid muttering or awkward stops and restarts. Evolve some sort of rhythm or logic in the way you speak.

The painting has a life of its own. I try to let it come through.
JACKSON POLLOCK

- **Feel free to pause at appropriate points and silently ponder what you've said already, or what you want to say next.** When you reach the natural end of a certain part of your talking, or when you're stumped about how to continue, give yourself a break for reflection, just as you might in the company of another person. Put off making any written notes until after you've finished the whole talking-aloud session.

  If you feel at ease with a tape recorder and want to record yourself, by all means do so, but use a model with a good, built-in microphone so that your hands and head have some freedom of movement. And don't rely entirely on the tape you produce to assess your performance. The main purpose of this activity is to listen to what you say as you say it, and then use your memory to recall it and refine it later.

- **End the session whenever you decide the time is right.** For concentration's sake, some people like to devote a preset timespan to this activity—anywhere from twenty minutes (my recommended minimum) to an hour or more. Others prefer a more casual, open-ended approach, with the freedom to talk as long as they want, and to stop whenever they feel they've accomplished enough.

  The point is to come to a definite end, rather than tapering off into a sort of half-talking. You can always engage in future sessions of talking aloud to work out yet-undeveloped or unpolished parts of your story.

I suggest talking out loud as the *ideal* way to spin out a story because, in reality, most storytellers I know (including myself) usually rely on a combination of methods to produce a single tale. No matter what expressive technique or combination of techniques you eventually use, first should come *imagining* key moments in your story—giving them visible, tangible, audible, olfactory, and tasty life within your mind, so that these moments can then speak to you with the power of fresh memories. Carl Jung, in his book *Word and Image*, calls this procedure "active imagination" or "dreaming the dream onward." We've already been applying it, during the three previous parts of the book, to individual images from our life experience.

After we perform this initial, internal act of storycreating, which we'll inevitably repeat numerous times as we develop the story, we can begin not only talking the story aloud but also jotting down notes for it, outlining it, doing research for it, and maybe even writing a rough draft of it. Most of us have been so well trained to work out whatever we want to say in writing that it can be very difficult—and sometimes, if our fingers positively itch for a pen or keyboard, senseless—to avoid doing so when we're putting together stories to tell. The point is to wean ourselves from our tendency to rely *solely* on writing as our story-creating medium, and especially from any inclination we have to generate a complete, word-for-word story script.

The secret to the whole enterprise of storytelling is to trust ourselves and, most especially, our vocal powers. If we start giving voice to a personal story idea, it's very likely that a complete and interesting tale will slowly but surely issue forth from within us. The chances are also good that this tale (which may, of course, go through several more revisions) will contain a host of surprising "new" memories that we might not otherwise have accessed. As we've all experienced during certain conversations in our life, the act of talking about an event in our past performs a kind of mental alchemy, whereby we find ourselves speaking of things we

Self-trust is the first secret of success.

RALPH WALDO EMERSON

haven't thought about for years—or things we don't recall ever having thought about before.

Another magic dimension of spontaneous storytelling is that the material we want to communicate often takes its own best shape in the course of the telling itself, as opposed to the shape it might have taken if we had confined ourselves to thinking or writing it out. As much as I believe in the speaking-aloud creative process, I have only developed a story *entirely* from talking it out on five or six occasions. But these have been by far my most exciting creative experiences and have spawned some of my most effective, intimate, and meaningful stories.

The most recent instance of this kind occurred during a communal retreat in upstate New York. Shortly before leaving home for the retreat, I learned that Jeanette, a friend from my Memphis days in the 1970s, was now mentally deteriorating from Alzheimer's disease. Something in the retreat reminded me of the time Jeanette kept a county-commissioned road crew from cutting down a beloved mulberry tree in front of her house. Overnight, she built a sturdy platform up inside the tree branches and attached a sign to the trunk claiming the tree as a community shelter. Starting the next morning, she and various recruits, including me, took turns occupying the "shelter" and announcing loudly to any observers (some of whom were also recruited as shills) why we depended on trees in general, and this tree in particular, for shelter. It was a clever and ultimately successful stunt that I thought might make a good story to pay tribute to Jeanette.

The retreat only allowed one full hour per day of free time, and I decided to use the time to develop my story. Wandering through the surrounding woods, a notebook and pencil in my pocket, I found a wonderful spot to compose: a bank of stones jutting out into the confluence of two heavily swollen streams, across from which was a natural mountainside amphitheater of pine trees, respendently green in full sunlight. The sound of the rushing water was so invigorating, and the alert treescape in front of me was so inspiring, that I wound up telling the story out loud instead of writing notes for it.

As if I were actually introducing Jeanette in conversation to

There are no new plots, there are only new people, new treatment, new reactions, new locations, new times.

ADELA ROGERS ST. JOHNS

Everybody needs his memories. They keep the wolf of insignificance from the door.

SAUL BELLOW

All paths lead to the same goal: to convey to others what we are. And we must pass through solitude and difficulty, isolation and silence, in order to reach forth to the enchanted place where we can dance our clumsy dance and sing our sorrowful song — but in this dance or in this song there are fulfilled the most ancient rites of our conscience in the awareness of being human and of believing in our common destiny.

PABLO NERUDA

the wilderness around me, I didn't begin my tale with the tree incident, as I originally planned, but with the first time I met Jeanette: something I hadn't thought about for a long time. It happened shortly after I moved to Memphis from Boston. I heard other people refer to her as a country-bred expert in local lore, so I arranged to drop by her farmhouse to swap stories. When I got there, her front door was wide open, and she yelled from deep within the house, "Walk straight on back, I'm just fixing us some soup." When I stepped into the kitchen, I saw a woman whom I guessed to be in her mid-fifties, wearing an Ole Miss sweatshirt and camouflage pants. She said, "Come on over here so I can sniff you." I did, and she did. And then she said, "You look so much like my nephew Marcus, I just had to find out if you smelled like him!"

Recalling this bizarre first encounter as I talked to the babbling streams in upstate New York, I suddenly remembered the soup Jeanette was making that day—what she called her three-shelf soup, meaning that she picked up random cans and jars from the three deep shelves in her larder and concocted whatever soup she could out of them and her many homegrown herbs and vegetables. I had forgotten all about that staple of her cooking until the words "fixing us some soup" flew out of my mouth, but over the next hour, it became the metaphor for my whole story: random scenes from Jeanette's random life, which had so recently been transformed into a different, more troubling kind of randomness. The final, twenty-minute story was created right then, right there, on that stony bank, and the tree incident, originally intended to be the whole focus of the story, wound up as one small, quickly sketched scene.

We need to remind ourselves over and over again that storytelling is a *vocal* art. What makes a told story appealing to its listeners differs considerably from what makes a written one pleasing to its readers, which is one of the main reasons I've chosen not to include word-for-word transcripts of told stories in this book. Were I to write a short story about Jeanette, I would certainly use a more literary style, in shaping not only individual sentences and paragraphs but also the story itself. A written story, because of how the mind reads through language to process it, tends to work best when it is organized around a single epiphany or turning point. Therefore, if I were to write a story about Jeanette, I would probably concentrate on elaborating the tree incident—or some other single episode—rather than trying to replicate the narrative string of events that gets spun in the tale I tell about Jeanette.

Aside from keeping in mind that storytelling is a vocal art, we also need to remember that it is a *folk* art, in the broadest sense of the term—an art that emerges naturally from being the "folk" that we are. Acting is also a vocal art, but there's a critical difference. Actors interpret a role from a script. They strive to bring a character to life within a theatrical context, which means speaking their parts verbatim, usually in careful concert with additional and separate elements in a precision-run production, including other actors, scenery, props, costumes, stage directions, lighting cues, and sound effects. Storytelling, in contrast, involves speaking from one's own heart, with one's own voice and style, to bring an entire story to life in a *human* context, as opposed to a theatrical one. The actor Jason Robards, also a much-admired raconteur backstage, explained the difference this way: "When I'm playing a Eugene O'Neill character, I'm playing the character best when Jason Robards disappears. It's exactly the opposite in storytelling. Storytelling is at its best when the story can't be separated from the teller."

In the case of telling a *personal* tale, the self-expressive component is all the stronger, which makes it all the more important for us to listen more closely and creatively to what we naturally have to say. The unique beauty and value of our natural, vocal story-making—as opposed to more formally organized creative efforts like acting or writing—is symbolically conveyed in a Jewish parable I first came across in Nikos Kazantzakis's novel *Report to Greco*.

Long ago, Rabbi Nachman, cherished by his followers for his wisdom and compassion, was asked by a disciple, "Instead of just telling tales like some old grandfather, why don't you produce great literary works, like other distinguished rabbis? That way, everyone can truly find out how wonderful you are!"

The artist is not a special kind of man; every man is a special kind of artist.

SRI COOMARASWAMY

135

As always, Rabbi Nachman responded with a story: "Once an adoring nettle asked a rosebush, 'Tell me, please, what's your secret for making a rose?' The rosebush responded, 'All winter I work the soil with love and hope, and keep just one thing in mind: the rose. The rains pelt me, the winds rip off my leaves, the snows try to freeze me to death, but I stay focused on that one thing: the rose.' "

Leap, and the net will appear.

JULIA CAMERON

Realizing that the rabbi had finished speaking, his disciple said, "I don't understand how your tale answers my question."

The rabbi said, "Whenever I have an idea, for a long time I silently work on it with love and hope. And when I finally open my mouth—what a wonderful mystery!—the idea comes out as a tale. Don't you see? We human beings call it a tale. The rosebush calls it a rose."

ACTIVITY
Writing on the Wind

Developing a story out loud combines the best of talking (giving free rein to your own voice) with the best of writing (putting your thoughts and feelings into pleasing order). Now's your chance to give yourself something to talk about, and find out how that combination feels.

Choose *three* of your favorite or most promising story ideas from among all the options that you've identified in previous activities and/or that occur to you now. Then, select *one* of them to talk out loud at the earliest opportunity. Follow the guidelines on pages 130–32.

You can use the same idea (and whatever you make of it by talking it out) as the basis for each of the story-developing activities in this part of the book. That way, by part V, you'll have a complete story to share.

If you decide to go further and talk out one or both of the remaining two ideas (a good way to determine which one might work best for you to develop as you continue reading this part of the book), be sure to talk out each option *at a separate session*, preferably on a different day, so that you don't exhaust your creativity—or your vocal chords!

CROSSING THE STREAM

15

Often, talking out a story gives us surprisingly fine images and a lot more self-confidence, but we don't come away with a clear sense of having made a retellable story. We're not exactly sure what's missing, but we're likely to assume that the missing element has something to do with *plot*.

Bill Joel, a storyteller based in Hyde Park, New York, and a fellow member of a monthly storyswapping group, once shared a "fool" tale that relates well in concept and imagery to my main belief about plotting out a personal story. A fool was sitting by a broad stream, his brow furrowed in consternation. He didn't know how to swim, couldn't tell how deep the stream might get, and wondered how he would ever get to the other side. A wise-looking man walked in front of the fool to the edge of the stream. The fool was amazed to see that the wise man didn't stop, but proceded to walk on top of the water, straight over to the other side! A short while later, along came another wise man, and he, too, strode right across the water to the far bank. A few moments passed, and a third wise man appeared and did the very same thing. The fool thought to himself, "Well, it must not be hard to cross that stream after all. If they can do it, so can I!" The fool started to walk into the stream and began to disappear below the surface, screaming and waving his arms as he sank. One of the wise men, watching from the other side, said to his companions,

There are just three essentials to a good story: humanity, a point, and the storyteller.

J. FRANK DOBIE

One must work with the creative powers —for not to work with is to work against; in art as in spiritual life, there is no neutral place.

MARY OLIVER

"If only we'd known he wanted to cross, we could have told him where the rocks are!"

When telling a story to others instead of only ourselves, we could blithely prattle on with little notion about where we're going, as we often do in ordinary conversation, and our story *might* turn out okay in our listeners' own and our own estimation. However, we might just as easily find our ourselves drowning in details, vagueness, forgetfulness, or self-doubt.

The primary goal of this book is to help you prepare your stories in advance, not only so that they can be more entertaining, insightful, and true to life, but also so that you can communicate them more skillfully, confidently, and enjoyably. An essential part of this preparation is having a clear sense of where you're going when you tell a story—what major "stones" you need to reach, in what order, to go from where you begin your story to where you want to wind up.

Much to my delight, I found out several years ago that storyteller Donald Davis uses a similar metaphor of crossing a stream on stones to describe navigating one's way through a story. In explaining his sense of the metaphor, Davis points out that it's not just a matter of the teller not needing a full-scale bridge (completely plotted text) to negotiate the stream (story). It's also a matter of the trip being more natural and lively for *both* teller and listener if the teller uses a few well-placed stones rather than a bridge.

In moving from stone to metaphorical stone, a teller becomes actively engaged in each step every time the journey is made. Furthermore, the pace, rhythm, and time span of each telling inevitably varies to suit the particular occasion. The crossing of a bridge, by contrast, is a much less dynamic act to perform or to witness. The teller can easily slip into a half-passive state and stride across the bridge in the same old way, time after time.

So at the other, problematic extreme from the storytellers who erroneously assume they can walk on water are the bridge-dependent storytellers who tend to be overly concerned with plot. These tellers often have trouble even developing a story idea precisely because, right from the start, they intimidate themselves needlessly with the daunting prospect of assembling the most substantial plotline they can. They fail to appreciate the value of simply portraying a person, evoking a place, illuminating an event, or breathing life into an abstraction—all of which are usually much easier points of departure for developing a story than thinking up a plotline.

Assuming that bridge-building tellers do manage to create a plotline that's sufficiently intricate, intriguing, and dramatic to satisfy them, it's also likely to make the telling experience itself more contrived and mechanical. Certainly the act of initially committing the story to memory—and keeping it there—becomes far more complicated and arduous. And if, during a telling, the teller should happen to fall from the bridge (that is, stumble on, or lose track of, the word-for-word plotline), it's much more difficult for him or her to recover and resume in a graceful manner than it is for a teller who simply slips on, or misses, a stone.

Extrapolating from my own bouts with bridge dependency, I suspect that plot-obsessed tellers in general are inclined to confuse the demands of a *written* story with those of a *told* story. A written story definitely requires some sort of carefully controlled, artistically consistent plotline to sustain a reader's interest. In fact, a written story is, by definition, a bridge: a carefully constructed word-for-word narrative that, in itself, never changes from reading to reading.

A told story, however, is meant to have a more open, interactive, lively, homespun quality. In presentation, it works best if it's made up not only of preconceived images (the key story scenes or "stones") but also of many other, spontaneously emerging elements: the teller's on-the-spot energy, mood, imagination, judgment, appearance, and gestures; the audience's perceived needs and cues; the circumstances surrounding the telling occasion; and the influence of the physical setting. Indeed, personal storytelling derives much of its virtue and charm from the "fluidity" that exists all around the stones in a story, and from the teller's freedom to move across these stones in a number of different, impetuous, and captivating ways.

Although a word-for-word bridge can often give a personal storyteller a welcome sense of security (especially a novice or

In Ireland, a writer is looked upon as a failed conversationalist.

ANONYMOUS

When you start a painting, it is somewhat outside you. At the conclusion, you seem to move inside the painting.

FERNANDO BOTERO

nervous teller), I strongly recommend taking, instead, a "major stones" approach to developing, remembering and telling a personal tale as often as possible. It's a delightfully simple process. After you talk aloud to help yourself generate raw material from a story idea, you identify several key moments or incidents—what I like to call key scenes—that you want to be sure to include in any full version of the story.

A key scene, at least by the time it's fully developed, is a specific event in the tale that you re-create in a fair amount of detail. You *depict* something happening instead of just saying that it happened. Typically, you narrate people acting or interacting, often conversing, in a vividly evoked setting. The scene occurs, as you tell it, in something close to "real time," so that the listener has the sensation of witnessing it—or reliving it—as it unfolds.

Scenes of this type are the most significant elements in told story. They magically bring to life a few moments in time and offer the listener unique, vicarious experiences. They're much more vital to a story's effectiveness than a clever plotline, a bunch of intriguing facts, an inspirational message, or a strong punch line. As much as these other elements can enhance a story, it's true value to the listener is the sensation of being "right there" in certain scenes as the teller creates them.

In terms of the stream metaphor I introduced earlier, the key scenes in your story are the big stones that you want to hit as you go from the beginning of the story to its end. These key scenes may or may not involve major plot developments. Suppose you want to create a story about your mother. Instead of spinning a plot around a certain event or period in her life, you may want to organize your story like a portrait gallery, where you offer your listeners, say, three favorite memories (which become key scenes or stepping stones) involving your mother. In simple chronological order, the first scene may be based on an anecdote your grandmother told you about the time your mother ran away from home when she was ten. The second scene may be taken from your parents' courtship: a critical afternoon when your mother, hoping to impress your father with her tennis game, lifted one foot behind her in returning his serve, caught her toe in a chain link fence, and fell. The third scene may be a time when your mother comforted you after you lost your first important career opportunity.

These episodes are worth telling all by themselves, without much interlinking, to give your listener a heartwarming, multidimensional appreciation of your mother. The beginning of the story could be a broad characterization of your mother that somehow fits each of the episodes you recreate: for example, "My mother is a woman who can understand—and heal—the big pains that even the little events in life can cause." The ending of your story could be a simple return to the same solid ground you started from: a restatement of your mother's capacity to bring herself and others through life's little catastrophes, or some sort of general testimony regarding what that talent of hers has meant to you.

Sometimes when you tell this story, you may want to offer additional scenes from your mother's life, or incorporate anecdotes from your own life as a parent, or intersperse humorous commentary on motherhood at different periods in history. These options exist as other, minor stones that you can sometimes step on when you make your way across the stream, depending on your mood and the situation. There may also be times when you may want to stay longer on one key scene (or stone) than the other two.

No matter how you tell the story from time to time, you want to be sure that *every* time you tell it, you touch base with each of the three key scenes. This strategy helps make sure that the story always has the same pleasing wholeness and symmetry in the ears of your listener that you originally designed it to have. It also helps you to keep the entire story together, fresh, and easily recoverable in your memory. Occasionally you can recast separate parts of the story into anecdotes or conversational material as you see fit, but the story as a whole needs to have its own integrity for full-scale storytelling purposes.

As an alternative to a loosely knit "portrait gallery" narrative, you may want to tell a tighter tale that *does* have major plot developments. In fact, we instinctively tend to shape all our stories into the same archetypal, four-step dramatic pattern, as follows:

You shall no longer take things at second or third hand, nor look through the eyes of the dead, nor feed on the spectres in books,/ You shall not look through my eyes either, nor take things from me,/ You shall listen to all sides and filter them from your self.

WALT WHITMAN

141

1. A *starting-point situation*, or status quo, is described.

2. Something changes in that situation or status quo to cause *drama or impending drama*: a catastrophe, a stroke of good fortune, a personal decision, a life passage, a small but potent outside development.

3. A *turning point in the drama* is reached and somehow experienced: a specific crisis, conflict, or challenge.

4. An aftermath, or *end-point situation*, is described.

We create stories and stories create us. It is a rondo.

CHINUA ACHEBE

In this way, you may want to tell a story about the time your mother finally sold the family house, where she was living alone, and moved to a smaller apartment. The key scenes—or "stones"— in this saga might each represent one of the four major parts of your plot. After you briefly describe your mother's life alone in the family house (step 1: all summary with no key scene), your first key scene could take place the morning when your mother struggled to cope with a flooded basement—an event triggering her decision to move (step 2). The next key scene could recall the actual day your mother was moving out and you came over to help her transport a few remaining treasures (step 3). The final key scene could re-create the afternoon when you and your mother returned to the house to check out the remodelling done by the new owner (step 4).

You might also develop a key scene in a story that does *not* represent one of the major developments in the plot. For example, one key scene in the "mother moves out" tale could be about a time when your mother rescued a stray kitten from a tree in the front yard. The scene doesn't directly relate to any of the four plot-development steps outlined earlier. The event itself didn't even occur during the same time period as the other events you're recounting. You simply want that scene in the story because it vividly portrays an aspect of your mother's personality, temperament, coping ability, or association with her home property that's important to the overall tale.

You might also develop a story so that all the key scenes occur during just one phase of the plot development. For example, you might communicate steps 1, 2, and 4 in a summary-style narrative, while step 3—the turning point—consists of three key scenes: the afternoon when your mother showed the house to the eventual purchaser; the evening you took your mother out to celebrate the sale; and moving day.

When you first face the task of developing a story idea into a full story, it often helps to give yourself an arbitrary—and figurative!—whack on the head. This head whack, *somewhat* like Newton's apple, might bring to light a perfect solution. I suggest a head-whack experiment I occasionally use in my storytelling workshops. Here's how it goes: After choosing a subject for a personal tale, you draw three big circles across the length of a large sheet of paper. Then, without worrying about the overall structure of the story, you fill in each circle with notes about *any* single scene that you can relate to your subject. You may be excited to realize in retrospect how interesting these three arbitrarily chosen scenes are, and how smoothly you can weave transitions from one to the other—maybe even in the same order—to tell a complete and satisfying story.

If you already know how you want to develop your story *before* performing this experiment, then you can more consciously fill in the circles in their proper order. You may even want to add two or three circles to accommodate other major scenes you know you want to include. Just be sure to confine your attention to major scenes, rather than drawing circles for every event relating to the story.

In most of my own experiments of this nature, I prefer to stick to a three-circle organization for the sake of practicality. As a professional teller, I have calculated that it takes at least two to three minutes to communicate a scene verbally in enough detail so that a listener can truly experience it, that is, so that the scene is a key one in the story. For print-oriented people, here's a translation: It takes about two minutes to read aloud, at a relaxed, storytelling pace, a single $8\frac{1}{2}$- by 11-inch page of typed, double-spaced print. Thus, three key story scenes are going to take up at least six to nine minutes of telling time. Add at least a minute of introduction, a minute of transition between scenes, and a

I believe [storytelling] to be something that transcends method, technique—the hows and the whys. It is, in the main, spiritual experience which makes storytellers.

RUTH SAWYER

minute of conclusion, and the minimum time for telling the entire story becomes at least ten to thirteen minutes, which, in my opinion, is a good average length for a told story to be: not too short, so the listener has time to settle into it, and not too long, so the listener doesn't get tired of it.

It's not important to be too concerned about time factors when we're first creating a story. We can always expand or cut back a story later on, when it's more secure in our mind. In some cases, it works out very well to create a long story that can be then be customized (and, thereby, shortened) to suit specific occasions. Furthermore, different telling circumstances involve different interest and tolerance levels among listeners. A story that's a long haul for paying customers sitting on stiff folding chairs in a hot tent might be over too soon for loved ones listening while lounging around a cozy den.

My life belongs to the world. I will do what I can.

JAMES DICKEY

ACTIVITY
Stepping Stones

In this activity, you literally draw your own path through a personal tale by going in circles. If this sounds irrational, then all the better! Your main purpose is to have some fun and then look back and see for yourself how much sense it made.

Using the story idea you talked out in chapter fourteen––or any other idea you want to pursue throughout the rest of this part of the book—follow these guidelines:

1. On a large sheet of paper—at least 8 1/2 by 11 inches—draw a big circle for each major scene in your story. The circles should go from left to right in order, so that the first circle represents the first-occurring major scene; the circle to its immediate right, the next-occurring major scene; and so on. If you run out of space, use a second sheet, joined to the righthand side of the first sheet, to continue.

    Be sure to leave some writing space all around each circle. After you've finished drawing circles on an 8 1/2- by 11-inch sheet, for example, there should be a solid band of writing space across the top and the bottom approximately two inches wide.

If you haven't yet developed an overall sense of how you want your story to flow, simply draw three circles and then think of three different scenes that relate to the story. Assign one circle to each scene without worrying about the overall structure of the story.

2. Fill in each circle with pertinent details: what's going to happen in the scene, what sensory images you can use to enliven the scene—whatever notes you want to make. For now, don't worry about writing down everything that occurs to you. Just fill in the circle itself, so that it's well-covered with small but legible words. Don't make any notes *outside* a circle. They come later!

In your notes, avoid indicating options—for example, a note saying, "Max and I either swimming in Logan Lake or climbing Mt. Hugo." Instead, for the "just do it" sake of this activity, make any such choices *before* you write.

3. After you've filled in each circle, think for a few moments about the following:

- How you might *begin* a story with these particular scenes in it

- How you might *make transitions* in the story from one scene (or circle) to another

- How you might *end* the story

Don't make any notes on the sheet until after you have thought through all three things for a while and have arrived at one "final" story line.

And for the sake of the activity, don't change anything you've already written in the circles. Assume these scenes are final. You can revise this sheet any way you want after the activity.

4. At the top of the sheet, write a brief note about how you've decided (at least for the purpose of this activity) to begin the story. Then, underneath the first circle, write a brief note about how you've decided to make the transition from this scene to the next one. Do the same with each circle until the last one. At the bottom of the sheet, write a brief note about how you've decided to end the story.

16

STORYBOARDING

Whether or not a picture's worth a thousand words, a comic book can tell a pretty good tale, as any storyloving kid well knows. Once we've identified and, to some extent, planned the key scenes in a story, we may want to structure it in a more thorough and systematic way by creating a comic book–style storyboard.

The word *storyboard*, coined by filmmakers, commonly refers to a large board holding sketches that depict step-by-step plot progressions in the early stages of developing a movie. Like its cinematic counterpart, a storyboard for tale-plotting purposes is a series of images that represent not just the key scenes in a story but each and every significant shift of scene, perspective, or subject from the beginning of a tale to its end.

We can evolve a storyboard solely in our imagination, or we can also write it out, using an outline format with short phrases for each shift. If we really want to be authentic and give ourselves some valuable, right-brain exercise, we can even make sketches for each shift. Symbolic images—for example, an apple or a dollar sign to represent a point in a story where we go to a grocery store—are generally easy to remember and, therefore, can function as excellent memory aids. More realistic sketches can help us, as we're drawing them, to "see" all the more deeply into that moment of the story.

After we create a storyboard that satisfies us, we can then deposit it in our memory bank, so that it's there to help us revisualize the tale whenever we want to enhance it or retell it. In a sense, the storyboard serves as a compromise between keeping in mind the key stepping-stones in our tale (which is simpler to do, but may not offer enough guidance for longer stories or more formal telling occasions) and, at the other end of the spectrum, memorizing a complete script (which offers more support, but is much more work and may ultimately make our delivery sound staged).

At this point in our exploration of the storycrafting process, we need a complete, fairly long sample personal tale as a basis for further discussion and illustration. Because this is a book and not a live workshop, I'll make an exception to my policy of not transcribing told stories and offer a written version of one of mine.

The stories have grown the storytellers, grown them into who they are.
CLARISSA PINKOLA ESTES

SARA

My puberty began in the spring of 1957, though I didn't know it then. I was just finishing sixth grade in a wealthy suburb of Columbus, Ohio, called, with endearing pretension, Upper Arlington (there is no *Lower* Arlington). One day, I decided to take a closer look at the school I'd be attending for the first time that fall: Upper Arlington Junior and Senior High School.

I rode my blue English racing bike from my home at one end of Upper Arlington to the junior-senior high school at the other end. As usual, it took a half-hour. I braked my bike outside the door to the auditorium. It was propped wide open, and I could hear . . . calliope music! . . . coming from inside. Then, out through the doorway, ran—a gypsy woman! She had bright red lips, purple eyelids, and curly brown masses of hair, and she wore a patchwork jacket and a swirly dress all colors of the rainbow. She laughed, and spun around, and completely took over the scene in front of me. Only when she stopped to catch her breath did I see that she was not a gypsy woman at all, but a girl my age wearing makeup! I really don't know why, but at that instant, I was consumed from head to toe with hatred for this creature. To me, she was outrageous, ridiculous, infuriating!

Then, into the doorway, stepped a high school goddess. She began talking to the infuriating creature. Overhearing scraps of their talk, I realized that the creature was the goddess's little sister. And she was playing the role of a little girl, the smallest of parts, in the high school's production of the musical *Carousel*. The creature and the goddess went back indoors. I peeked after them into the auditorium, and there, on the stage, was a real carousel, slowly spinning around and around and playing "The Carousel Waltz."

I couldn't care less. I was too outraged at the nerve of that creature to exist. I pedalled furiously toward home, standing all the way, my spine positively stiff with indignation. I made the half-hour ride home in a record seventeen minutes!

Summer also went by in record time. That fall, I walked through the door of my new, seventh grade homeroom for the first time, and my world turned to hell—there she sat, that infuriating creature! And by a fluke of alphabetical order, but also by the sheer logic of nightmares, she sat directly across from me on my left. I heard the homeroom teacher call out her name: "Sara Jennings?" It didn't sound bad enough! Then I made the fatal mistake of getting up too fast from my unfamiliar seat. Out from my left pocket fell my tube of Butch Wax!

What, you might ask, is Butch Wax? Well, it was a green, waxy substance in a circular, pushup tube, sort of smelled like limes, that all the guys used back then to prop up their hair across the front, so that their mandatory, GI-style crew cut would look more like a rebellious flat top. Anyway, my tube rolled across the aisle to my left—clackety-clack, clackety-clack—and stopped directly beneath Sara Jenning's glittering, brown, catlike eyes.

She pounced on that Butch Wax like a hyena on a field mouse! "What's this? WAX!" she howled. She pointed to me with a phony look of terror: "Are you *really* the incredible WAX MAN! Did you *really* escape from the incredible WAX MUSEUM?" And she whooped and shrieked with laughter, and so did everyone else.

Except me. I went cold with the manliest, most murderous contempt I had ever felt in my life. I gave it right back to her, I sneered: "What's it to you, Snakehead!" But instead of being stunned into silence by my scathing wit, she laughed, and whooped, and shrieked all the harder!

So began weeks and months of venomous back-and-forth badinage that, I admit, didn't start out very clever, but soon got better, thanks to things going on in the outside world. The Russians launched the first satellite into space that year. It was called *Sputnik*. So Sara and I would call each other things like, "Boogernik!" and "Cootienik!"

Also, Jack Kerouac's book *On the Road* was published that year, and so there was all this new beat language. I would say to Sara, for example, "You crazy chick!" and Sara would say back to me, for example, "Like . . . man, what a weirdo! What a square!" There was also a kind of beat rap, a rhyming way to talk, like "See you later, alligator," to be answered, "After a while, crocodile." So Sara would say to me things like, "Get the facts, ball of wax," and I would answer, "Take a break, rattlesnake."

Anyway, as the year progressed, and the duelling dialogue between Sara and me escalated, something else was going on that really fascinated me. For the first time in my life, I began to realize that everyone around me saw me in a different way:

My mother seemed to think I was her terrible two-year-old come back, only this time wilder and definitely woolier.

My father, I could tell, saw me as a kind of funhouse mirror. When he looked at me, he seemed to catch distorted glimpses of himself: some hilarious, some horrifying.

To my eight-year-old brother, I was a giant force to be reckoned with: sometimes a benevolent giant, like Paul Bunyan; other times, an ogrish adversary—Goliath, Godzilla, or the big Red Communist Menace.

Our neighbor, Mrs. Kirk, clearly saw me as the wild-dog master of our family dog. He was a cairn terrier named Rocky, after the world champion boxer Rocky Marciano, and he was much given to barking, escaping from his yard, and attempting to mount any large female mammal in the neighborhood, including Mrs. Kirk.

My peers and I regarded each other as magical shapeshifters. Our bodies seemed to mutate daily ("mutate" was a big concept in the dawning atomic age; one of Sara's and my favorite insults was, "You mutant!"). We could change our whole image with the flick of a collar or a button. Our personalities were in a constant state of flux. So was life itself! From hour to hour, it could be a blast, a rumble, a Cold War, a Cuban revolution, the Brooklyn Dodgers turning into the Los Angeles Dodgers, a black-and-white standoff in Little Rock: all of which were images very much in people's minds that year.

Most of all, though, life for us kids was a dance. Almost every kid I knew had gone to a cotillion club since the fifth grade to learn how to dance. I myself went to the Frank and Elisha Potts School of Social Dancing. Those years were exceptionally ugly ones in the history of dance. There were three competing cross-currents that had to be acknowledged in every ballroom and cotillion class: (1) the traditional fox trot and waltz, (2) the Latin American dances that remained popular all through the 1950s like the samba, the mambo, and the cha-cha-cha, and (3) the new rock-and-roll, which simply couldn't be ignored. And so a typical evening at the Frank and Elisha Potts School of Social Dancing might include "The Blue Danube Waltz," "Besame Mucho," and "You Ain't Nothin' but a Hound Dog."

At Upper Arlington Junior and Senior High, we were encouraged to dance in the gym during the lunch break—a way of keeping us constructively busy since we weren't allowed to leave the building. The deejays were high school boys, and they played the latest hits. Almost always, fast dances, like "Jailhouse Rock" or "Great Balls of Fire." Very rarely slow dances. Many students, especially in junior high, considered slow dances too mushy to mess with.

Sara Jennings and I both liked to dance. Sara Jennings and I were the same height (girls tended to be taller than boys in the seventh grade, at least back then). Sara Jennings and I were well-known partners in repartee. So Sara Jennings and I occasionally became dancing partners, even though we officially couldn't stand each other. But only for fast dances.

Then, one lunchtime, the last dance was Pat Boone's big new hit, a slow fox trot called "Love Letters in the Sand." I don't know why, the music got to me somehow, I was feeling . . . cool, so I asked Sara to dance. We did, nothing remarkable, but then afterward, as we were heading back to our homeroom, Sara turned to me and said, "Do you want to go to the Sadie Hawkins Day dance with me?" That was an *evening* dance named after a character in the comic strip *Li'l Abner* who ran after men. It was the only evening dance all year when the girls could ask out the boys. I said to Sara, "Okay," and walked away completely flabbergasted: not that she had asked me, but that I had said, "Okay."

In the weeks leading up to the Sadie Hawkins Day dance, nothing changed between Sara and me. Same old enemies. I'd seen enough TV westerns to know I couldn't back out of the dance. Instead, I just kept quiet about it. Of course, word got out—you know how the grapevine is among teenagers. Kids teased me, but I teased right back: standard, daily, junior high warfare.

Then, somehow, my father got wind of it! I swear, I'd said nothing yet at home. But one Saturday, I came in the kitchen for lunch, and my father had stuck into my hot dog a pennant made from a toothpick and a piece of paper, and on the pennant he'd written a single word: "Sara." I fumed, he burst out laughing, I said, "For your information, I am *not* in love with Sara Jennings!" And then, to really zing him, I said, "You . . . don't . . . know . . . what . . . love. . . is!" and stormed off.

The night of the dance came. Sara's father had died a few years before, so my father had to drive. I begged him not to let my little brother ride along in the front seat. On my one previous date, for the graduation dance at the Frank and Elisha Potts School of Social Dancing, my brother had come along and suddenly, apropos of nothing, blurted out to my date, "Jack took a *bath* today!"

My father assured me he wouldn't bring my little brother. Then he said, "Would you like to borrow five dollars to take Sara out afterward for a soda or something?" (Five dollars was a lot back then—I could have bought two steak dinners with that.) I rolled my eyes and said, "No, Dad! I don't want to spend one minute more with Sara Jennings than I absolutely have to!" My dad was sort of exasperated with me. He said, "Jack, what's wrong with Sara? Why are you acting this way?" I thought, "Wow, this is a real man-to-man moment!" I pondered the most . . . worldly answer to give. Finally I said, "Well, she's a little fat in the chest for me."

That night, my father and I pulled up in the car in front of Sara's house. I went to the door and rang the bell. Mrs. Jennings opened the door and ushered me into the front room. Then, in through the opposite doorway, came Sara. A shock bolted right up my spine, just like that first time I saw her. She had on the same swirly dress of many colors she'd had on then. She wasn't wearing the patchwork jacket, though. Instead, she was wearing . . . breasts!

I sailed out of the doorway in her wake. We floated into the back seat of the car. I leaned forward toward the driver's seat and said, "Dad?" He turned around. He looked very . . . owl-eyed. "Yes?" he said. I whispered, "Can I borrow five dollars?"

That's the night I knew that my puberty had definitely begun.

A number of factors coalesced one spring to give birth to "Sara." Among them were a niece's bat mitzvah, dinner party chat regarding how men, unlike women, don't get any clear signal of puberty's onset, and my study of Zen Master Dogen's "Mountains and Rivers Sutra," which talks about the same thing appearing differently to different people and to the same person at different times. However, the ultimate catalyst was a week I spent conducting an Elderhostel workshop on personal storytelling (Elderhostel is a nonprofit educational organization that offers learning and travel programs geared toward people over age 55).

I initially envisioned "Sara" as having four key scenes (or stepping-stones)—the ones that were most vivid in my memory:

1. Riding my bike to check out the junior-senior high, seeing Sara as the gypsy woman, being overwhelmed with fury, and racing home

2. Walking into my homeroom for the first time and seeing Sara, dropping the tube of Butch Wax, being taunted by her, and taunting her back

3. Dancing with Sara to "Love Letters in the Sand" and her asking me to the Sadie Hawkins Day dance

Storytelling is where we share what we've discovered, all of us have discovered a little secret about life.

MICHAEL COTTER

4. The night of the dance: refusing my father's five dollars, seeing Sara in the tight-bodiced dress, responding with a shock similar to my fury on first meeting her, sailing out the door in her wake, asking my father for the five dollars

I could have just ended my "formal" story development as soon as I'd brought these four scenes to sufficient life in my imagination—recalling more details, adding explanatory or transitional passages, and thinking about the ways I could pace, inflect, or "gesturize" my telling. However, because I wanted to develop and tell this story within the context of my Elderhostel workshop, I decided to give it an even tighter structure by devising a written storyboard.

The underlined phrases that follow are my original storyboard notes for "Sara." I've added commentary underneath each note, in brackets, that describes why or how I included that part in the story as a whole and, in some cases, the different ways I've dealt with it in subsequent tellings.

1. **Puberty begins: finishing sixth grade** [I decided to introduce the general concept of puberty right up front, to catch the listener's attention and to give the story a universal point of reference that I could return to at the end of the story.]

2. **Ride my bike to UA jr-sr: see Sara — gyspy woman, then girl my age in makeup — outrageous!** [To accommodate the Dogen-related theme of "appearing differently" that I mentioned above, I wanted to emphasize that I saw Sara first as a gypsy woman, then as a girl my age—something that wasn't clearly thought out in my original memory.]

3. **Sara's sister in doorway: realize she's "little sister," little girl in Carousel** [At first, I wasn't going to include the appearance of Sara's sister. The incident did happen, but it seemed extraneous. However, I decided to incorporate it into my storyboard (representing the "official" full version) to reiterate the theme of "appearing differently":

As I'm telling stories about my life, I'm holding up a mirror to my listeners — trying to jog their memories, getting them to look at their stories, the tales that lace their lives.

ELIZABETH ELLIS

153

Sara being not only a girl my age but also a little sister and an actress playing a little girl.

In some tellings of this story, I eliminate the older sister to save time or to tighten the focus. While I believe it's important always to touch base with the four key scenes of this story when I'm telling it, I feel comfortable eliminating or altering individual storyboard elements from time to time.]

4. **Peek in doorway and see actual carousel** [I included this actual event in my storyboard to add another, puberty-appropriate "spinning" image to the story (like the image of the spinning "gypsy woman" that occurs earlier), as well as to inject, subliminally, the haunting tune of "The Carousel Waltz" into the mind's ear of listeners who might know it. Nevertheless, it's an expendable image if I want to save time.]

5. **Pedal furiously home** [A storyboard doesn't necessarily incorporate all the parts that might be included in a single telling of the story. Sometimes when I tell this story, I add a part about the streets of Upper Arlington being named in alphabetical order after tasteful English towns: Abington, Brixton, Canterbury, Dorset, Edington, Farleigh, and so on. I do this when I want to make the story evoke more about life in a suburb, or when I feel like contrasting more strongly the notion of alphabetical order (as in the homeroom seating that puts Sara next to me) with the notion of overall chaos in puberty.]

6. **I enter homeroom, see Sara, sit next to her, drop my Butch Wax, she picks up, we trade insults** [Everything's true in this story except Sara's name (to protect her privacy, I used a distant sound-alike), Mrs. Kirk's name (same motive), and the precise words that Sara and I exchange on various occasions (although "Waxman," "Boogernik," and "Cootienik" are genuine quotes).]

7. **Refer to Sputnik, Kerouac** [In some tellings, I skip this part to save time.]

8. **Realizing others see me in different ways: mother/two-year-old . . . father/funhouse mirror . . . brother/giant . . . Mrs. Kirk/wild-dog master . . . peers and me/shapeshifters** [This part furthers my "seeing differently" theme, so it's very important to me, but I sometimes skip it, reluctantly, to save time. To help remember the sequence of people, I think of symbolic images: a Madonna and child, next to a funhouse mirror, next to Paul Bunyan, next to Rocky (my dog), next to a pack of shamans (shapeshifters). I do remember realizing, as a twelve- to thirteen-year-old, that different people were seeing me in different ways, but I developed the actual images in my story from present-day hindsight.]

9. **Life constantly changing** [If students are listening, or if I'm telling the story for some sort of commemorative event, I sometimes extend this historical part—adding other images from 1956–57 (for example, the movie *Around the World in 80 Days* or Nevil Shute's anti–nuclear war novel *On the Beach*) or offering more commentary on individual images.

   Rather than recall a fixed list of events each time I tell the story, I trust my memory to recall a sufficient number of "change" events from this year. There are plenty! I didn't originally remember all of them until I consulted reference books.]

10. **Life as a dance—cotillion: waltz-samba-rock-and-roll** [In some tellings, to save time, I go right from saying something like "life for us kids was a dance" to the lunchtime dancing at school, deleting the part about cotillion class.]

11. **Dances at school—"Love Letters"—Sara asks me to Sadie Hawkins** [Sometimes, particularly if there are teenagers in the audience, I add a few details about the lunchtime dances, like the fact that we took off our shoes to protect the gym floor (hence the phrase "sock hops") or how Sara and I would indirectly go about positioning

ourselves near each other, or sending out signals, in order to "become" dance partners.]

12. **Weeks before dance: I keep quiet, but father finds out— hot dog incident** [This story is a family legend, so the dialogue is verbatim from my memory, and the scene itself is especially vivid—perhaps more so than any other single scene in the story. Although my memories of first seeing Sara and, later, realizing she had breasts are also strong, I don't think I ever shared them with anyone until I started developing this story, so I had to work harder to reimagine them in detail.]

13. **Night of dance: no little brother!, five dollars?: no!, Dad: what's wrong?** [In some tellings, to save time and sharpen the focus, I reluctantly drop the part about my brother. The dialogue between me and my father—often recounted when we got together and especially meaningful to me at the time—is exactly as I remember.]

14. **We pull up at Sara's house—I see her in the same dress, but with breasts—I ask father for the five dollars** [This scene is quite memorable and significant to me, so I do a lot with voice, gesture, and pacing to re-create that isn't very well reflected in the written words themselves.]

ACTIVITY
All-Aboarding!

In this activity, you make your own storyboard. It's great practice in creativity. And afterward, you'll have a tool to help you enrich and remember at least one personal story!

Create a step-by-step storyboard for the story idea that you developed in the previous activity, "Stepping-Stones." Feel free to use any outline, graph, chart, or comic strip format you want for your storyboard. You can model it after the one I made for "Sara" (bold-type phrases only), or you can create your own format using words and/or sketches.

ENLIVENING WAYS
AND MEANS

A good story for telling is never static. It constantly changes as it's relived by its teller and its listeners.

As soon as you've established major stepping stones for a personal tale (and, if you decide to do so, a storyboard), you can start playing with methods for expressing individual parts of it more effectively. As time goes by and you continue to think about the story, tell it in different contexts, and get feedback from new listeners, more and more options will inevitably occur to you for handling certain scenes, expanding or contracting the story's overall length, breaking it into smaller anecdotes, or building in segues to other related tales or anecdotes.

"Sara," the story I transcribed in the previous chapter, belongs to a category of especially pliable, adaptable stories that I call knapsack tales, because a knapsack easily takes shape according to the volume of stuff it carries. Knapsack tales can furnish material for a variety of telling situations—from casual chats to concerts, from family dinners to boardrooms, from sickbeds to campfires.

Whenever I've been given permission and space to tell "Sara" as a full story, I always include the four major stepping-stone scenes, but I sometimes delete other scenes that are on my

Each story that we tell is a journey. Each journey we take is a story. Each is an adventure in which we discover our own individual story and the story that is Everyman's.

JENNIFER MUNRO

The role of the storyteller is to awaken the storyteller in others.

JACK ZIPES

The art of storytelling is a co-creative process, requiring both the teller and the listener, working together, to weave the whole fabric of tale, the warp and weft of it. While the teller tells the story, allowing it to unfold, the listener creates an image of what's happening— conjuring up mind pictures— and the story comes alive.

JIMMY NEIL SMITH

official storyboard, or add on to them, or make substitutions. For example, when sharing "Sara" with members of a particular club, I may weave in a related account of my mock-torturous initiation into a secret society for seventh grade boys. Sometimes this additional material replaces my usual references in "Sara" to current events and to other people seeing me differently. On other occasions, I may leave out certain scenes or add others depending on the perceived interest of my listeners or my own whim at the time. I may also borrow parts of this story to use in general conversation. For example, when the talk turns to the subject of father-son relationships, I might share an anecdote derived from the end of "Sara": the part about my father wanting to loan me five dollars for the date, my initial refusal, and my later request.

There are various techniques you can use to enliven the basic storyline you've just developed through storyboarding. (I again refer to examples in "Sara," not because they're especially good, but because they're specific and available.)

- **Add dialogue.** Nothing works better in a story than dialogue to snag a listener's attention, convey the personalities and feelings of characters, and lend a sense of immediacy and authenticity to the events taking place. Since you are, after all, speaking aloud simply to tell the story, you're in a perfect situation to speak aloud (or think aloud) on behalf of its people.

  In "Sara," I made sure to re-create a few examples of teasing between Sara and me, even though it meant putting some words in our mouths that I don't actually recall. Donald Davis says, "When we return to the time of a story, we become the same age we were then." In that spirit, what I say to Sara truly reflects who I am as I tell the story. And what Sara says back to me truly reflects who she is in my memory.

  I chose to portray my father primarily through dialogue because that approach most economically reveals the quality of our relationship, without my having to offer much commentary on it. My brother has such a small part in the story that I give him a spoken line to make him more vivid. Sometimes, to inject my mother's voice and humor into the story, I quote a line I remember her saying once—"Won't you just *try* to act a little more like a human being?"—when I mention her seeing me as her two-year-old come back.

- **Show, don't tell.** This advice is commonly applied to everything from creative writing to behavior modeling, relationships, and Zen koan study. In the context of storytelling, it has two meanings.

  The first meaning is to focus on *re-creating* events rather than simply *reporting* them, as we're inclined to do in ordinary conversations. For example, instead of merely announcing, "I found her hiding behind the garage," guide your listener to see this happen by saying something like, "I went out to the back yard to look for her. I rummaged through the spirea bushes. She wasn't there. I struggled up the beech tree—climbing six tiny wooden blocks nailed into the trunk—until I reached the treehouse. It was empty. The sun was beating down hotter by the minute. I was getting more and more sweaty and angry. Then, out of the corner of my eye, I glimpsed a piece of red cloth disappearing behind the garage. I ran on tiptoe around the other side of the garage. I rounded the corner—and there she stood, frozen in a running stance!"

  The other meaning of "show, don't tell" in storytelling involves using vocal tones, pacing, facial expressions, gestures, and body language to animate certain points, rather than simply stating the points out loud. This important aspect of face-to-face telling is another thing that makes transcripts or written versions of told stories so inadequate and misleading. When I tell "Sara," for example, I literally roll my eyes when I talk to my father, instead of actually saying, "I rolled my eyes." And when I *do* say in the story, "I was consumed from head to toe with hatred," I also show it, in my body lan-

Storytelling is like sailing on a thin silk thread. I'm the ferryman. My listeners make the scenery.

LAURA SIMMS

159

[A] story must be judged according to whether it makes sense. And "making sense" must . . . be understood in its most direct meaning: to make sense is to enliven the senses.

DAVID ABRAM

guage. Elsewhere in the story where it fits, I recommunicate the same hatred by repeating the same body language.

• **Appeal to all five senses.** Incorporate in your story details that stimulate all five senses in your listeners' minds: sight, sound, smell, touch, and taste. You can appeal to a different sense in each of several different images, but it's even more effective to invest a single image with several different sensations.

In "Sara," for example, I appeal to the sense of sight in particular when I refer to "my blue English racing bike" (a stronger visual image than just "my bike"). I create a more potent, multisensory image when talking about my Butch Wax. First I describe its tubular shape and waxy texture (senses of sight and touch). Then I mention that it has a limelike smell (which, like many smells, also suggests a taste). Finally, I mimic the sound of the tube ("clackety-clack, clackety-clack") as it rolls across the floor.

You may find that you have to expand or change your original story line so that it *can* invoke all five senses. In a story about your grandmother, for example, you may have to include, somehow, her favorite food in order to have an image that appeals to the senses of smell and taste. This addition may seem rather mechanical when you first make it, but, in fact, it helps to guarantee that your portrait of your grandmother has a well-rounded life of its own when you share it, and can come to a similarly full life in your listener's imagination.

Now that I've encouraged you to use sensory images in your tale, I have to urge you to do so judiciously. Including too many descriptive details can weigh down your narrative, making it sound more like a written story. A told story needs to be livelier and more action oriented to hold the attention of its listener. This means being selective about details, choosing only ones that are especially clear and compelling.

- **Include ear-catching words and phrases.** Every now and then, drop into your story expressions that are appropriately (or, for comic effect, inappropriately) colorful, humorous, crude, sophisticated, or poetic. These special uses of language not only bolster or reward your listener's attention, but also help you remember the parts of the story where they occur. When telling "Sara," for example, I make it a point always to use the expressions "endearing pretension" and "venomous, back-and-forth badinage." The somewhat affected quality of these expressions communicates that the story is being filtered through a particular personality—one that would make distinctive, slightly awkward word choices.

    Interesting metaphors or comparisons can also add more flavor to a story. Suppose you want to say that the "puka," an exotic fruit you once ate at a friend's house, tasted sour. As if you were a stand-up comic, imagine voices shouting from your audience, "How sour *was* it?" In this case, you might say, "It was so sour, that just to talk about it makes my tongue go dry." A comparison can also be more conventionally explicit, as when I say in "Sara," "She pounced on that Butch Wax like a hyena on a field mouse."

- **Add interesting facts or allusions.** Often, a story is doubly valuable to a listener if it includes interesting pieces of relevant historical or educational information. For instance, a tale involving a turtle's special meaning in your life could refer to the fact that its shell always has thirteen shields, which has special meaning to Native Americans because they associate them with the thirteen annual moons. In "Sara," I mention symbolically relevant current events during the year my puberty began.

    You could also make allusions to other works of art—paintings, musical compositions, novels, movies, poems, folktales—that are similar in theme to your story, or that help to capture the quality of something you mention in the story. In some respects, alluding to another tale can

Our eyeminded society has forgotten the power of the spoken word and emphasized the visual . . . but in storytelling, the full range of language is possible.

AUGUSTA BAKER

161

become a miniaturized variant of the story-within-a-story format discussed in chapter 12.

Colorado-based storyteller Jan Cooper tells a story about dating the prettiest girl in high school in which he uses an extended "Sleeping Beauty" analogy. Alluding to the hundred-year paralysis that the whole kingdom endures between the time Sleeping Beauty falls into a coma and the time the prince kisses her, Cooper speaks of the house where the girl lived as being frozen in a spell, surrounded by thorny hedges, empty streets, and silent, neighboring houses with their curtains pulled shut. He says he worried about what might happen when he finally worked up the nerve to kiss the girl on her living room sofa. He feared that at the first smack of their lips, her never-used fireplace would burst into flames, her drab walls would spew forth wedding bunting, her elderly parents would dash from their rockers to get the preacher, her lethargic hounds would start dancing around them, and her neighbors would rally in front of the house, cheering, waving gift-wrapped toasters, and blocking his escape.

By using an allusion in a satiric way, Cooper gives his personal story a mock-heroic perspective that personal storytellers often adopt, for two main reasons. First, the listener, conditioned since childhood to love the grand, larger-than-life sweep and tone of an epic adventure, gets all the more caught up in wonderment. Second, the teller is thereby able to talk about him- or herself with more detachment, adding to the story's humor and avoiding the pitfalls of being too sentimental, self-important, intimate, or boring.

In addition, satirical allusion to a better-known story accomplishes what *any* kind of allusion does: It conjures up images from the culture at large that help make the teller's own story deeper, more resonant, and more universal.

- **Build in repetitions and catalogues.** Repeating important or interesting words, phrases, facts, or sentence struc-

While we are alive, we tread the same earth on which the ancient shamans danced and sang their spirit songs, and King Arthur's men rode in quest of the Holy Grail. Can it be that our journey through life is to be no less wonderful than theirs?

STEPHEN LARSEN

tures during the course of your story can lend it a pleasing sense of structure and familiarity. It can also add to the story's humor. But perhaps best of all, it can help both you and your listener remember things. Children especially value repetition in stories for all these reasons.

In "Sara," I repeat the full name "Sara Jennings" a lot— partly so people will be more likely to remember it, but also because it suits the way my seventh grade mind obsessed over it. I repeat the name "The Frank and Elisha Potts School of Social Dancing" because it now sounds so quaint.

A catalogue is a quick series of images, like, in "Sara," "a blast, a rumble, a Cold War, a Cuban Revolution," and so on. Sometimes when I'm telling "Sara" to listeners who are around my age, I recount longer catalogues of song titles than I do in the written version given earlier. In a told story, catalogues of specific items or details offer listeners a wealth of images to savor; the mere fact that you, the teller, can provide such a list reassures them that you know what you're talking about.

If you connect with your own mind deep enough, it reverberates for everyone. That's what we call art.

NATALIE GOLDBERG

• **Plan appropriate pacing and inflection.** The best possible equipment for telling personal stories is your own natural voice and vocal style. At this stage in story development, when you've just finished putting your story together, it helps to note the parts of it that you think—or feel—should be told especially slowly or swiftly, loudly or softly, seriously or comically, insistently or tentatively.

Review your story carefully and ask yourself, Where might I pause for a few seconds to let what I've just said linger in the listener's mind? In some cases, pauses help emphasize a point—or set one point distinctly apart from another. In the Butch Wax episode of "Sara," for example, I pause between saying (swiftly), "she whooped and shrieked with laughter, and so did everyone else" and, seconds later, adding (slowly), "Except me." In other cases, pauses can build suspense, reflect the passage of time, change the mood, provide a transition from one subject to

Even if you don't consider yourself an artist, to make something that is beautiful and not destructive, or to make something that is useful and not destructive, that is the healing power of the artist.

ALICE WALKER

another, give the listener a chance to realize something, or offer you *and* your listener a brief opportunity to rest.

Pauses can be some of the most effective moments in a tale. They can also be some of the most difficult to deliver. As speakers taking a pause, we tend to get more and more antsy as each microsecond of silence passes. For this reason alone, it's good to plan certain significant pauses in advance. Another reason to include at least a couple of pauses in your story is to give yourself some remembering space, just in case you need it. In addition, if you've already paused once or twice in a natural (albeit preplanned) manner as you're telling a story, it's easier to insert yet another *unplanned* but still natural-seeming pause when you need to buy time to recall something you've forgotten.

ACTIVITY
The First Official Telling

In this activity, you'll be telling yourself the "final" version of the personal tale you've been developing during this chapter, thereby officially launching it into the airwaves.

As you tell your story, you'll also be listening to it. Primarily, you should simply enjoy feeling the story come to life in your voice and hearing it come to life in your ears. Secondarily, however, you can be listening for ways to enhance it, either as you go along—provided you can do so without interrupting its natural flow—or later, as you reflect on your telling.

Follow these guidelines:

1. Reread each of the story-enlivening techniques already discussed:

   - Add dialogue.
   - Show, don't tell.
   - Appeal to all five senses.
   - Include ear-catching words and phrases.
   - Add interesting facts or allusions.

- Build in repetition and catalogues.

- Plan appropriate pacing and inflection.

2. Choose *one* of these techniques to be especially mindful about as you tell your story.

3. In your usual telling-out-loud place, or some other quiet spot where you can be alone and undistracted, assume a comfortable standing or sitting position, and tell yourself your story as naturally as possible from beginning to end, without stopping, repeating yourself, or jumping ahead.

   If you make a mistake, handle it as best you can without breaking the tale's momentum. Pretend you have other people listening and therefore need to provide a fairly smooth delivery, even if it means sacrificing or changing certain story details on the spot.

If you want, you can think about one or more of the other enlivening techniques during future retellings.

Anytime you tell your story, to yourself or to others, it's best to tell the whole story—rather than just part of it—and then to wait for a while (at least a couple of hours, preferably a day or more) before telling it again. In this way, you preserve the natural, overall flow of the story and allow yourself some time after each telling to reflect on what you've heard.

PART V

YOUR STORYTELLING POWERS IN ACTION

Enough fleas can stop an elephant.
Storytelling is to change the world.
BROTHER BLUE

EMBODYING A STORY

18

After a concert of telling stories about her childhood, Elizabeth Ellis was approached by two young boys from her audience. One of the boys asked in amazement, "Did you memorize all those stories?" The other boy poked him in the side before she could answer, and said, "No, stupid, she knows them by heart!"

Once we give a personal tale a life of its own in our imagination, we then proceed to incorporate it into our larger life, the one we live as we move through, and interact with, the outside world. It's an ongoing process of *embodying* the story—or coming to know it by heart—that differs greatly from the mechanical task of *memorizing* it, or coming to know it by mind.

To memorize a story is to brand it word for word into our conscious, short-term memory so that we won't forget it. Only if we're lucky, and repeat the branding often enough, will the tale burn its way into our long-term memory. The implication (and often, sadly, the reality) is that we aren't familiar enough with it to trust ourselves to remember it any other way.

To embody a story involves living with it, taking pleasure in it, and learning from it, until its every twist and turn has been naturally engraved into our consciousness. It then survives in our memory forever, like a beloved, especially intense life experience that we relive time and time again.

If I were a tree, each story I would tell would be like a new root growing deep into the ground—nurturing, nourishing, and grounding me. What a gift a story is!

DIANNE MACINNES

18

To truly own a story, you must fashion it and shape it, as you would a garment, to fit your frame.

ROBIN MOORE

Memorization is a shortcut, an expedient, a substitute for the slower experience of developing intimacy with a tale. Like any tool, it has its virtues. Memorizing a tale may be dull and frustrating in itself, but at least it's relatively quick and clear-cut: Cast the story into visible words on paper, and repeat these words until we no longer need the paper to recall them.

Coming to know a tale by heart is definitely more relaxing and inspiring, but it's also more prolonged, ambiguous, and intangible—attributes that our cultural conditioning trains us to reject. Instead of actively forcing a story into our memory, we passively allow it to make its own, indelible impressions there.

In order for this memory process to occur, we need to carry the story gently in our minds for several weeks as we go through our daily life, which means taking greater responsibility for "nursing" it. Furthermore, we must check in with it every now and then to make sure it's still there, to deepen our sense of its qualities (literally, its sights, sounds, tastes, smells, and textures), and to examine its meanings in the light of whatever else is happening in our lives.

The full course of embodying a tale requires us to do things that we don't ordinarily do on a regular basis, such as put aside our rush to the finish line, exercise patience with ourselves, and talk to ourselves repeatedly about the same subject matter—each time speaking with a fresh voice and listening with fresh ears. When we do these things, we eventually come to the most satisfying reward we can have as storytellers: *knowing* we have a story to share, instead of *hoping* we can recall it.

Even better, this process of embodiment breeds a very rich, flexible, and multifaceted tale that we can then more easily adapt, in whole or in part, to fit a wider range of telling situations, from conversations to on-stage performances. By keeping a story in our mind, and revisiting it there again and again over an extended period of time, we grow to realize its different images, aspects, dimensions, and possibilities so well that it turns into a knapsack tale: a piece of our storytelling luggage that adjusts to suit any kind of traveling.

Memorization, on the other hand, commits us to one rigid story script that we can't change nearly as easily or comfortably to fit the situation at hand. And, if we forget, fumble, or deliberately alter any one part of this script, we break the preprogrammed rhythm of our delivery and increase the odds that we'll lose track of what comes next. In any event, we can suffer a momentary loss of self-confidence ("I didn't tell the story the *right* way") that, however slight, can mar the rest of the storytelling experience for ourselves and our listeners.

Obviously, I believe that coming to embody a tale—to know it by heart—is better than memorizing it. In actual practice, however, most personal storytellers I've asked, like me, rely to varying degrees on *both* embodiment and memorization to help ensure they can recollect and retell a story for other listeners.

When I broach the subject of embodiment versus memorization in workshops, almost invariably a participant will say something like, "I'm not a natural-born storyteller. I *have* to memorize a story." Aside from the issue of self-defeating behavior (being quick to dictate to yourself what you can or cannot do), there's another problem involved in this attitude—the common misconception that some people are natural-born storytellers and others are not.

Many individuals who have this misconception claim that natural-born storytellers come into the world with a better memory for narratives or a greater facility for delivering them (often referred to as "the gift of gab"). Unlike their less fortunate counterparts, natural-born storytellers don't have to memorize their personal tales to feel capable of, or confident about, telling them well. Other misconceivers make different, more subtle claims that still betray their belief that they lack a natural ability to tell: "My style is more polished [or reserved, sophisticated, urbane, individualistic] than theirs is, so I have to work from a text that I memorize," or "Unlike *them*, I've always been trained to memorize things, so now I need to go through that procedure to really learn a story."

Filling up blank sheets of paper is, indeed, not the same as the sound of your own voice shaping a tale as it wells up out of your memory and as your own fancy plays with all its twists and turns. And the best part of it is that finally by some mysterious process you find that you are listening to the tale yourself as much as the listeners around you.

RICHARD CHASE

Everybody likes to tell a story. Little children do it effortlessly. Great artists do it with native talent and years of practice. Somewhere in between stand you and I.

SYLVIA ZISKIND

171

Capacities clamor to be used and cease their clamor only when they are well used.

ABRAHAM MASLOW

These objections may have a certain degree of merit on a case-by-case basis, at least as entry-level situations, but the overall premise on which they're based is false. We are *all* natural-born storytellers. What makes one teller more effective than another is a matter of commitment, practice, and experience. In other words, it's an *acquired* proficiency, not a built-in one.

One person may have been born, for example, with better vocal equipment than another person, but storytelling is not just a matter of vocal equipment. The person who lacks this endowment can more than make up for it with spontaneity, charm, stateliness, pep, empathy, a flair for drama, intelligence, sensitivity, imagination, an ability to mimic, charisma, humor, physicality, an ear for dialogue, or simply intriguing life material to talk about. This fact renders the concept of a natural-born storyteller as ludicrously redundant as the concept of a natural-born human being!

Storytelling is a simple and exceptionally broad-based art, not a specific, inherited talent. We each have certain innate gifts that we can bring to storytelling, but we each also have to work at developing the craft as a whole. Embodying a tale is a way of *becoming* a storyteller—of living the storytelling life—instead of merely being someone who occasionally spins tales.

On the other hand, while embodying a tale means enhancing our ability to remember things without necessarily memorizing them, it doesn't mean refusing to memorize at all. Suppose you were raised among storytellers, or were well schooled along "whole language" lines (communicating beyond just writing), or enjoy good powers of visualization, or have an extroverted, talkative, risk-taking personality. Because of any one of these factors, you may find it delightfully liberating to give up the drudgery of memorizing written words for the more natural process of embodying a tale. However, you would still be wise to memorize certain key phrases in each tale. It's a means of providing yourself not only with a quick-recall system, but also with an insurance policy against forgetting things during a telling when you're unusually tired, exuberant, or distracted.

On the other hand, if you experienced little storytelling as a child, or grew up addicted to reading or writing, or can't visualize things easily, or have a shy, quiet, order-loving personality, you may find it very scary and difficult *not* to rely heavily on memorization to learn a tale. Memorization can, indeed, offer invaluable support, reassurance, and smoothness of delivery, especially if you're telling in a context that's formal, intimidating, or otherwise out of the ordinary. However, to imbue your storytelling with a more homespun or intimate quality, it would still be a good idea to avoid word-for-word memorization when possible. This means striking a reasonable balance in each tale between words and phrases that you want to tell exactly as you created them, and other passages that you feel comfortable communicating in whatever specific language occurs to you during a particular telling.

I offer below my recommended process—deliberately loose and open-ended—for learning a tale by heart. Note that it includes *both* embodiment and memorization. It's entirely up to you to determine, story by story, the proportion of time and energy you devote to each approach.

Embodying a story is a very personal process that you need to pursue in your own way and at your own pace. Please accept each guideline as a general one, despite the occasionally blunt, directive language that I've used for the sake of clarity. The numbering indicates an approximate sequence of initiating certain activities, not a step-by-step action plan. Many of the numbered activities can be conducted simultaneously or intermittently throughout the period of embodying a tale.

The first time you follow this process, I suggest doing so conscientiously over a period of at least two weeks, preferably three. In the future, with the same tale, you'll find yourself automatically reenacting certain parts of the process at different times, as things happen in the outside world that remind you of the story, or as you tell it to more and more people.

LEARNING A STORY BY HEART

1. After you feel you can recall the story's overall flow (or, if you have one, its storyboard) in your mind, establish and memorize the first words of each major part—the transition passages that take you from one scene to another. (In the written version of my story "Sara," these passages would be the first few words—or even the first full sentence—in each paragraph.)

   If there are other key words, phrases, or passages that you want to be sure to recall verbatim every time you tell the tale, then establish and memorize them as well—each one in its proper sequence.

   No matter how much of the tale you wind up memorizing, always keep an open mind about the possibility of changing things, or of leaving yourself free to use whatever words come naturally as you're telling it.

2. As soon as you can, stop using any written text to remind yourself of what comes next, even if it means not telling a word-perfect version of what's on paper. As soon as you do this, you may discover that you're well satisfied with almost any spoken version that does the job. Cut free from the script, you may even spontaneously give voice to several variations that you like better.

3. Think about your tale every so often during each day. Once you've remembered to do so, let your thoughts evolve naturally. Don't worry about organizing them, or getting anything out of them, or going over the entire tale, or thinking exclusively about it, or keeping your thoughts on it for any particular length of time. The only purpose of this "checking in" activity is to keep you mindful of the tale in a very general way.

4. At least once every three days, review your tale all the way through in your mind. At first, just concentrate on *envi-*

sioning it, scene by scene, as if you were re-showing a movie without paying too much attention to the sound. Gradually, as the reviewing process becomes more comfortable, you can start focusing more closely on actually *telling* the tale in your mind as you're seeing it.

5. At least once every three days, tell your tale *out loud* to yourself, from beginning to end, without undue stopping, pausing, repeating, or skipping around.

   Every now and then when you're telling the story out loud to yourself, make it a point to assume a position that you're likely to use in the future when you're telling the story to other people: for example, sitting in a chair, or standing with freedom to move around, or standing in one place as if you were behind a podium or a stationary microphone. Practicing in this way helps you figure out different physical movements you can make in that posture to support what you're saying, and gives you a "body memory" of having told it in that position before.

   It's also beneficial if you can somehow replicate the larger storytelling environment that you anticipate telling in. For example, if you eventually want to share this tale with your family around the dining room table, tell it once or twice to yourself at the table—or an equivalent—as part of your embodiment process.

6. As you go through your daily life, take mental note of things you think, do, see, hear, smell, taste, or feel that remind you of the tale, or any of its parts. You may get an idea for making a specific moment in the tale more vivid. Even if you don't, you're likely to deepen your appreciation and memory of many of the story's images.

7. Be aware of times when it may be especially appropriate for you to tell the tale to yourself in a more personal, spiritual, ceremonial way: as a source of peace, inspiration, enlivenment, consolation, celebration, grounding, centering, or self-affirmation.

[S]torytelling [is] one of the oldest traditional arts, having its roots in the beginnings of articulate expression. . . . Every traditional storyteller I have heard . . . has shown above everything else that intense urge to share with others what has already moved him deeply.

RUTH SAWYER

8. Think about individuals or groups of people with whom you might share the story in the near future, or occasions in the near future for which the story might be appropriate.

9. Contemplate possible additions, substitutions, or digressions you *could* make in telling the tale. Don't worry—at least for now—about whether you actually would or should do so.

    The purpose of this activity is to broaden your sense of the story's potential scope and interconnection with other images and tales. As a side benefit, it also prepares you for possible expansions or modifications of the story in the future, as the telling challenge or opportunity arises.

    While contemplating different options, consider the following:

    - Related memories from your own life

    - Related incidents or images from the lives of individual characters in the tale

    - Facts or historical events that relate to any part of it

    - Analogies, allusions, or examples that relate to any part of it

10. Contemplate possible deletions or condensations you *could* make in telling the story. Also, consider what parts of it could potentially stand alone as shorter anecdotes. The purpose of this activity is to give you advance practice in trimming—or borrowing from—the story in case the challenge or opportunity arises in the future.

11. When the process of embodying your tale is well underway—that is, when you've dabbled in all the activities just listed and you feel that your heart, as well as your mind, is getting to know the story—time yourself once with a watch or clock as you're telling it aloud to yourself. Then, think-

ing about the lengthening and shortening options you've contemplated (activities 9 and 10), ask yourself:

- What if I had *twice* as much time to tell my story? What might I add? How might my particular listening audience influence my choices?

- What if I had *half* as much time to tell it? What might I leave out? How might my particular listening audience influence my choices?

And the end of all our exploring/ Will be to arrive where we started/ And know the place for the first time.

T. S. ELIOT

The process of embodiment may look daunting in print, but it flows gently in practice. Most of the thinking, noting, and contemplating steps (numbers 3, 6, 7, 8, 9, and 10) come automatically in the aftermath of creating a story, whether or not we intend to do them.

The more unusual and demanding steps are the actual rehearsals: going all the way through the tale in your mind (number 4) and telling it out loud to yourself (number 5). These two steps are the most essential ones in the embodiment process. We gear ourselves up to do them because we value the story, ourselves, and our future listeners. And in time, we discover that we glean a special enjoyment from them—and maybe even a life-sustaining pride.

In her essay "Stories as Equipment for Living," anthropologist Barbara Myerhoff recalls an assignment she once gave to a student: Get a life history from a person who was part of your life but to whom you never paid much mind. The student chose to interview his family's maid—a quiet, illiterate woman. He ultimately taped eighteen hours of her tales about growing up poor, putting a brother through school, being a prostitute, and grappling with hunger. Afterwards, he thanked her profusely for sharing so much of herself. She said, "Oh, you mustn't thank me. You know, every night when I go to sleep, I lay here on my narrow cot, and I memorize my life, in case anybody should ever ask."

In the terms I'm using, the maid was not memorizing but *embodying* her life stories. And the long-awaited time finally came when her stories embodied her.

ACTIVITY
Slow and Easy

This activity will help you begin the process of embodying a story, and will help you appreciate the full beauty of your natural telling voice.

First, go to your usual telling-out-loud place, or some other similarly quiet and private spot. Assume a comfortable position and proceed to tell your story out loud *at a slower pace* than you would normally use. Don't say the words so slowly that it sounds as if you're playing a tape at the wrong speed, or that you lose track of the story's flow. Simply take a second or two of extra time to say each word, phrase, or sentence more resonantly, to listen more closely to its sound, and to derive more pleasure from its feel in your throat, mouth, and ears.

In addition to giving you a greater, more physical awareness of your voice in the story, this activity has a secondary purpose. The most common mistake people make in telling stories is speaking too fast. This tendency is even stronger among tellers who rely on intensive memorization to learn their story. Maybe they want to rush through the story because they're anxious about forgetting anything, or because that's the tempo they've grown used to: the memorizer's "whiz-through-to-see-I've got-it" pace. Rushing may also be due to nervousness, embarrassment, stage fright, overeagerness, or fear of boring or exhausting the listener.

Telling your story out loud and slowly gives you practice in moderating your pace so that listeners can fully get used to, and enjoy, what you're saying. Remember, your story may sound familiar to you, but it's new to them. They need more time to process it than you do! Furthermore, if you learn to tell your tale *on any occasion* just a bit more slowly than you might otherwise be inclined to do, you give yourself more time and space during the telling to recall and re-imagine each scene.

The trail is the thing, not the end of the trail. Travel too fast and you miss all you are traveling for.

LOUIS L'AMOUR

We need to look hard at the stories we create, and wrestle with them. Retell and retell them, and work with them like clay. It is in the retelling and returning that they give us their wisdom.

MARNI GILLARD

19

THE VOICE OF
YOUR BEING

In his classic autobiography *Meetings with Remarkable Men*, spiritual teacher G. I. Gurdjieff shared a story that was told to him by one of his mentors, Father Giovanni. Two traveling brethren used to stay at Father Giovanni's monastery in central Asia every now and then. Although the men were similarly devout and held identical beliefs, their sermons during these visits had profoundly different effects on everyone in the monastery, including Father Giovanni. Brother Sez spoke in a beautifully modulated voice—"like the song of the birds in Paradise"—that mesmerized his listeners as it purled along. By comparison, Brother Ahl, his traveling companion, spoke badly and indistinctly.

Nevertheless, the results were the opposite of what one might expect. The strong impact originally made by Brother Sez's words quickly faded afterward until little or nothing remained in the listener's memory. Meanwhile, Brother Ahl's words, so unimpressive when he uttered them, gradually took on more and more meaning in the listener's memory until finally they were enshrined there forever. Father Giovanni explained: "When we became aware of this and began trying to discover why it was so, we came to the unanimous conclusion that the sermons of

When the heart overflows, it comes out through the mouth.

ETHIOPIAN PROVERB

Brother Sez proceeded only from his mind, and therefore acted on our minds, whereas those of Brother Ahl proceeded from his being and acted on our being."

By extrapolation, this anecdote suggests that what matters most in the sheer physical expression of a story is not a *good* voice, but a voice that *proceeds from one's being*. A voice with a timbre and range that enthralls listeners is definitely an asset, but it is not a requirement. It may get a very gratifying reception during and immediately after the telling, but it can't create an abiding impression all on its own. Just as a personal tale must be true to our selves to ring true to our listeners, so must our storytelling voice be natural—or true to our being—in order to move our listeners in a lasting way.

I often compare good storytelling to the act of inserting a timed-release explosive charge deep within the listener's psyche. It may not go off at the time of implant. As a matter of fact, such a quick explosion may defeat its purpose. Instead, the change may remain quietly, but palpably, where it's been targeted, and only go off later, at a time when the listener is more open to it.

This dynamic usually occurs when a teller communicates a good story of any kind in an essentially "ordinary" voice. The tale sneaks into the listener's mind, rather than making a dramatic entrance, and therefore has a better chance of finding just the right spot to settle down for a while until its optimum time to register has come. So tellers of autobiographical stories, who seek to impart the wisdom or wonders of their lives in a manner that will endure in their audience's memory, tend to speak in their natural voice, one that proceeds from the heart of their being.

Out of respect for our own inner storyteller, we need to relax and value our own natural voice as the proper and best vehicle for our personal tales. However, there are guidelines you can practice as you see fit to make the most of your voice, as well as your tale, during any storytelling venture:

- **Choose a time and environment for telling that works well.** For the sake of both your voice and your story, the time and environment should be relatively quiet, peaceful, and free from distraction or interruption, at least for as long as it will take you to spin your tale. If you're telling to a group that's spread out, ask your listeners to move in closer to you and to each other so you won't have to strain your voice or eyes. If you're telling outdoors, find a secluded spot where the acoustics are good.

It's also best when your listeners can give you their full attention. If, for example, they are wrapping pennies or darning socks when you're about to tell—or if you feel they might start doing so during the tale—ask them in a polite way, before you start, to take a break for a few moments. Emphasize that you have something you'd really like to share with them. Also, as a general rule, avoid storytelling around a dining table until *after* the meal is over, or storytelling to a driving companion until *after* you're out of the car.

Sometimes, the right time and place for one of your personal tales can suddenly come together without any advance planning on your part. It can happen in the course of a conversation. Instead of slipping in a brief anecdote that relates to what's just been said, you realize you can tell an entire story that's appropriate.

Other times, you need to plan the right time and place. You could decide in advance to share a personal tale on a certain special occasion that has already been scheduled— or that you yourself could set up—such as an anniversary party, a picnic with friends, a Halloween gathering, a romantic tryst, or a club meeting (see page 182 for other ideas). If so, give thought to when and where, exactly, would be best to tell, and how to settle your audience into a comfortable listening mode.

You could also aim more generally toward telling a personal tale in the future as a means of dealing with a situation more creatively, or enhancing a relationship with another person or group of people. For example, you could think about the possibility of sharing a story with a convalescing friend, the class you teach, the circle of

GOOD TIMES TO TELL
(A PARTIAL LIST)

anniversary or commemoration	hospital visit or healing ceremony
St. Patrick's Day	Buddha's birthday
retirement party	vigil, watch, or waiting period
Christmas	Memorial Day
bridal or baby shower	vacation
bar/bat mitzvah	Fourth of July
confirmation or coming-of-age celebration	fund-raiser or benefit
Thanksgiving	Labor Day
fireplace, campfire, or bonfire gathering	new moon or full moon night
reunion	Rosh Hashanah
Passover	welcoming party
birthday	Martin Luther King, Jr. Day
farewell or bon voyage party	picnic
Earth Day	christening, baptism, or naming ceremony
dedication, groundbreaking, or startup ceremony	funeral, memorial service, or wake
spring or autumn equinox	saint's day
congratulations party	Veterans Day
Halloween	pep talk
awards banquet	Ramadan
Midsummer Night	house-, apartment-, or officewarming
May Day	Valentine's Day
wedding reception	graduation party
Easter	Kwanzaa
engagement party	roast, testimonial, or tribute
Father's Day	Hanukkah
victory, accomplishment, or good news celebration	sports banquet
	induction, initiation, or investiture ceremony
Mother's Day	Sukkot
winter solstice	commencement party

cronies you meet with on Thursdays, the son who's drifting away from you, or the coworkers you'll be responsible
for motivating over the next six months. The more advance
thought you give, however speculative it may be, to "who,"
"when," and "where," the more easily you will find your
voice as the right listeners, times, and places present themselves.

• **Prepare your listeners.** First, say something short and
simple that lets other people know what you're going to do
and, ideally, asks their permission, such as, "I'd like to tell
you a story—may I?" or "Would you like to hear a story?"
If it's already been established that you're going to tell, or
if asking for permission seems inappropriate or awkward,
just say something transitional like, "I have a story to share
with you that means a lot to me."

Next, offer a *brief* statement that more directly intro-
duces the tale: letting your audience know its subject,
or something relevant about it (without actually explaining its meaning), or any simple reason why you like to
tell it. You don't want to go on too long with introductory remarks or your audience will grow restless. Nor do
you want to devalue or apologize for your voice, style, or
story in any way; for example, by saying things like, "I'm
not very good at this," "This is new to me," or "Bear
with me." The purpose of your introduction is to give
your listeners (and, for that matter, yourself) a few seconds to shift gears and get used to your more personal
voice and rhythm as a storyteller before you actually
begin the tale.

• **Speak mainly in your firm, low-pitched natural voice.**
Aside from talking too fast, the most common storytelling
mistake is speaking in a voice that's too high-pitched, ten-
tative, and thin. It happens because the teller consciously
or subconsciously adopts an artificial, sing-song manner—
much like the one stereotypically associated with story-

*Draw your chair up close to the
edge of the precipice and I'll tell
you a story.*

F. SCOTT FITZGERALD

*A call in the midst of the
    crowd,
My own voice, orotund sweeping
    and final.*

WALT WHITMAN

telling to kids—rather than trusting in his or her own best natural voice.

This unfortunate habit is especially prevalent among women, who are culturally conditioned to avoid asserting themselves when speaking in public, and to cultivate a soft, fragile voice that is presumably more attractive and deferential. However, the habit is also widespread among male storytellers. General shyness or fear can just as easily crimp the chords of one gender as the other.

To counteract any tendency you may have toward a thin, high-pitched voice, listen to yourself as you tell a story, and make a conscious effort to speak audibly and use the full register of your natural voice, including your lower tones. This may require you to speak more formally or thoughtfully—even when you're telling a comic tale—than you normally do, but it doesn't mean you need to speak any the less *naturally*. Chances are you will still be speaking naturally because your voice will proceed from your full being, rather than merely from your throat.

- **Vary the pace, emphasis, and tone of your delivery as appropriate.** Another common fault among storytellers is speaking in a monotone. Practice shifting the manner of your speech in accordance with what you're communicating. For example, active passages should be told more swiftly than reflective, poetic, or descriptive ones. The word "exciting" should sound *!!!EXCITING!!!*; the word "dull," . . . duuullllll . . .

There are other things you can do with your voice that can help give your tale a better structure. Use pauses to create suspense, humor, or narrative breaks. Vocally punctuate parts of the story that are especially important for your listeners to remember. Soothe their ears in moments that are especially tranquil. And build up interest as you approach the climax.

184

- **Create distinctive vocal styles for each speaker in your story.** Another way to avoid monotony in a story is to speak each character's words in a slightly different voice—if possible, one that's based on a quality of his or her real-life voice; if not, one that's somehow appropriate for that person in the context of your tale. This technique also augments your listeners' interest in each character and helps them keep better track of who said what.

  Creating these distinctive vocal styles does not mean radically changing the natural voice you use to narrate the story. You simply exercise different parts of it to bring different characters to life. One person in your tale might speak more laconically, with a more pronounced twang, than you or any other character does. Another person may have an overall vocal mode that's a shade deeper, higher, raspier, sillier, more abrupt, or more cynical.

  Don't strain yourself to create these imitative voices. If you do, you may sound as if you're performing a theater piece, which, though splendid in itself, might disconcert listeners who expect a more homespun, personalized tale. Instead, imagine that you are having fun recalling and mimicking different characters with a close friend. That may, after all, be exactly what you're doing!

- **Include gestures, body language, and postures in telling your story.** Think of your body as having another, coordinate voice that you can bring to your tale. Plan to use it in expressing things that are especially appropriate for its voice, rather than for your throat's voice.

  For example, instead of saying, "He shook his finger at me and snarled, 'You'll pay for this!'," shake your own finger in the same way and say, "You'll pay for this!" in a snarly voice. Shrug your shoulders when you talk about not knowing what to do (or *instead* of talking about it). Close your eyes and smile when you allude to being in love. Imitate handing a letter to someone else when you describe doing so. You may even want to give each character a distinctive gesture or posture as he or she speaks.

Don't strain yourself to create physical images or moves that don't suggest themselves naturally, either when you first create the story or anytime afterward. If you're not very expressive with your face or body in everyday life, then you're very likely to feel and look weird morphing into a mime to deliver a story.

Alternatively, you don't want to turn rigid or develop nervous mannerisms when you tell—something that often happens to people who are self-conscious or self-restrictive about physical movement. Making sure that you have a few simple different things to do with your face, hands, and body in the course of spinning a tale helps prevent these problems.

Think of physical activity as what naturalist David Abram calls the bodying-forth of emotion. It shouldn't be utterly wild or completely contrived but should be modulated into your own form of human expression, as your voice is. In fact, Abram claims the voice is, in essence, a bodily gesture: "a vocal gesticulation wherein the meaning is inseparable from the sound, the shape, the rhythm of the words." Therein lies the unique beauty of a told story as compared to a written one.

- **Maintain rapport with your listeners as you tell.** Stay in contact with their eyes, looking away only briefly to "see" things that you're narrating. If you're telling to a group, regularly scan all the faces, so that you look at each individual listener from time to time while you're speaking.

  As you tell, note how your audience is responding to your tale—not just with your eyes, but also with your ears and your intuition. Appearances can be deceiving. However, if your listeners' attention *seems* to be wandering, it won't hurt to inject a little more energy or drama into your delivery. If they're obviously responding well to a certain part—laughing or looking spellbound—let yourself enjoy

In my stories, I want to prompt my listeners to visualize—to go places with me, back to places they know, places they have been. And if I can get them laughing at their own memories, laughing at things in their own lives, then they are protected, and they'll go anywhere and see anything with me.

DONALD DAVIS

it too. Then put special effort into sustaining that interest or rekindling it during other, similar parts of the story.

- **Bring the telling to a gentle but definite close.** Last impressions are important in storytelling. You don't want to end too abruptly, or taper off too listlessly, or create an annoying series of false endings, when the tale appears to be over but really isn't. To avoid these pitfalls, use your voice, language, and pacing to help your listener know when the end is coming up and, finally, when it's been reached.

  Different stories may require—or benefit from—different strategies, but here are some general recommendations:

  - Set up the ending by alluding to it earlier in the story: for example, as the climatic event you're anticipating, or as the third of three escapades you want to describe.

  - State directly that the end is coming; for example, by saying, "The final outcome was a little sad," or "There was one last thing she had to do."

  - Gradually slow your pace as you speak in an increasingly firm, distinct voice.

  - Put special emphasis on the final few words.

  As soon as you've finished your tale, it's often a good idea to say so point blank: for example, "And that's how Aunt Madge caught the elephant!" (repeating the opening line) or simply, "And that's the end of my story." Ending this way prevents any awkwardness or embarrassment that might otherwise occur if your listeners don't realize you've finished. Remember: You know your story far better than they do, so what strikes you as a clear ending may only seem like a pause to them.

  It's always appropriate to thank your audience for listening. Depending on the situation, you may also want to invite them to tell *their* tales, either right away or at some

The telling of stories, like singing and praying, would seem to be an almost ceremonial act, an ancient and necessary mode of speech that tends the earthly rootedness of language.

DAVID ABRAM

Although setbacks of all kinds may discourage us, the grand, old process of storytelling puts us in touch with strengths we may have forgotten, with wisdom that has faded or disappeared, and with hopes that have fallen into darkness.

NANCY MELLON

later time. It's a great way to build community and to gain new storytelling insights.

I offer these vocal guidelines only to give you some options and ideas to play with in your own storytelling endeavors. Just in case they've had the opposite, unintended effect of intimidating you, let me share a moment from one of my favorite mythic tales that says something very comforting and inspiring about the simple, natural "voice of your being."

The tale is "The Children of Lir," an ancient narrative from the Irish oral tradition that survives today in several written versions. In Welsh mythology, the Celtic god Lir became Llyr, the prototype for Shakespeare's tragic King Lear, who seeks to divide his kingdom among his three daughters. In Ireland, he has been known for centuries as the grieving father of four children turned into swans by their jealous stepmother.

In the version I tell, the Irish goddess Brigid, Lir's sister and (like her later Christian incarnation, Saint Brigid) the patron of storytellers, is the one who discovers the terrified swan-children afloat on Lake Darvra soon after their transformation. Overcome with sorrow, she cries out to them from the shore, "Oh my dear children, I cannot undo the spell that has changed you. But I hereby give you the power to sing what is dearest in your hearts, and those songs shall bring beauty and hope to all who hear them." And so the swans live a worthy existence, despite what has happened to them.

We have each been shaped by our experience, for good or for ill, in ways that we cannot change. But, as part of the bargain, we each have the power to sing from our heart about our life in ways that bless our listeners.

ACTIVITY
Giving the Gift of Story

This action-planning exercise is a means of committing yourself to give a person or group of people the gift of one of your personal stories. Thinking of the tale you brought to life in part IV—or any other one you've created or can develop in the near future—follow these directions:

1. Identify people or groups of people who might enjoy hearing your tale. Generate at least two possibile audiences. For each one, ask yourself:

   • Why would this person or group enjoy my story? (If you're not certain, give possible reasons.)

   • When and where, specifically, could I tell my story to this person or group? (Consider special situations that you could arrange, as well as situations that are already established or routine in your relationship with this person or group.)

   • How, specifically, could I let this person or group know that I want to tell a personal story? (Consider different options for each person or group.)

2. After pondering all your responses to step 1 above, choose at least one person or group to hear your story.

3. Before contacting this person or group, choose at least one specific time and place to suggest for the telling. If your story is new, be sure to allow enough time before the telling to learn the story by heart (preferably two to three weeks: see the guidelines in chapter 18).

4. Contact this person or group and agree on a time and place for the telling—unless, of course, you want it to be a surprise and can arrange for it to happen all on your own.

Stories are "love gifts."
LEWIS CARROLL

Sharing a story stirs the imagination, pulls a heartstring, tickles a funny bone; it allows us to give the greatest gift — a part of ourself.
JOAN BRANYAN-WARD AND
JOHN WARD

20

THE MANY WORLDS OF PERSONAL STORYTELLING

[W]e ourselves are characters within a huge story that is visibly unfolding all around us, participants within the vast imagination, or Dreaming, of the world.

DAVID ABRAM

Our lives consist of worlds within worlds within worlds: private domains and public sectors; family circles, business rounds, and social spheres; fantasy realms and brutal realities; present, past, and future scenarios. Through personal storytelling, we can journey among all these worlds in a host of new ways that benefit ourselves and everyone around us.

In part III, I made a distinction between big stories (about major, self-defining life events) and little ones (about smaller-scale dramas). Often tellers find themselves specializing in one category rather than the other. There's nothing wrong with that. However, if we become habituated to telling *only* one type, fearing or discounting the other one entirely, we limit our true potential. In this case, growing as storytellers means learning to love communicating *both* kinds of tales.

An even more prevalent and possibly more crippling phenomenon is the tendency to tell personal stories in only a few contexts. We may tell to our family members and friends but never to our coworkers; in our homes and offices but never in our community; for getting laughs and making points but never for inspiring the soul; when we're with people we know but never among strangers.

It is crucial for us as storytellers to learn to love bringing our tales into every major context of our lives. Only then can storytelling evolve into an integral aspect of who we are. Only then can who we are totally blossom within our storytelling. And only then can storytelling perform its full magic in our own lives and those of our listeners.

In this and the next three chapters, we'll explore three major life contexts for storytelling:

- **Family storytelling**: to our immediate family, other relatives, extended family, and family of close friends

- **Storytelling at work**: to our coworkers, staff members, bosses, trainees, clients, and business associates

- **Storytelling in the community**: to individuals and groups in our neighborhoods, towns, cities, countrysides, ecological niches, and spiritual congregations

As you read these chapters, you may well think of other contexts for storytelling, or different ways of parsing or describing the ones I offer here.

Equipping ourselves to tell personal stories in each of these three contexts may require us to develop and embody three distinct varieties of tales: some about domestic or family matters, others relating to the workplace, and another batch involving local, regional, or spiritual issues. It's far more likely, however, that the same tale will work in two or all three contexts, with only slight modifications in the way it's introduced or delivered. This is especially true of knapsack tales, which are highly flexible in their structure, length, wording, emphasis, and tone.

I'll give you an example of how a knapsack story can be adapted to fit each of the three contexts. A tale I often tell concerns an exceptionally long, cold, and snowy winter a few years ago, during which both the local wildlife and I had to stretch ourselves to survive.

That winter, I spent more time than usual in the dining

We have before us the question not simply of physical survival but of survival and development into intelligent, affectionate, imaginative persons thoroughly enjoying the universe about us, living in profound communion with one another.

THOMAS BERRY

We cannot live only for ourselves. A thousand fibers connect us with our fellow men; and among these fibers, as sympathetic threads, our actions run as causes, and they come back to us as effects.

HERMAN MELVILLE

room of my house near the woodstove, the sole source of heat. By the middle of January, the snow was so deep in the yard that I couldn't reach the birdfeeders or tree-mounted suet holders. All I could do was repeatedly clear a long swath of the outside deck railing nearest the house and leave birdseed there. Sitting at my dining room table, I would look out the window at this feed-strewn space about twelve feet away and witness such normally incompatible critters as squirrels, blue jays, cardinals, and tufted titmice (small gray birds with jaunty crests) eating so closely together that their bodies sometimes touched.

But I wasn't always watching. Occasionally the space would empty of feed or fill with snow without my noticing it. One morning, after yet another blizzard, I was lingering over a mug of coffee at the dining room table when I heard a sharp tapping on the window beside me. I looked, and a titmouse was banging on the pane with its beak! As soon as we made eye contact (we were inches apart), it flew over to the snow-covered deck railing, zigzagged back and forth above it, and then darted back to the window. I knew for sure that it was asking me to put out new feed, so I did. Within seconds, birds and squirrels converged from all directions to chow down.

When I want to gear this story toward a particular context, I introduce and tell it from a slightly different, expressly appropriate perspective—adding, subtracting, minimizing, or maximizing details accordingly. I never actually change the core of the narrative or stray from the truth of what happened. I simply choose my emphasis, tone, language, and interpretation to fit the telling situation.

Here are some of the adaptations I make for each context:

- **Family storytelling:** I spend more time talking about my home environment, daily rituals, and personal "hungers" that winter. The point of view centers more around how I dealt with the unusually severe weather: sometimes comically or ineptly, other times stoically or resourcefully. I gradually come to focus on the wildlife—and, ultimately, the titmouse—as fellow sufferers.

- **Storytelling at work**: Because I'm a storyteller and writer by profession, I more pointedly use words and images that evoke the themes of isolation (an aspect of both trades), communication (between the bird and me), and inspiration (the simple but impressive tapping episode evolving into a tale). In the larger field of business in general, the tale can be told as a parable of supply and demand, customer service, attentiveness to signals in the environment, and/or management challenges and responsibilities.

- **Storytelling in the community**: I add references to how other people in the area where I live coped with that horrendous winter. The tale as a whole is more geared toward the subject of the individual versus the group (me versus other, similarly homebound neighbors; me versus the local wildlife; and the individual animal versus the starving collective). I also spend more time describing the physical region (mid–Hudson River valley)—its weather, flora, and fauna.

    To give the story a more spiritual cast, I dwell on how moved I was by the titmouse's intelligence, bravery, and trust, as well as by the fact that we connected so strongly at that moment of tapping, despite being members of different species. I create a dramatic contrast between the starkness, severity, and lifelessness of the winter and the beauty, tolerance, and liveliness of the animals. The story talks about nourishment on a number of different levels.

Each of these storytelling contexts—family, work, and community—offers its own unique learning experiences and enrichment opportunities, which is why we have so much to gain from applying ourselves to all three. We'll be exploring them individually in the next three chapters.

In my life, the stories I have heard from my family, my friends, my community, and from willing stangers all over the world have been the true source of my education. They have taught me humor, compassion, and courage.

HOLLY NEAR

ACTIVITY
Shifting Perspective

Examining how you might alter the introduction, content, or delivery of a personal tale to fit different contexts helps you to recognize and take advantage of more opportunities to tell it.

Think about the story you developed in part IV, or any other personal tale you want, and ask yourself these questions:

1. What aspects of the story (or its background) might especially interest family members or close friends?

2. What aspects might especially interest people with whom I work?

3. What aspects might interest different people or groups who live in my community or who attend the same religious institution I do?

4. How could I introduce the story, modify it, or adjust the way I tell it to better appeal to each of these three audiences?

We are all humans — and stories remind us of our humanity, our sense of fun and wonder and struggle. The stories you begin to collect can be personal . . . but tell them, tell them, tell them.

JAY O'CALLAHAN

21

FAMILY STORYTELLING

O̲ur families—the people related to us by blood, marriage, or love who are intimate parts of our ongoing lives—are the best possible source for our storylistening and storycreating endeavors. It's only logical, therefore, that they also represent the best possible audience for our storytelling ventures.

Because bonds of care and common experience already connect us to family members, we can easily shape our personal narratives to appeal specifically to them. We can also be more confident that our tales will get a warm reception. And because we know, and frequently share, the rhythm of our family members' day-to-day existence, we can more easily anticipate, schedule, and encounter opportunities to tell stories. We can even develop regular traditions for it—on holidays or whenever there's something to celebrate.

Throughout human history, storytelling has played a vital role in easing communication within families and in perpetuating family history, identity, and solidarity from person to person and generation to generation. It's a singularly effective way to honor what's special in the family experience: a birth, an adventure, a victory, an act of heroism, a cause for laughter.

Perhaps even more important, storytelling may be the only practical and humane means of talking, however indirectly,

[F]amilies are united more by mutual stories — of love and pain and adventure — than by biology. "Do you remember when . . ." bonds people together far more than shared chromosomes. Stories are thicker than blood.

DANIEL TAYLOR

21

about difficult but profound matters that might otherwise silently fester in the family closet and pollute the family atmosphere: a divorce, a business failure, a mental illness, a suicide, a betrayal, a crime, a feud. In *A Celebration of American Family Folklore*, Steven Zeitlin notes:

> [Storytelling] stimulates healthy family interaction, it provides a technique for influencing and managing family members, it serves as a "family engineered canal" through which culture flows from one generation the next. Yet storytelling serves one function apart from other traditions. . . . [it] serves to make the critical, the disturbing, the tragic breaks in the cycle of rituals part of the smooth, ongoing life of the family.

Storytelling within the family is especially beneficial for children. Today's kids typically spend a disproportionate amount of time being entertained or preoccupied by machines, and the result can be a certain loss of humanity. Modern children desperately need a live art form like storytelling that offers more symbiotic, sympathetic, and mutually responsive links between one person and another. Telling personal tales provides more of what Daniel Goleman, in his 1995 bestseller *Emotional Intelligence*, calls education of the heart: the face-to-face, interactive demonstration and learning of patience, sensitivity, empathy, self-awareness, and self-management that's so lacking in the average contemporary child's daily life.

The storyteller Ron Evans talks about a friend who visited an African village shortly after the first television set was introduced there. He learned from one of the villagers that they adored this modern marvel for two weeks, hovering around it whenever they could spare the time, but one by one they gradually abandoned it. When he asked his informer why, he was told, "Oh, we don't need it. We have the storyteller."

"But don't you think the television knows many stories?" Evans's friend asked.

"Oh, yes," the villager replied. "The television knows many stories, but the storyteller knows me."

Hearing and telling stories about their own family and heritage helps kids figure out how they fit in — at home and in the world.

HOLLY GEORGE-WARREN

By hearing the emblematic tales that spring from your heart and your love, your child will sense his or her own worthy being in your eyes, and perhaps sense a worthiness in the broader sweep of the human race.

CHASE COLLINS

Here are tips for being a well-known storyteller among your family members:

- Help ensure that storytelling opportunities arise with predictable frequency by associating the activity with certain regularly occurring events, for example:

  - Birthdays (everyone could recount a favorite memory of the honored person from the past year)

  - Bedtime (you could relax a child by telling a tale that occurred to you that day)

  - Holiday gatherings (you could tell tales of past holidays or gatherings)

  - Walking or hiking excursions (you could stop along the way to tell any kind of tale you want)

  - Sunday supper (you could swap tales of the week immediately after eating)

- When asked how your day was, instead of sputtering vague adjectives or reciting your hour-by-hour schedule, practice "storying" one or more key events. Remember, all polite inquiries don't have to be answered mechanically, nor do all personal stories need to be about yesterdays!

- Whenever you tell stories, allow time for your listeners to tell them, too, if they so desire. When appropriate, encourage them by asking, "Would you like to tell me a story?" By swapping tales with each other, your listeners will learn more about who you are, and, at the same time, you will learn more about who they are.

- Whenever appropriate, develop a simple ritual to mark off storytelling time from the time surrounding it. For example, always tell in the same place, or dim the lights, or replace them with candles, or ask everyone to remain silent for a few moments, maybe even keeping their eyes closed, before the actual telling begins. You decide what specific measures might work best for your particular listeners.

• Whatever you decide, turn down the phone and answering machine and make sure that everyone is prepared to give their full attention to storytelling. Creating a distinctive, conducive atmosphere for telling tales works especially well to engage the attention of kids (who enjoy ceremonial events), but it helps people of any age to shift mental gears from what they were doing before.

• Remain alert and prepared for storytelling opportunities that emerge unexpectedly: a rainy afternoon when you're all trapped indoors with nothing to do; a spontaneous party to celebrate good fortune; a sad moment when your spouse or close friend might value some gentle, heartfelt tale-sharing; an evening alone with a relative you don't often see.

• Always bear in mind that telling a personal story within a family or close circle of friends is an excellent means of resolving tensions and overcoming communication barriers. In an article in *Creation Spirituality* (November/December 1992) entitled "Don't Argue, Tell a Story!" Jean Lanier, theologian and mother of six, remarks:

Most of us are reluctant to say how hurt we feel, how angry, how jealous, or how disappointed. Instead, we resort to accusations and blame which distort genuine feelings, and only serve to arouse hostility and fear. We all know how such recriminations, excuses, and even lies undermine personal relationships and leave us feeling lonely and misunderstood. How much more of a chance we would have if we could say, "I'd like to tell you a story," and then tell our story without accusing or blaming the other people involved.

The tale we share under such circumstances could be one that we create on the spot to depict our experience of the problematic situation, without rendering any judgments. It could also be one we've already developed that somehow relates to, or alleviates, the situation.

• It's easy to take family members or friends for granted—to expect their attention and overestimate their patience. Bear in mind that a story is a gift, to be given to others in a careful and caring manner, no matter how well—or how little—you know them.

• Remember as you spin your tale that you are offering your listeners a slice of your life, not a piece of your mind. This means guarding against preaching or editorializing. Don't say, for example, "Let me tell you a story that shows how wrong that is," or "In those times, people were a lot more friendly to their neighbors," or "When I was kid, I wouldn't dare talk back to my parents the way kids do today." Also, don't expect or demand any particular response: for example, by saying afterward, "Now, do you see why I feel the way I do?" or "What did you think about that?" or "Did you like my story?"

• Over time, keep track of what seems to interest individual family members and close friends about your life, or what you'd like to let them know about it, given the chance. Then develop personal tales based on these topics. In a home environment, you might even designate a special box or jar as a place to drop in story suggestions.

• Every now and then, conduct special storytelling projects. Among immediate family members, for example, one project could be to interview elder relatives to learn their tales. Or a group of friends might decide to share tales of their fathers on Father's Day.

Without preaching or moralizing, stories sum up our beliefs and principles. And there's no better way to communicate your family's values — whatever they may be — than to create and tell tales to your children.

CHASE COLLINS

ACTIVITY
All in the Family

In this activity, you'll be identifying not only what you can pleasurably do to help your family members—whether they're relatives or dear friends—but also what they can pleasurably do to help you.

Follow these guidelines:

1. Think about living members of your family in the more traditional sense of the word: your spouse or mate, your children, your parents, your siblings, and other people who are related to you by blood, marriage, or home-sharing. Identify the individuals and groups in your family with whom you *regularly* spend time. Then, for each individual and group, ask yourself the following questions:

   - What kinds of personal stories would I like to tell this individual or group?

   - What kinds of personal stories would I like this individual or group to tell me?

   - What particular times and places might be best for storytelling with this individual or group?

2. Think about your "family" of friends—the people who are not related to you by blood, marriage, or home-sharing but by affection and common interest. Focus on the individuals and groups in this category who *regularly* participate in your life. Then, for each individual and group, ask yourself the following questions:

   - What kinds of personal stories would I like to tell this individual or group?

   - What kinds of personal stories would I like this individual or group to tell me?

   - What particular times and places might be best for storytelling with this individual or group?

STORYTELLING AT WORK

22

Long ago, before the printing press, when communication among people almost always went directly from mouth to ear, telling personal stories was a major means of conducting day-to-day business. After all, when human beings themselves are the medium, even work-related messages tend to be narrative in style and experiential in content.

Today, a wide variety of machines—presses, cameras, photocopiers, fax machines, computers, satellites, and so on—have done much to make overall business communication far more technical in style and data-based in content than it used to be. That doesn't mean, however, that personal storytelling no longer has a function in the workplace. It continues to play a more vital role in work-related operations than we acknowledge, and it could serve us even better if we'd let it.

Certain jobs intrinsically call for *some* kind of oral story-telling—for example, teaching, journalism, selling, counseling, preaching, and tending bar. The same goes for certain activities that are common to many different types of jobs, like giving speeches, making presentations, participating in workshops, networking, and entertaining clients. There's no reason why job-appropriate *personal* tales shouldn't be included in the mix of stories that are told. In the working world in particular,

You could say that the story is the pretext for getting together in a personal way.

NANCY RAMBUSCH

201

*[T]he flow of stories is
medicine — similar medicine to
listening to the ocean or gazing at
sunrises.*

CLARISSA PINKOLA ESTES

personal tales can relate the teller to the work, the listener to the teller, and the listener to the work in lots of fresh and constructive ways.

If you are self-employed, or engaged in a small, entrepreneurial venture, or perform some sort of specialized service for a living—whether it's brain surgery, computer repair, or chimney-sweeping—personal tales may be your best vehicle for rendering the demands, experiences, and motivations of your unconventional work life more comprehensible to others. If you are employed in the corporate world, where individual identities tend to get lost, personal stories may represent not only a life-saving means of humanizing your work relationships but also a vital tool for communicating your unique wisdom, needs, and goals to others.

Superficially, the corporate environment may seem the least likely place for telling personal stories. In fact, the activity already thrives there under other labels. Some are respectable, such as mentoring or training by example. Others seem somewhat negative: schmoozing, gossiping, or trading "war stories."

Regardless of the label or how it's regarded, the simple act of sharing personal tales in an otherwise impersonal environment always helps individual tellers and listeners invest more of themselves in each other. This ultimately means that they can apply themselves to their jobs more wholeheartedly, which benefits them *and* their company.

David Boje, associate professor of management at Loyola Marymount University in Los Angeles and editor of the *Journal of Organizational Change Management*, advises, "Think of an organization as a big conversation. People are conversing all day long. An organization is an ongoing storytelling event." Given this situation, it pays for corporate employees to put extra effort into crafting personal stories that are interesting and more germane to their jobs, and therefore more effective in improving the quality of their day-to-day work life.

David Armstrong, vice-president of Armstrong International and author of *Managing by Storying Around: A New Method of*

Leadership, knows from firsthand experience that storytelling can do wonders within a corporation to forge partnerships and teams, to pass along ideas and information, and to enhance workplace reporting, interviewing, evaluating, and recruiting processes. He has virtually institutionalized storytelling in his company, taking it upon himself to be one of the key tellers, listeners, and spreaders. "I average only about one meeting a week," he told Larry Pike, a writer for *Storytelling* magazine. "Ninety percent of the time I'm walking around, talking to people."

Armstrong also firmly believes in the value of developing good stories in advance, rather than leaving matters to chance. Comparing story communication to marketing, he states, "Too many people think, 'I don't have much time; I'm just going to blurt it out real quick.' Well, if you want to sell somebody an idea, you've got to present it properly. If you want to sell a story, you've got to present it properly, too."

Here are suggestions for getting down to business with your personal storytelling:

- In a workplace atmosphere, it's best to tell tales that are relatively short, realistic, and plainspoken. It's also nice if they clearly illustrate a specific point.

- Because work is so achievement oriented and workers are so often overstressed, give special consideration to developing and telling personal stories that can somehow empower your listeners: ones that offer them new information, or trigger fresh ways of thinking, or encourage them to realize their goals, or validate what they're doing, or simply put them in a better frame of mind.

- Be alert for problematic workplace situations, issues, projects, or relationships that might benefit from the novelty of personal storyswapping. Quite often, the activity in itself—apart from the actual content of the stories—can lead to more innovative points of view.

Inside the world of story, our minds run free — to do what children do when they are drawing — to color beyond the lines, all over the pages.

JIMMY NEIL SMITH

John Ward, a corporate consultant in what he diplomatically calls "creative communication" rather than "storytelling," believes that stories develop a businessperson's "peripheral vision." He describes this visionary asset as the ability to see beyond the dots, referring to the famous puzzle involving a nine-dot square (three rows of three dots), where you're asked to connect all nine dots using no more than four lines, with no backtracking or lifting the pencil off the paper.

Ward's theory is that stories set in motion a different way of thinking that can result in workplace breakthroughs: "Stories can potentially support thinking beyond the dots by arousing emotions and awakening the imagination." He believes that storytelling is particularly effective in helping to resolve those problems in a corporation that somehow relate to communication. He therefore offers this suggestion: "As a storyteller, think about or discover where an organization might be vulnerable in the area of communication, then find a story to suit the situation—or search out one from inside the organization that gratifies the communication need."

· Consider proposing a creative-thinking or team-building program or retreat for your work group that includes sharing personal tales. Possible topics for storyswapping might be: success, failure, leadership, problem-solving, work versus home, your toughest assignment, your best working relationship, lessons learned, ethics and values, quality and service.

ACTIVITY
Working with Personal Stories

Here are some questions that will start you thinking about how storytelling might benefit you, the people who work with you, and your business:

1. Thinking about your work history—not just your present job, but all the jobs you've held in your life—ask yourself these questions:

   • What experiences did I enjoy the most? Why?

   • What experiences were the most difficult to handle? Why?

   • What important lessons did I learn? How?

2. Thinking about individuals or groups that are involved in your present work situation, ask yourself:

   • What kinds of personal stories would I like to tell this person or group?

   • What kinds of personal stories would I like this person or group to tell me?

23

STORYTELLING IN
THE COMMUNITY

Listening is a magnetic and strange thing, a creative force. The friends who listen to us are the ones we move toward, and we want to sit in their radius. When we are listened to, it creates us, makes us unfold and expand.

KARL MENNINGER

As Richard Stone says, "Story has the power to invite us into the growing circles gathered around community fires." Today, more and more people seek to overcome feelings of isolation, emptiness, and frustration by participating more actively in human society. At the same time, human society, challenged by increasing fragmentation, discord, and impotence, is ever more in need of creative individual involvement.

Storytelling ably assists both processes. It gives the teller a means of connecting more vitally with people at large, and it offers people at large a context for re-experiencing collectively the wonders of being human.

On a very basic level, a repertoire of personal tales equips us with interesting and worthwhile things to say virtually anytime we're among others. We may not tell entire ten-minute personal tales to new acquaintances, but at least we can share with them certain parts of those stories to help inspire more lively conversation. For example, instead of mechanically discussing such topics as the weather, the recent election results, or the rug we're standing on, we can tell acquaintances about the horrendous summer in our past when it was so hot the swimming hole dried up, the memorable hometown mayoral election that ended in a three-way tie, or the wonderful braided rug a friend made out of her children's outgrown clothes.

On a deeper level, the concept of personal storytelling can provide us with a rationale for creating community-building occasions that otherwise might never take place. For example, a storytelling friend of mine, wanting to help a newly settled family of four feel more at home in the area, invited them and all the other neighbors to a welcoming party, during which people took turns telling stories about when they moved there or, if they grew up there, what it was like during their childhood.

Storytellers Lee-Ellen Marvin and Doug Lipman devised an even more ambitious project along the same lines. Shortly after they both moved to Somerville, Massachusetts, they collected oral histories from townspeople whose families had lived there for at least three generations. They transposed that material into a thirty-five-minute tandem (or "two-teller") story that they performed locally and in surrounding towns to stimulate even more storyswapping about regional lore. It was a way for Marvin and Lipman to learn more about the area, for their neighbors to get to know more about them, and for everyone involved to value each other and their "common ground" more interactively.

This more profound kind of participatory tale-sharing is one of the best and brightest uses of personal storytelling. Glenn Morrow, editor of *Museletter*, a publication of the League for the Advancement of New England Storytelling, wrote on this point in an editorial in the May 1997 issue, "Spinning a Yarn from Common Threads":

> There is a superficial equating of "personal" and "community" these days, when people who like the same rock band or ball team, or surf to the same web site, are referred to as a "community." But a group of consumers, of stories or anything else, is not a community. Community requires an act separate from listening and being entertained, or telling and being impressive. It requires a small surrender of self—of that part of self that stands above and outside, the same part that started this process of turning your life into a story to begin with. For when a

Life gets life. Energy creates energy. It is by spending oneself that one becomes rich.

SARAH BERNHARDT

personal story is told in community, the audience cares about the story. They care because the teller cares more about the audience than s/he cares about the tale.

In other words, telling personal stories is a way of building a *sense* of community between or among individuals who may otherwise feel solitary, regardless of what they may have in common. It's a means of *enlivening* people by restorying their basic humanity. Jackie Torrance compares this kind of storytelling to sharing "pot likker" among friends. In the rural South where she grew up, pot likker is the nutrient-rich liquid left over from cooking vegetables—a prized, homemade health tonic. Elizabeth Ellis calls the process of storytelling in the community "blowing on the embers of a fire": the embers being the listeners' hearts. She points out that we have to "get down on our knees," or humble ourselves, as tellers to do a good job of "stirring the fire."

Through sharing our personal tales and, by extension, ourselves, we can stimulate this warm, communal sensation in almost any public forum: from an apartment complex or neighborhood park to a community or cultural center, school, library, concert hall, retirement village, restaurant, clubhouse, conference room, church, temple, mosque, ashram, or zendo. We can seize a spontaneous moment during a party for a tale or two, or we can plan a one-hour performance as a volunteer or paid teller at a rally, fundraiser, arts festival, company banquet, or holiday celebration. We can share whatever stories strike us as right at the time for the group in front of us, or we can organize in advance a program of stories around a single theme: say, "heroes and sheroes," "encounters with nature," "living and learning," or "giving and receiving."

An especially good environment for personal storytelling is a hospital or hospice, where patients and staff members are ever in need of relief from stress, loneliness, fear, and depression. During the telling itself, the healing effects of the stories may not be readily apparent. Individual listeners may suffer physical or emotional problems that keep them from expressing their feelings noticeably or impulsively. The true blessings of the event may not manifest themselves until later, after the teller is gone.

In the National Storytelling Association anthology *Homespun: Tales from America's Favorite Storytellers*, Kathryn Windham recalls hearing about this kind of reaction from the director of a hospital where she told stories:

> She said after I had left the cancer ward that the patients stayed in the day room, and for the first time, they talked to each other about the things that mattered to them. They talked about dying, about their fears, about their faith, and about how they wanted to be remembered. Storytelling had broken down the walls that divided them, and for once they were free, open, and honest with each other so they might share fully the deep feelings they each had.

How do you get started in community-oriented storytelling? First, repeatedly ask yourself two basic questions; and, each time you ask them, put together your answers as specifically as you can:

1. What gifts do my personal tales have to offer: what joys, cares, values, interests, and special life experiences do they convey?

2. Where, how, and why in my community might these gifts be needed or appreciated?

Finally, contact people in your community who might be able to help you set up some storygifting opportunities.

There's also another, intermediary step you can take: starting or joining a local group that meets regularly to swap tales, discuss stories-in-progress, and share plans or information relating to storytelling events. As it happens, the time is ripe for finding or forming such a small, organized community of like-minded people. A "small-group movement" is now sweeping the country, giving rise to salons, drumming circles, dreaming networks, meditation societies, and, yes, storytelling groups everywhere.

We are here to hand one another on.

WALKER PERCY

209

Patty McGrath, a financial systems manager for a Virginia-based global communications company and a member of three small groups (for dreaming, worshiping, and dancing), offers an explanation (in *Common Boundary*, July/August 1997) for the popularity of small groups *and* storytelling:

> Why does it sometimes take a circle of people to *get* it? Look at the species. We have evolved by sitting around a fire, telling stories, sharing dreams. The groups bring the richness of other people's experience. It's very nourishing and warm. Everything that happens is, in a sense, enriching.

To find a storytelling group near you, consult local periodicals, arts groups, bookstores, libraries, community centers, wholistic studies organizations, and the National Storytelling Association (see the appendix). To create and conduct your own group, you can follow these recommendations:

- Start small and intimate. Draw up a list of people you know fairly well who might be interested in the possibility of meeting regularly to share personal tales. Then call these people and arrange a time for everyone to get together and make plans for the group.

  If you can identify or pin down only one other person who's willing to join you, that's fine. The two of you can meet and plan your ongoing "story buddy" relationship. As time passes, you are almost certain to think of and attract other participants.

- Begin the initial planning session on an inspirational note by telling a short, simple personal tale. Then invite others to tell their own. A topic that works well for spontaneous personal story-sharing—especially if some people don't know each other—is: "Tell a story about your name (first, middle, last, nickname, whatever): how you got it, what it means, how you feel about it, or any way it's figured in your life experience." Emphasize that the story doesn't have to be long or polished.

If actual storysharing seems inappropriate at the beginning of this session, then do it later in the session, or at the next, "first official" meeting.

- Acting as the leader of the business part of the session, first explain your vision of the group. Briefly touch on all of the following issues:

  - Why you contacted the individuals about forming a personal storytelling group

  - What things the group might do or accomplish

  - How its members might be recruited, organized, led, served, and utilized

  - Where and how often it might meet

  - How each meeting might proceed and be governed

After you've finished, ask each member of your group to offer his or her commentary on the same topics. Work toward a final agreement on all these issues.

- Avoid being overly ambitious. For example, if you're evenly divided on the issue of whether to meet biweekly or monthly, choose monthly. If you can't decide between meeting for dinner *and* storytelling, or just meeting for storytelling, choose the latter. The more obligations you impose on yourselves, the greater the chances of not fulfilling some of them and, therefore, feeling a sense of failure.

- Each meeting should be conducted by someone who's been designated in advance: either the group leader, the person hosting the meeting, or a volunteer. The conductor is in charge of making sure that everyone knows and gets reminded about the meeting, devising alternative plans if the original ones fall through, determining the general content of the meeting (if appropriate), and keeping it on track.

- Each meeting should offer a number of people a chance to tell stories and, if desired, to get help in developing stories.

  To make sure there's enough time for everyone interested, the conductor can circulate a "sign-up" sheet at the beginning of the meeting. Everyone who wants to tell or get help can then jot down (1) what he or she wants to do, and (2) approximately how much time it will take. The conductor can then review the completed sheet and make sure there's enough time to accommodate everyone's request, as well as to perform any other business—such as making announcements, planning future meetings, discussing general storytelling-related topics, and/or taking a short, mid-meeting break.

- In addition to storytelling, each meeting might feature a particular discussion or activity that somehow relates to storytelling.

  For a *discussion theme*, you might choose "favorite foods," "pet peeves," "family lore," or "a magic moment in my life since the last meeting." You could share anecdotes on this topic, generate possible story ideas or story-developing strategies, and—thinking ahead—identify possible reasons, occasions, and venues for telling such stories. For an *activity*, you might choose one from parts II or III of this book. If appropriate, the topic or activity for a given meeting could be established in advance—at the previous meeting or even earlier—so that members can come prepared.

- Each meeting needs to be considered by all members as a time of mutual respect, support, safety, and confidentiality. This means adopting the following general guidelines:

  - Give each teller undivided attention, without interrupting.

We are all wedded to our stories. It doesn't mean we are each hermetically sealed in our own little worlds, impervious to the influence of others. It does mean the only way to avoid such isolation is to listen, compassionately, to the stories of others.

DANIEL TAYLOR

- Afterward, thank the teller, praise the strengths of the telling and the story, and give the teller a chance to make any comments or requests he or she wants. Don't rush immediately to the next story or order of business.

- If a teller wants constructive criticism, he or she should ask for it. If desired (either to save time or to avoid being overwhelmed), the teller can ask that the discussion be confined to certain aspects of the story or its telling.

- Listeners should only offer constructive criticism when it's invited by the teller. When they do so, they should base their remarks on how *they* responded to the telling, not on what the teller presumably did.

     For example, instead of saying something like, "You lost me just before the trial part," "Your voice is too soft at the beginning," or "You're a little harsh on your sister" (all three remarks presumptive and accusatory in tone), say, "I got confused about what was happening just before the trial part," "I couldn't hear you well at the beginning," or "If this were my story, I'd go a little easier on my sister" (each of these three remarks is nonjudgmental and informative in tone).

- Stories heard at a meeting—or personal information learned there—should not be told elsewhere without permission.

ACTIVITY
The Common Cause

This activity helps you to figure out ways to extend your personal tales and storytelling activities out into the communities that surround you. Follow these guidelines:

1. Thinking of the town, city, or region where you live, ask yourself:

   - What groups of people, issues, or aspects of life here do I most care about?

   - What personal stories do I have—or could I develop—that relate to these groups of people, issues, or aspects of life?

2. Ask yourself: Who could I contact in my area that might know more about storytelling events or possibilities?

3. Ask yourself: Who might be interested in meeting regularly with me to swap stories and storytelling ideas?

TAKING THE TELLING LEAP

I n surveys of what people fear, "speaking in public" always gets a high rating. Personal storytelling is not quite the same thing as public speaking, but it comes close!

In the first place, telling personal tales does not always involve speaking *in public*. Often it takes place in relative privacy, among family members and close friends. Nevertheless, it's a more preplanned, complex, and emotionally laden mode of private communication than we ordinarily engage in, so we can easily become more nervous about it.

Second, personal storytelling that does occur in public (in other words, before groups that contain at least some strangers) is almost never subject to the same hard scrutiny and demand for perfection that are associated with public speaking. People usually accept it more tolerantly and even gratefully as homemade entertainment. Nevertheless, it's a more self-revealing act than we usually perform in that context; and the prospect of being judged, however indulgently, by so many different minds can often be alarming.

Sometimes we may not consciously realize that we fear the public speaking aspects of personal storytelling as much as we actually do. Rather than acknowledge such vulnerability, we convince ourselves that we're just lazy, or that storytelling is a waste of our time, or that we don't have any tales or telling talents worth

I say, follow your bliss and don't be afraid, and doors will open where you didn't know they were going to be.

JOSEPH CAMPBELL

215

sharing. We fail to appreciate the incredibly self-damaging nature of these excuses because, in our minds, they somehow protect us from facing our arch enemy: fear. Thus, we paradoxically remain all the more in fear's thrall because we never actually engage it in battle.

Once we recognize that we may sometimes be afraid to tell, we can give ourselves better pep talks. As speechmakers, athletes, artists, soldiers, and lovers have always done, we can keep saying to ourselves that fear is just the flip side of excitement, or that anything worth doing is bound to involve a certain amount of worry about doing it well. We can remind ourselves that we're not really having an adventure unless we're a little bit scared, and that only fear can give us the adrenalin to achieve what we desire, to transform the possible into the fully real.

These pep talks can help us weather our storytelling fears when they strike. But what's even more effective is to prepare ahead of time not only to avoid or minimize such fears but also to channel them into productive energy. We can accomplish this self-liberating mission in a number of different ways:

- **Always give special care to developing and embodying your personal stories.** More than anything else, this attention will ensure that each tale gains a strong, invincible life of its own and, therefore, that you can bring it to life for others without much difficulty. Giving special care means staying focused on how the tale is going and growing inside you, instead of fretting in advance about how others will like it, or when, where, how, and to whom you're going to tell it.

- **Realize and respect the independent value of the story, the teller, the telling, and the listener.** You *think* your tale is worthwhile, so why not *believe* it? You know you're qualified to tell it, so why not grant yourself permission? The telling itself can be fun, so why not let it be? And the lis-

A man who has a vision is not able to use the power of it until after he has performed the vision on earth for the people to see.

BLACK ELK

216

tener wants to enjoy your story—and wants you to enjoy telling it—so why not act accordingly?

The success of a storytelling venture doesn't hinge entirely on any one of these elements, in which case that single element would need to be near-perfect. Instead, it draws on all of them, and each has its own intrinsic value to contribute.

- **Commit yourself to storytelling ventures.** What can really stir your blood as a storyteller is anticipating specific occasions when you know you'll be telling. If you're looking forward to an actual event, rather than simply waiting around for a chance to tell spontaneously, you can more actively plan specific ways to make your tale and its delivery all the more appealing to your audience. And, in the process, you can confront your specific fears and overcome them.

    Set a time and a place to share a personal tale or two with a particular person or group of people: for example, after Thanksgiving dinner at your sister's house, at your monthly club meeting, next Thursday evening when your son is home, during your upcoming talk at work, as part of the community's annual talent show. Whenever appropriate, let your listener(s) know what you intend to do, so your commitment is all the stronger.

- **Identify in advance the potential problems or issues that bother you most, so that you can deal with them more effectively.** Fear is a great exaggerator. Instead of allowing yourself to become afraid of storytelling in general, work toward pinpointing the specific, more manageable aspects of telling stories that really worry you. Once you've named your fears, you're well on the way to mastering them!

    Here are the concerns that participants in my workshops most often express:

It is not because things are difficult that we do not dare; it is because we do not dare that they are difficult.

SENECA

We are the hurdles we leap to be ourselves.

MICHAEL MCCLURE

I may omit or transpose facts, or make mistakes in dates. But I cannot go wrong about what I felt, or about what my feelings have led me to do; and these are the chief subjects of my story.

JEAN-JACQUES ROUSSEAU

- *How do I handle my fear of sounding like I'm bragging, or begging for sympathy, or trying to be the center of attention by telling a personal tale?* In my experience, the people who worry about such matters usually have the least cause for concern. They tend to be normally considerate, self-effacing, and deferential around others. One of the major virtues of personal storytelling is that if provides essentially shy people a safe, gentle, and welcome means of opening up to others and taking charge of the moment at hand—something everyone in a group has a responsibility to do occasionally.

  Whatever your basic temperament or usual conduct may be, the best guarantee that you won't appear to be boasting, pleading, or grabbing the limelight when storytelling lies primarily in the care you put into developing your tale ahead of time. As long as you keep in mind both your concerns and your listeners' enjoyment during this process, you'll be okay.

  If you're worried about putting too much "I" focus in a tale, devote more attention to the other characters in the tale. If you think you appear too heroic, temper this image with some appropriate glimpses of your more human side—thoughts that were less than noble, or actions that were somewhat selfish.

  As for mistakenly thinking that the sheer act of telling in itself is a pushy one, remember that your goal is to express yourself in a natural manner that pleases your listeners. If you throw yourself into it in good spirit, they're bound to as well!

- *What if I forget or accidentally leave out part of my story?* If you're suddenly stopped in your tracks, wondering what comes next, then chances are you have relied too heavily on word-for-word, passage-by-passage memorization. After all, the story is about your life: You should know, at least in general terms, what comes next, and thus be able to proceed accordingly, whether or not it's the way you planned to go.

To handle the actual moment of forgetfulness, you can pause as naturally as possible (maybe giving yourself time to remember), and perhaps say something like, "Now, I don't recall exactly what happened next, but . . ." (going on to summarize or take a slightly divergent track).

Remember that storytelling is a homespun art. Many times when your memory suddenly goes blank, you can handle the episode as you would in casual conversation, saying, for example, "Isn't it strange? Some days, I can remember all this as if it just happened, other times, like now, the memory just comes and goes as it will," and then make some transition to a part you can remember.

As for leaving out a certain part of your story, in most cases your listeners won't even realize it. Later you may wish you'd included that part, and you may be haunted by a feeling of not having told the full tale; but as long as the partially complete story makes sense to your listeners, they can still thoroughly enjoy it.

If, while you're actually telling your story, you realize that you left out an essential, earlier part of it, you can say at the next natural stopping point, "Now, there's something I didn't tell you before," and go on to offer the skipped segment. Chances are it will seem as if you intended this structure, perhaps to increase the suspense, humor, or drama.

- *What should I do if I get interrupted while I'm telling?* Deal with it as naturally and efficiently as you can, somewhat as if you were simply carrying on a conversation with your listener(s). Remember: It's more important to maintain rapport with your audience than to keep your story going forward, come hell or high water.

If the interruption is simply a loud noise or a passing distraction, give it the barest possible acknowledgment—preferably nonverbal—and resume. Simply to ignore it may not be possible without seeming as if you're completely off in some other world.

If it's a longer noise or distraction, like a passing train, offer some transitional, good-humored remark, like, "Let's just hold that image while the train passes," and wait it out. If it takes quite a while, you can offer a brief remark every now and then to sustain your audience's attention, like, "My grandfather always hated train noises (if your story's about your grandfather)" or "This reminds me of another story, but I'll save it for another time." When you do return to the story, offer a brief summary of what happened just before the interruption to reorient your listeners toward what comes next.

If you're interrupted by a question from a listener that you can't just politely refrain from answering, then answer it as briefly as possible, in the same voice that you're using to tell the story, and then say something like, "but let's finish this story," to forestall any future questions.

If your story is completely disrupted by another person or event (for example, someone bursting into the room with an important announcement or a storm breaking directly over your heads), then you have two options: (1) If the disruption is short enough and doesn't require you and your audience to disband altogether, you may decide that you can gently guide your audience back into the story. If so, first settle them down with some transitional remarks and then review what you were saying before the disruption. (2) If you decide you have to stop telling altogether, then say something brief and simple, like "We'll have to get together again soon to finish the story."

- *What if I don't get any response to my story, or my listeners don't seem to have enjoyed it?* Telling a story works best when we do it in the spirit of giving a gift. For the sake of ourselves *and* our listeners, we want to avoid attaching any expectations to the exchange.

We can't really judge how well a listener liked our story simply from how he or she looks or reacts immediately after it's over. Listening to a story is an act of retreating inside oneself. In many cases, listeners will remain somewhat inward after the tale is over and therefore relatively undemonstrative. Far from being a sign that they did not get much out of the story, it may well indicate that the experience really grabbed them.

We must also bear in mind that a person's true response to a tale may not come until later. Many of the stories my grandmother told me when I was a kid have only recently hit home in my imagination, as I find myself becoming the same age that she was then. When you tell a story, you are giving your listener something to think about, so you may as well give him or her the *time* to think about it as well—even if it's a lifetime!

Another dimension of this "no response" issue involves cultural conditioning. In today's society, people are used to getting their entertainment from TV, movies, and books. They don't need to respond physically to these media. In fact, there's no point to responding physically, unless they simply can't suppress a laugh or a groan.

Faced with a live storyteller—something that doesn't happen to the average person very often—even the most appreciative listeners can be unsure how to respond, and, therefore, hesitant about doing so, especially if they've just been simultaneously amused, impressed, entranced, moved, and thrown back into their own thoughts and memories. This is especially true of people

And the trouble is if you don't risk anything, you risk even more.

ERICA JONG

221

who habitually hide their emotions, or who are coping with an unusual amount of stress in their life.

- *What if someone gives me negative feedback?* This is a difficult situation for almost any teller, no matter how seasoned, because three complex factors are involved:

  · No one likes to get negative feedback.

  · The effect of negativity on the teller, who has just been very open and generous, is almost certain to be greater than the critic intended or than the teller would experience in other contexts. The surprising strength of the impact can be very confusing and therefore disturbing.

  · Unless the teller has explicitly invited criticism, such remarks on the part of a listener are thoughtless and rude, regardless of his or her intentions, which adds an additional fillip of embarrassment and possible resentment to the situation.

Bearing in mind that you run a high risk of overreacting to negativity, the best way to respond overtly to your critic is to say and show as little as you can, so you can quickly put the moment behind you. A simple, "Thanks, I'll think about that," accompanied by a thoughtful look, is sufficient. Getting involved in a dialogue about the criticism can overshadow the memory of the storytelling itself, which should be allowed as much space to develop in your own and your listener's mind as you can give it.

As for your internal response, remember that you can't please everyone, and that you have full freedom to take or leave whatever anyone says. And there can be a virtue in taking. Every now and then, an unsolicited critical remark—unpleasant as it is at the time—may lodge in your brain and eventually enlighten you with a better way to tell your tale.

As for *solicited* criticism, that's another matter altogether! You can benefit a lot from asking other people to serve as sounding boards for your story, telling you what they like and what they think needs more work. However, choose these times and critics wisely.

It's best not to ask for feedback on a tale until you already feel that you've worked it into fairly good shape on your own. Pick people you really trust as critics, and give them honest guidelines on how you'd prefer them to deliver their responses so that you don't get offended or overwhelmed. Also, prepare yourself to take seriously whatever they say. Of course, that doesn't mean you have to do anything with it!

- *What if I tell a story about someone who's still alive and he or she finds out?* The underlying issue here is sometimes the teller's fear of being embarrassed ("I don't want this person to know how I feel about him or her"), sometimes the teller's fear of embarrassing the other person ("I don't want this person to feel self-conscious about being in my story"), and sometimes the teller's fear of being confronted by the other person ("I don't want this person to accuse me of being inaccurate or unfair").

  The solution to all these issues is the same: As long as you make it clear that you're telling a personal story ("This is how I remember it . . .") rather than offering an objective case history, you protect your right to speak as well as the other person's right to privacy (or to a different opinion). And as long as you speak from the heart—respecting yourself, your story, your listener, and the humane nature of storytelling—you're highly unlikely to say anything that would embarrass or offend the people you talk about. They're much more likely to be flattered, honored, and touched simply to be in your tale.

We can't do great things. We can only do small things with great love.

MOTHER TERESA

It is only in adventure that some people succeed in knowing themselves—in finding themselves.

ANDRÉ GIDE

- *What if my story about a person, place, or event doesn't agree with a listener's memory of the same person, place, or event?* Again, if you're especially concerned about this issue, make it clear beforehand that your tale reflects how you remember things, not necessarily how they (f)actually were.

This issue is most commonly associated with telling a family story among other family members. In such a situation, each listening member may recall a particular person, place, or event mentioned in the tale in an entirely different way—partly because of his or her unique role, perspective, and experience within the family.

But whether you're concerned about family members, friends, or other kinds of listeners challenging your memory, if you refer to the phenomenon of "everyone seeing things differently" when you introduce your story, you may not only defuse criticism, but also inspire follow-up stories.

We've now reviewed some *specific* worries about personal storytelling. I also hear from people who can't reduce their fear to a specific question, instead expressing a much broader concern like, "What if I make a fool of myself?" They often go on to give an equally sweeping answer to their own question: "If I do, I'll just die!"

Storytelling derives much of its virtue from being a simple, easy, and, yes, even a *little* thing to do. But there's no denying it can sometimes seem like a fearsome undertaking, and any fear can loom disproportionately large.

Whenever I have anxiety about storytelling, I find powerful encouragement in recalling traditional tales about meeting a great challenge and rising to the occasion. Fortunately, there are many of these stories to choose from. One of my favorites is a Zen tale called "The Teaching," which I learned from Pat Jikyo George, a monk at Zen Mountain Monastery. It speaks symbolically of the value of knowing in advance what we're going to do when we tell—that is, of *embodying* a tale—and of staying wholeheartedly involved in each moment of the storytelling process, instead of being distracted either by fear or by hope. In this tale, fear takes the appropriate form of a samurai: a terrifyingly well-trained warrior in ancient Japan.

THE TEACHING

The early morning market in Kyoto is unusually crowded. And so it happens that a poor farmer accidentally bumps against a samurai—a horrible breach of etiquette—something that the samurai cannot tolerate. And so he says to the farmer, in a voice loud enough for others to hear, "I must avenge my honor against your grave affront. I challenge you to a duel by sword. If you fail to meet me in the market courtyard tomorrow at noon, have no doubts, I *will* find you!"

The farmer is appalled. He knows nothing of the way of the sword. However, he does know of a retired swordmaster and teacher who lives just outside the city, and he goes to him and asks, "What can I do?"

The teacher replies, "Put out of your mind any thoughts about winning. The best you can hope to do is to kill your adversary at the same time that he kills you. To do this, you must fight with all your heart, even though you know that you will die."

The teacher then instructs the farmer to meditate for a few hours before making his decision. The farmer goes home, meditates, returns to the teacher, and says, "I am resolved to fight my best. After all, there's no way for me to escape from the samurai. I want to do what I can to preserve my honor, knowing I cannot hope to live."

So the teacher takes the farmer to the market courtyard, where the duel will be fought the next day. There, the teacher looks around for some distinctive mark on the ground. Seeing a reddish patch of grass, he says to the farmer, "Tomorrow, arrive early and take up your position there, with your left foot on the reddish patch. This will be your starting point. I don't have time to show you how to hold the sword properly, so hold it any way you want. I only have time to demonstrate how you should move. Stand a little distance away and watch. You need to imitate my movements exactly."

Now, there is a certain master stroke in Japanese fencing that depends on taking two very large steps very quickly, without hesitation. It's aimed at coming right underneath your opponent's thrust to make your own strike. Even masters in the way of the sword sometimes hesitate out of fear of the oncoming blade: Their muscles contract, their steps shorten, and the stroke is ruined. Again, it is not because the stroke itself is difficult. What is difficult is making it without any hesitation, with the whole heart, undistracted by any hope of surviving.

The farmer learns to make the basic moves, and as the hours of practice go by, the teacher gets him to lengthen the two steps more and more. Near the end of the day, while the farmer is still practicing, the teacher excuses himself for a moment. He hurries around a corner, kneels down, picks up two pebbles at random out of the mud, wipes them off, puts them in his pocket, and returns. He tells the farmer to move aside, and he himself stands with his foot on the reddish patch. He makes two giant strides fast as lightning and gives a tremendous shout as he executes the deadly thrust.

Then he says to the farmer, "You see the two places on the ground where my feet trod? I am now going to embed a magic pebble in each place. The places will then be charged with a special power. Leap upon them, and you will feel the powerful magic and make the same deadly cut that I did!" And he takes the two pebbles out of his pocket—the same ones he just picked from the mud—and embeds them in the two places. He has the farmer continue to practice leaping and, by the end of the day, the farmer is hitting the same two spots, feeling the power, and making the stroke.

The next day, the farmer comes early to the market courtyard and takes his position on the reddish patch. The samurai arrives and faces the farmer at the prescribed distance. The referee gives the signal. At that precise instant, the farmer, with no hope of living, but with his whole heart, leaps forward, hits the two peb-

At a certain point, you have to go to the edge of the cliff and jump — put your ideas into a form, share that form with others.

MEREDITH MONK

Set forth thy tale, and tarry not the time.

GEOFFREY CHAUCER

bles, and pierces the samurai's heart—before the samurai has even moved his sword into position. Imagine the farmer's wonder and joy!

Now, if you believe the pebbles in this story were magic, you are wrong. However, if you believe the pebbles were *not* magic, you are also wrong.

A similar paradox applies to telling personal stories. If you believe that it takes magic to spin tales of yourself, you are wrong. But if you believe that spinning tales of yourself does *not* involve magic, you are also wrong.

May you get right to it!

APPENDIX
OTHER STORYTELLING ACTIVITIES

This appendix offers supplementary activities for developing and telling more effective personal stories. It's organized into five sections reflecting the five parts of the book.

After you read each part of the book, you can consult the relevant section here to gain a better sense of how to extend the knowledge and skills you've acquired so far. After you complete the entire book, you can do any of the activities suggested here at any time to refresh your knowledge and skills.

PART I: WHY TELL PERSONAL STORIES?

- Buy, make, or designate a notebook for personal storytelling. You may want to use one with built-in dividers, or make your own organizational tabs, so that you have separate sections for different purposes: for example, activities from this book; your own story ideas and outlines; research notes; action plans; to-do items; resource lists.

- Start keeping a personal storytelling "image file" in a folder, scrapbook, box, or large envelope. In this file, collect photos, maps, correspondence, and memorabilia that directly relate to people, places, or events in your life that you might like to feature in tales you create.

  Also include in this file any images that you feel might *indirectly* relate to your personal storytelling endeavors, such as magazine photos or postcards that capture an era, a setting, or a mood you might want to evoke, or prints that depict an animal, building, or object you might want to describe.

If nothing else, these direct and indirect images can often provide general storymaking and storytelling inspiration. For this reason, it's a good idea to display a few of these images—on a rotating basis—in places where you can easily see them, such as a mantel, refrigerator, side table, or bulletin board. You can use either images associated with a specific story idea you're developing, or images chosen at random, in the hopes that they will eventually induce story ideas.

- Find a place, indoors or outdoors, where you can speak in a normal tone of voice without disturbing others or being disturbed. You can use it to start telling aloud informal, spur-of-the-moment stories however and whenever you want.

    Choose any subject you want for a story, and then make up what you say as you go along, as if you were speaking to a good friend, yourself, or an imaginary, ideal interviewer. Avoid being judgmental about the quality of your voice or your tales. Your goal at this point is solely to get used to the process of telling with, and listening to, your voice.

- Start telling aloud the same kind of informal, spur-of-the-moment stories, and then listening to them, with a small tape recorder that has a good microphone and earphones. Again, keep yourself from critiquing what you do. Just allow yourself to get comfortable with the process.

- Spend an entire day conscientiously listening to people more attentively than you normally do. Also, encourage people to speak—especially to share their stories—more than you normally do, so that you'll have plenty of listening opportunities. The three R's of good listening are:

- **Remain silent** until the other person has finished speaking ("silent" is an anagram for "listen").

- **Respond** to the speaker with appropriate verbal and nonverbal cues (for example, a nod of approval, an "ah!" of amazement, or a brief phrase like, "tell me more"), so that he or she is encouraged to continue.

- **Remind yourself** afterward of what you've heard so far that day—a memory-bonding act that should be repeated every couple of hours that day.

- Recruit another person—or a group of people—to read this book with you, do the activities, and swap stories. Guidelines for a formal storytelling group (that is, one that meets regularly and follows an agenda) are offered in part V, but you can start your own, informal learning-telling-listening exchange right now!

- Research local periodicals for storytelling performances you can attend. For the purposes of this book, make sure ahead of time that the event features at least some literal telling of stories—that is, does not exclusively consist of reading aloud from a text, acting, reciting, lecturing, puppeteering, or singing. If possible, find out what kinds of stories will be told: personal ones, original fictions, folktales, myths, legends, or literary tales. For the purposes of this book, personal stories are most appropriate, but listening to *any* told tale can give you subject, plot, character, or delivery ideas—not to mention entertainment!

- Start listening to tapes or CDs of storytellers—preferably tellers of personal tales. Ask librarians and other likely sources for recommendations, and consult the list of resources in part V of this appendix.

PART II: RECLAIMING YOUR STORYLOVING SELF

- Reread books that you liked when you were younger, going all the way back to childhood. Any book has something fresh to offer every time you re-enter its world, if only because you yourself have changed in the meantime. Therefore, rereading a favorite book from your past not only revives memories from that period, but also stimulates new ones to harmonize with the old. Your total experience of the book thus gains a multidimensional depth and texture that can make for a great personal tale or for an impressive retelling of what you've read.

- Listen to music you liked when you were younger, going all the way back to childhood. As you listen, let your thoughts and feelings wander back to that particular period in your life. Ask yourself, What was I doing then? What was going on in my life? In the lives of people around me? In the world as a whole? Your answers may give you some good material for personal tales.

- Take another look at movies or television shows you liked when you were younger, going all the way back to childhood. To find them—and to trigger your memory for titles—regularly check out TV listings, video stores, and local revival theaters.

  As you watch one of these movies or TV shows, keep track of the moments that you remember the best. For each of these moments, ask yourself, Why do I remember this so well? Why did it impress me so much when I saw it before?

  Keep track of any moments that are different from the way you remember them—either in actual fact, or in the way in which they impress you. For each of these moments, ask yourself, Why do I remember this differently? What might have influenced me back then to remember this in the particular way I did?

- Gather favorite possessions from the past (especially from your childhood or adolescence) in a place where you can see, touch, smell, and play with them regularly. While James Joyce was writing *Finnegan's Wake*, he surrounded himself with objects molded by the sea—like shells, rocks, driftwood, and seaweed—to prompt memories of seaside environments he wanted to put in his book, and to make his descriptions of these places all the more real to his readers. As you ponder and develop personal tales, the nearby presence of past possessions might work a similar magic for you and, eventually, your listeners.

- Pay closer attention to your night-time dreams for possible story triggers or ideas. There are numerous techniques you can use to improve your ability to recall your dreams. The most potent one is simply to tell yourself several times during the day that you intend to remember your dreams, and, finally, to repeat this intention especially strongly just before you fall asleep.

  You may want to experiment with inducing dreams on a particular subject—such as "my childhood" or, even more specific, "the red wagon I had as a child." To do so, restate to yourself your chosen subject every time you repeat your intention to remember your dreams.

  You may want to keep a pencil and paper close to your bed for jotting down notes as soon as possible after you awake from dreaming—even if it's in the middle of the night. The sheer fact that you go to sleep knowing the pencil and paper are there and then see them again right after waking up may subliminally help you keep conscious tabs on your dreams.

  Other things you can do to increase your chances of "catching" dreams are:

- Don't move or speak for a while after awakening. Instead, concentrate on remembering your dreams. Engage for a few moments in loafing: giving your mind freedom to roam back into your dreams in any way it chooses. For a stronger focus, perform the "thinking and feeling backward" activity: following any particular thoughts or feelings you have on awakening back into your dreams.

- Drink a glass of water before retiring. It will help you wake up faster—or more often.

- Write down your last thoughts (and a few notes regarding your chosen dream subject, if you have one) immediately before retiring. This activity will help settle your mind for dreaming and may influence the content of your dreams.

- Set your alarm for an earlier time than usual. You may surprise your mind in the middle of a dream! If you can get by without using an alarm to wake up, do so. The noise of an alarm can easily scare off lingering dream images or feelings.

- Place an object with a scent—a bag of herbs, a sachet, a room deodorant—near your bed for the deliberate purpose of "inspiring" dreams. The fact that you have consciously associated the scent with dreaming may trigger recall of a dream during the fuzzy moments of waking up.

    Smell is an especially powerful memory evoker! The French novelist Marcel Proust claimed that the genesis of his entire multivolume autobiographical masterpiece, *Remembrance of Things Past*, was the smell one afternoon of a Madeleine—a cookie he'd loved as a child.

- Practice creative visualization to reimagine a specific person in your past who you feel might offer good personal story material: a former playmate, a favorite teacher, your mother when you were sixteen, your first love—whoever!

    If you want, you can follow the same activity directions you used in part II to meet your inner storyteller, up to the point in step IV when the voice says, "In a moment the curtain will open." At that point, just substitute for your inner storyteller whomever you want to visualize. Then go on to see that person and to pose any questions you like. You can even ask for a gift!

PART III: GETTING STORY IDEAS

Experiment with different story-idea triggers in the four categories listed below: *people*, *places*, *objects*, and *events*. For each trigger you choose, think about what you remember from your past—related either directly or indirectly to the trigger itself—that might make a good subject for a personal tale.

Also start keeping regular track of triggers that occur to you but that you're not ready to pursue at the time. You can either add each new trigger to a written list, or, better yet, write each new trigger on a separate slip of paper and store them in a special story idea bowl, jar, box, or bag. Then, when you're ready to do some story-generating, simply pull out one of the trigger slips and surprise your creative mind. You may even want to start telling a tale to yourself right away based on the trigger you've drawn!

This activity can also be turned into a game for families, friends, or other groups to play. You can make separate slips for each trigger listed here or use other triggers tailored more specifically to the group. Take turns drawing triggers from a bowl, jar, box, or bag and telling spur-of-the-moment stories. Don't judge the results in any way. Simply enjoy them!

PEOPLE (AND ANIMALS)

- A teacher to whom I owe a lot
- Someone I once imagined marrying, but didn't
- Someone I once wanted to be like
- A relative who fascinates me

- Someone I very much envied, or was jealous of
- Someone I once taught something
- A memorable past house guest or roommate
- A past boss or supervisor that I especially liked
- A celebrity I once encountered
- A pet I once had but don't have anymore
- An animal who was not a pet but with whom I had a relationship

PLACES

- A special hideout or getaway place in the past
- A friend's home
- The first place I lived on my own
- My favorite store
- A place I originally didn't like but grew to love
- A place where I learned a lot about nature
- A place I was scared of
- My favorite relative's home
- A place I once considered to be especially magnificent
- A school I once attended
- A place that's sacred to me

OBJECTS

- A car I once owned
- A piece of clothing I thought would give me a new image

- Something I thought gave me magic powers when I was a child

- My favorite food

- Something of my own that I broke or lost and sorely missed

- Something belonging to someone else that I broke or lost

- Something that has great sentimental value to me

- Something I associate with my mother

- Something I coveted for a long time

- A tool or device I had trouble mastering

EVENTS

- A reunion I once had

- A time when I narrowly escaped disaster

- The time when I first began to feel like an adult

- A pageant, play, or theatrical event in which I participated

- A time when I felt something supernatural was going on

- A memorable birthday

- A time when I moved from one home to another

- A strange party I attended

- A historical event I took part in

- A time when I felt especially free

PART IV: BRINGING STORIES TO LIFE

• A more formal means of structuring personal tales is to think about your past experiences in terms of plots that commonly appear in traditional tales. Borrowing one of these plots is somewhat like creating a hybrid story—a story that features, or refers to, both a personal and a traditional tale (as discussed previously in this book). Instead of incorporating a specific traditional tale into your personal story, you can simply follow a traditional plot pattern to shape your personal experience into a story.

A very common theme in traditional tales is for the hero to undergo some kind of transformation from a negative state to a more positive one. In a personal story, the hero could be you or anyone else in your life.

Here are some transformational possibilities:

from	to
clumsy	graceful
sick	healthy
selfish	sharing
weak	strong
unpopular	popular
boastful	modest
cruel	kind
wild	tame
follower	leader
unreliable	trustworthy
ugly	beautiful
foolish	wise
poor	rich
harmful	helpful

Here are some other common plot features in traditional tales:

- A sympathetic character in a bad situation

- A warning from an unusual source

- An accident, event, or miraculous factor that causes a personality change

- A deathbed promise

- A child searching for a lost parent (or vice versa)

- A would-be champion seeking to correct a horrible injustice

- An evil character seeking revenge

- The redemption of an unpleasant character

- A mysterious power that can cause either fortune or misfortune

- The surprising intervention of fate or magic to resolve a problem

- The reconciliation of enemies

- The effects of a certain lifestyle on a character's personality or body

- The consequences of intractable behavior

- The loss and recovery of a valuable object

- The restitution of a character's, place's, or object's deserved state of being

- A quest to discover fame, fortune, or love

- The solution of a mystery

- Learning to work hard for something that once came easily

- Making a seemingly simple decision that winds up changing one's life entirely

PART V: YOUR STORYTELLING POWERS IN ACTION

For storytelling support, information, and inspiration, contact the following organizations:

National Storytelling Association (NSA)
(formerly the National Association for the Preservation and Perpetuation of Storytelling [NAPPS])
P.O. Box 309, Jonesborough, TN 37659; 1-800-525-4515

NSA is a nonprofit organization to encourage the practice and application of all types of storytelling. It markets books (including a nationwide directory of professional storytellers, organized by state), produces videotapes and audiotapes, and performs national and regional networking services for storytelling events and groups.

NSA also sponsors a large and wonderful storytelling festival each year that spotlights some of the country's most popular tellers of personal and traditional stories. The festival usually takes place over the first weekend in October in the historic Appalachian hilltown of Jonesborough, Tennessee.

If you become a member of NSA, you receive a copy of their bimonthly magazine, *Storytelling*, which publishes stories (usually traditional tales) as well as articles on a wide range of storytelling techniques, issues, events, contexts, and possibilities—involving personal as well as traditional and modern fictional tales.

August House Publishers
P.O. Box 3223, Little Rock, AR 72203; 1-800-284-8784

Yellow Moon Press
P.O. Box 1316, Cambridge, MA 02238; 1-800-497-4385
Both August House Publishers and Yellow Moon Press publish and distribute a wide range of books, audiotapes, and videotapes relating to personal and traditional storytelling. Ask for their catalogues and, if desired, talk with company personnel for specific suggestions that suit your interests and needs.

Storytelling World
ETSU Box 70647, Johnson City, TN 37614–0647
This seasonal magazine offers articles for many different kinds of storytellers and storytelling purposes. It also has excellent resource bibliographies and reviews.

International Order of E.A.R.S., Inc.
12019 Donohue Ave., Louisville, KY 40243
The order provides a good book- and tape-ordering service and publishes a lively magazine, *Tale Trader*.

I suggest you read more books relating to personal storytelling, traditional storytelling, or life contexts for storytelling. I recommend the following books on the basis of their general interest and their appropriateness for readers of this book. A more extensive bibliography follows.

Armstrong, David. *Managing by Storying Around.* New York: Doubleday, 1992. This book offers many different examples of personal stories relating to business.
Davis, Donald. *Telling Your Own Stories.* Little Rock, AR: August House, 1993. A concise, user-friendly guide for family and classroom storytelling, public speaking, and personal journaling, this book offers stimulating idea prompts and story-developing discussion from a grandmaster of the art.
Feldman, Christina, and Jack Kornfield, eds. *Stories of the Spirit, Stories of the Heart.* San Francisco: HarperSanFrancisco, 1991. This book is a compelling anthology of spiritually enriching parables and stories from various traditions around the world. Included are a few personal stories as well.
Greene, Bob, and D. G. Fulford. *To Our Children's Children.* New York: Doubleday, 1993. This book consists of hundreds of good questions to pose when interviewing family members for their personal stories.
Maguire, Jack. *Creative Storytelling.* Cambridge, MA: Yellow Moon Press, 1992. This book is about how to choose, invent, and share tales for children. It mostly concerns traditional tales or fictional stories that you make up yourself, but it also features discussion of personal tales.

Moore, Robin. *Awakening the Hidden Storyteller*. Boston: Shambhala, 1991. A very clever, hands-on guide to assist you in making personal storytelling a family tradition. It's filled with activities the author uses in his own workshops, and appeals especially to people seeking a spiritual, self-help path toward storytelling and relationship-building.

Smith, Jimmy Neil, ed. *Homespun: Tales from America's Favorite Storytellers*. New York: Crown, 1988. Edited by the founder of the National Storytelling Association, this book contains written versions of more than thirty stories—most traditional, but some personal and modern fictional—told by America's most well-known and well-respected tellers. It also offers good how-to and resource sections.

Stone, Elizabeth. *Black Sheep and Kissing Cousins*. New York: Penguin, 1989. This book discusses how our family stories shape us. It doesn't directly address how to fashion or tell personal stories, but it can provide a great deal of inspiration for doing so.

Stone, Richard. *The Healing Art of Storytelling*. New York: Hyperion, 1996. Drawing heavily (and helpfully) from the author's own professional and life experience, this book offers many valuable guidelines for building storytelling relationships with our family members and friends.

Taylor, Daniel. *The Healing Power of Stories*. New York: Doubleday, 1996. This book is very motivational and spiritually oriented. It focuses on the theme of personal storytelling, especially as narrative therapy; and features many how-to tips.

Yolen, Jane, ed. *Favorite Folktales from Around the World*. New York: Random House, 1986. This anthology contains some of the most beloved and enchanting traditional tales from all over the world, organized according to a number of different themes, such as "true loves and false," "tricksters, rogues, and cheats," and "heroes: likely and unlikely." It's one volume in the outstanding Pantheon Fairy Tale and Folklore Library, a series that also includes such books as *African Folktales*, *American Indian Myths and Legends*, *Russian Fairy Tales*, *Italian Folktales*, *Irish Folktales*, and so on.

Zeitlin, Steven J., Amy J. Kotkin, and Holly Cutting Baker. *A Celebration of American Family Folklore*. Cambridge, MA: Yellow Moon Press, 1982. This book offers an exceptionally lively and thought-provoking selection of family stories and photographs collected by the Smithsonian Institution, which sponsors a folklife festival in Washington, D.C., every summer.

BIBLIOGRAPHY

Abram, David. *The Spell of the Sensuous*. New York: Pantheon, 1996.

Aftel, Mandy. *The Story of Your Life*. New York: Simon & Schuster, 1996.

Andersen, Marianne S., and Louis M. Savary. *Passages: A Guide for Pilgrims of the Mind*. New York: Harper & Row, 1972.

Armstrong, David. *Managing by Storying Around*. New York: Doubleday, 1992.

Baker, Rob, and Ellen Dooling Draper, eds. "ARCS." *Parabola*, vol. 17, no. 2, 1992.

Barnes, Kim. *In the Wilderness*. New York: Doubleday, 1996.

Brody, Ed, Jay Goldspinner, Katie Green, Rona Leventhal, and John Porcino, eds. *Spinning Tales and Weaving Hope*. Philadelphia: New Society, 1992.

Byrne, Robert. *The Fourth 637 Best Things Anybody Ever Said*. New York: Fawcett Crest, 1990.

———. *The Other 637 Best Things Anybody Ever Said*. New York: Fawcett Crest, 1984.

———. *The 637 Best Things Anybody Ever Said*. New York: Fawcett Crest, 1982.

Caduto, Michael J., and Joseph Bruchac. *Keepers of the Earth*. Golden, CO: Fulcrum, 1988.

Cameron, Julia, and Mark Bryan. *The Artist's Way*. New York: Tarcher/Putnam, 1992.

Catford, Lorna, and Michael Ray. *The Path of the Everyday Hero*. New York: Tarcher/Putnam, 1991.

Chase, Richard, ed. *Grandfather Tales*. Boston: Houghton Mifflin, 1976.

Coles, Robert, interviewed by Christopher Woodhull. "The Man Who Listens to Children." *Storytelling*, vol. 4, no. 4, Fall 1992.

Collins, Chase. "Stories from the Heart." *Storytelling*, vol. 4, no. 4, Fall 1992.

Cowan, Tom. *Shamanism as a Spiritual Practice for Daily Life*. Freedom, CA: Crossing Press, 1996.

———. *How to Tap into Your Own Genius*. New York: Simon & Schuster, 1984.

Cushman, Anne. "The Spirit of Creativity." *Yoga Journal*, September/October 1991.

Davis, Donald. *Telling Your Own Stories*. Little Rock, AR: August House, 1993.

Donaldson, O. Fred. *Playing by Heart*. Deerfield Beach, FL: Health Communications, 1993.

Dooling, D. M., ed. "ARCS." *Parabola*, vol. 4, no. 3, 1979.

———. "Focus." *Parabola*, vol. 4, no. 4, 1979.

Edwards, Betty. *Drawing on the Right Side of the Brain*. Los Angeles: J. P. Tarcher, 1979.

Eliot, Alexander. "Focus." *Parabola*, vol. 21, no. 1, 1996.

Feldman, Christina, and Jack Kornfield. *Stories of the Spirit, Stories of the Heart*. San Francisco: HarperSanFrancisco, 1991.

Gersie, Alida. *Earthtales*. London: Merlin Press, 1992.

Gillard, Marni. *Storyteller Storyteacher*. York, ME: Stenhouse, 1996.

Goldberg, Natalie. *Writing Down the Bones*. Boston: Shambhala, 1986.

Greene, Bob, and D. G. Fulford. *To Our Children's Children*. New York: Doubleday, 1993.

Gurdjieff, G. I. *Meetings with Remarkable Men*. New York: Dutton, 1974.

Halifax, Joan. *The Fruitful Darkness*. San Francisco: HarperSanFrancisco, 1990.

Handley, Helen, and Andra Samuelson, eds. *Child*. New York: Norton, 1992.

Hillman, James. "A Note on Story." *Parabola*, vol. 4, no. 4, 1979.

Keen, Sam, and Anne Valley-Fox. *Your Mythic Journey*. New York: G. P. Putnam's Sons, 1989.

Lanier, Jean. "Don't Argue, Tell a Story!" *Creation Spirituality*, November/December 1992.

Larsen, Stephen. *The Mythic Imagination*. New York: Bantam, 1990.

Ledoux, Denis. *Turning Memories into Memoirs*. Lisbon Falls, ME: Soleil Press, 1993.

Leggett, Trevor. *Zen and the Ways*. Rutland, VT: Charles E. Tuttle, 1987.

Lewis, Deborah Shaw, and Gregg Louis. *"Did I Ever Tell You About How Our Family Got Started?"* Grand Rapids, MI: Zondervan, 1994.

Lipman, Doug. "Discovering the One and Only You." *Storytelling*, vol. 4, no. 1, 1992.

Maguire, Jack. *Your Guide to a Better Memory*. New York: Berkley, 1995.

——. *Creative Storytelling*. Cambridge, MA: Yellow Moon Press, 1992.

——. *Night and Day: Use the Power of Your Dreams to Transform Your Life*. New York: Simon & Schuster, 1989.

——. "Sounds and Sensibilities: Storytelling as an Educational Process." *Children's Literature Association Quarterly*, vol. 13, no. 1, 1988.

——. *What Does Childhood Taste Like?* New York: William Morrow, 1986.

Maguire, Jack, with the Philadelphia Child Guidance Center. *Your Child's Emotional Health*. New York: Macmillan, 1993.

Maisel, Eric. *A Life in the Arts*. New York: Tarcher/Putnam, 1994.

Martin, Rafe. *The Boy Who Loved Mammoths*. Cambridge, MA: Yellow Moon Press, 1995.

Martin, Suzanne. "Hearing Other People's Voices." *Storytelling*, vol. 5, no. 1, 1993.

McDarrah, Fred W. *Kerouac & Friends*. New York: William Morrow, 1985.

Mellon, Nancy. *Storytelling and the Art of Imagination*. Rockport, MA: Element Books, 1992.

Metzger, Deena. *Writing for Your Life*. San Francisco: HarperSanFrancisco, 1992.

Moore, Robin. *Awakening the Hidden Storyteller*. Boston: Shambhala, 1991.

Morrow, Glenn. "Spinning a Yarn from Common Threads." *Museletter*, vol. 10, no. 1, 1997.

Nasr, Seyyed Hossein, interviewed by Jeffrey P. Zaleski. "Echoes of Infinity." *Parabola*, vol. 13, no. 1, 1988.

Novak, Michael. *Ascent of the Mountains, Flight of the Dove*. New York: Harper & Row, 1971.

O'Callahan, Jay. "How Jay O'Callahan Created 'The Herring Shed.'" *Storytelling World*, Winter/Spring 1997.

Oliver, Mary. *Blue Pastures*. New York: Harcourt Brace, 1995.

Pike, Larry. "When Stories Mean Business." *Storytelling*, vol. 4, no. 3, 1992.

Rambusch, Nancy. "As the Twig Is Bent . . ." *Parabola*, vol. 4, no. 4, 1979.

Ramer, Andrew. *Revelations for a New Millennium*. San Francisco: HarperSanFrancisco, 1997.

Rothenberg, David. "Sound Traces." *Parabola*, vol. 22, no. 2, 1997.

Safransky, Sy. *Sunbeams*. Berkeley, CA: North Atlantic Books, 1990.

Sanders, Scott Russell. "The Most Human Art." *Utne Reader*, September/October 1997.

Sawyer, Ruth. *The Way of the Storyteller*. New York: Penguin, 1970.

Simms, Laura. "Summoning the Realm of Dream." *Storytelling*, vol. 8, no. 5, 1996.

Simpkinson, Anne A. "Sacred Stories." *Common Boundary*, vol. 11, no. 6, 1993.

Simpkinson, Anne A., and Charles Simpkinson, eds. *Sacred Stories*. San Francisco: HarperSanFrancisco, 1993.

Simpkinson, Anne A., Charles Simpkinson, and Rose Solari. *Nourishing the Soul*, San Francisco: HarperSanFrancisco, 1995.

Smith, Jimmy Neil, ed. *Homespun*. New York: Crown, 1988.

Snyder, Gary. *The Practice of the Wild*. San Francisco, CA: North Point Press, 1990.

Spiegelman, Art, and Bob Schneider, eds. *Whole Grains*. New York: Douglas Links, 1973.

Stone, Elizabeth. *Black Sheep and Kissing Cousins*. New York: Penguin, 1988.

Stotter, Ruth, ed. *One Hundred Memorable Quotes About Stories and Storytelling*. Stinson Beach, CA: Stotter Press, 1995.

Taylor, Daniel. *The Healing Power of Stories*. New York: Doubleday, 1996.

Tsacrios, Nell Fuqua. "Memory: Our Personal Mythologist." *Storytelling*, vol. 8, no. 3, 1996.

Walljasper, Jay. "The Speed Trap." *Utne Reader*, March/April 1997.

Walker, Alice. "A Wind Through the Heart" (conversation with Sharon Salzberg and Melvin McLeod). *Shambhala Sun*, vol. 5, no. 3, 1997.

Ward, John R. "The Business of Communication." *Storytelling*, vol. 6, no. 5, 1994.

Watson, Bruce. "Before Electricity, There Was Storytelling." *Smithsonian*, vol. 27, no. 12, 1997.

Whitman, Walt. *Leaves of Grass*. New York: Bantam, 1983.

Winokur, Jon, ed. *True Confessions*. New York: Penguin, 1992.

———. *Zen to Go*. New York: Penguin, 1990.

Yashinsky, Dan. "Tellingware: A Headful of Stories." *Storytelling*, vol. 5, no. 3, 1993.

Yolen, Jane, ed. *Favorite Folktales from Around the World*. New York: Pantheon Books, 1986.

Zeitlin, Steven J., Amy J. Kotkin, and Holly Cutting Baker. *A Celebration of American Family Folklore*. Cambridge, MA: Yellow Moon Press, 1982.

Zipes, Jack. "Tales Worth Telling." *Utne Reader*, September/October 1997.

INDEX

Abram, David, 186
Abstractions, linking specific images
    to, 104–109
Achebe, Chinua, 81
Acting, versus storytelling, 135
Adapting stories, 157–58, 170, 192–93
Aesop, 105
Alexithymia, 60–61
Allusions, 161–62
Anxiety, controlling through
    storytelling, 27–28
Armstrong, David, 202–3
*Ascent of the Mountain, Flight of the
    Dove* (Novak), 106–7
Audience. *See* Listeners
August House Publishers, 240
Auschwitz, 78
Autobiographical stories. *See* Stories,
    personal

Baal Shem Tov, 30, 37–38
Bateson, George, 41
Benefits of personal storytelling,
    13–34
Big stories, 82–83, 190
    personal significance of, 82
Black Sheep and Kissing Cousins
    (Stone), 95, 99
Body, stories embodied by, 114
Body language, 159–60, 185–86
Boje, David, 202
Books
    from childhood, 94–95, 232
    recommended, 241–42

Brain hemispheres
    myth of Odin and, 40
    right, and visual images, 96, 110
    shift in balance of, 40

Catalogues, defined, 163
Cather, Willa, 49, 63
*Celebration of American Family
    Values, A* (Zeitlin), 196
Ceremony. *See* Ritual
Chapman, John (Johnny Appleseed),
    71–73
Childhood
    books from, 94–95, 232
    as common denominator, 49–50
    and family storytelling, 196
    hero of, as memory trigger, 69–74
    images from, 94–95, 96–97
    landscape of, 112, 113
    music from, 94–95, 232
    recovering memories of, 53–57,
        58–64
Chronological order, 140–41
Commitment to storytelling, 217
Communication
    within family, 195–96, 198–99
    at work, 201, 204
Community, sense of, 207–8
Community-oriented storytelling,
    191, 206–14
    adapting stories for, 193
    as community-building occasions,
        207
    small-group movement in, 209–13

Confidence, increasing, 26–28,
    33–34
    forced delivery and, 68–69
    talking story out and, 137
Contexts for storytelling, 190–94.
        See also Community-oriented
        storytelling; Family storytelling;
        Work, storytelling at
    various, fitting stories to, 191–94
Cooper, Jan, 162
Corporate environment, 202–3
Cotter, Michael, 9
Courage, increasing, 26–28, 33–34
Craighead, Meinrad, 38–39
Creating stories. *See* Story-
    developing process
Creative visualization, 234
Creativity, 132
    Newton model of, 128, 129
    Sisyphus model of, 128–29
    social conditioning and, 22–23
    in storytelling, 16, 21–24, 32–
        33
    at work, 203, 204
"Creator's block," overcoming, 57
Crises, handling through storytelling,
    27–28
Criticism, 222–23
Crossroads. *See* Turning points,
    personal

Dante, 25
Davis, Donald, 24, 138
Daydreams, 40

Decision making. *See* Turning points, personal
"Destorification," 43–44
Dialogue, 23–24, 158–59
Diddley, Bo, 77
Disruptions/distractions, 220
Drama/impending drama, 142
Dramatic pattern, four-step, 141–42
Draper, Ellen Dooling, 82
Dreams, 14, 15–16, 40, 233
    recording, 233–34

Einstein, Albert, 66
Eliot, T. S., 25
Ellis, Elizabeth, 85, 169, 208
Embarrassment, 223
Embodiment of story, 169–78
    adapting stories and, 170
    automatic elements in, 177
    contemplating optional changes in, 176, 177
    defined, 169
    guidelines for, 173–77, 178
    versus memorizing, 169–73, 177
    telling story out loud in, 175
Emotional Intelligence (Goleman), 196
Empathy, 196
Ending story, 187–88
End-point situation, 142
Enlivening people, 208
Enlivening stories, techniques for, 157–65
Evans, Ron, 196

Facial expressions, 159
Fairy tales, 6–7
Family members. *See also* Family memories; Family stories; Family storytelling
    guidelines for interviewing, 101–3
    preparation for interviewing, 103
Family memories, 93, 95, 98–103
Family stories
    embellished truth in, 42–43
    gathering, 98–103

questions for eliciting, 99–102
    researching, 98–103
Family storytelling, 195–200
    adapting stories for, 192
    communication within family and, 195–96, 198–99
    role of, 195–96
    special projects, 199
    tips for, 197–99
Family tree diagram, 99
Fears, minimizing storytelling, 215–27
Feedback, 222, 223
Feeling or thinking backward, 60–64, 66–67
Final version, first telling of, 164–65
Floorplans, as memory tool, 111–12
Fluidity in storytelling, 139
Folktales, 6
"Fool" tale, 137–38
Forced delivery, 68–69
Forgetting, fear of, 218–19
Formal storytelling, 9–10
Forster, E. M., 105
Franklin, Benjamin, 78

Gammel, Stephen, 111
Genogram, 99
George, Pat Jikyo, 224
Gestures, 159, 185–86
Goleman, Daniel, 196
Gray, Spaulding, 122–23
Groups, contacting, 189
Groups, storytelling, 137, 209–13, 231
    constructive criticism in, 213
    discussion themes for, 212
    meeting guidelines for, 212–13
Gurdjieff, G. I., 179

Harley, Bill, 51
Healing Power of Stories, The (Taylor), 21
Heroes
    childhood, as memory trigger, 69–74
    ourselves as, 67

Hillman, James, 44–45
Homespun: Tales from America's Favorite Storyteller (Smith), 209
Horizontal thinking, 92–93
Hospitals and hospices, 208–9
Human experience
    collective, 206
    little stories and, 83–84, 190
Humanizing situations, 4, 21
    work relationships, 202
Humor, 161
    developing sense of, 25–26, 33

Ideas. *See* Story ideas
Images. *See also* Pictures
    keeping file of, 229–30
    as plot development aid, 146
    right brain hemisphere and, 110
    sensory, 107–8, 160
    specific, linking to abstractions, 104–9
Imagination, 21–22. *See also* Creativity
    using to deal with crisis, 27–28
Imagining key moments, 132
Individuality, 65–66
Inflection, 163–64
Inner self, listening to, 5
Inner storyteller
    making audible, 127
    meeting, 234–35
    reconnecting with, 45–46
    visualizing, 46–48
Integrity of story, 141
International Order of E.A.R.S., Inc., 241
Interruptions, 219–20
Intimacy, recapturing, 44
Introductory remarks, 183
Isolation, overcoming, 206, 208–9

Joel, Bill, 137–38
Johnny Appleseed. *See* Chapman, John
Journal of events, 27

Juditz, Vicki, 123
Jung, Carl G., 132

Kazantzakis, Nikos, 135
Keillor, Garrison, 29–30
Key scenes, 140–44
    chronological order of, 140–41
    in four-step dramatic pattern,
        141–42
    and plot development, 140–44
    storyboard representation of,
        146–47, 152–56
    in stream metaphor, 140
    time to communicate, 143
    time to read aloud, 143
    unrelated to plot development, 142
Kinslow, Michele, 121–22
Knapsack tales
    adaptation of, to fit context,
        191–93
    defined, 157
    embodiment and, 170
Koan, 85–86, 159

Landscape of childhood, 113
Lanier, Jean, 198
League for the Advancement of New
    England Storytelling, 207
Learning stories by heart, 169–78
    guidelines for, 173–77, 178
Legends, 6
Legwork. See Memory legwork
Length of story, recommended, 144
License in storytelling, 23
Lifelines, 84–86, 87–88
    crossroads, 90–91
    defined, 84
    parallel, 92, 93
    sample, 87
Life review, 84, 177
Life stories. See also Lifeline
    big and little, 82–84, 190
    embodying, 177
    prompts for, 68–69
    restorying, 78–81
    translation options, 78–81
    as whole, sense of, 67

Lipman, Doug, 207
Listeners
    generating, 189
    lack of response from, 221–22
    preparation of, 181, 183
    questions from, 220
    rapport with, 186–87
    in storytelling, 17
    storytelling as connection to,
        18–21
Listening, 3–12
    to inner self, 5, 11–12
    to others, 5, 10–11, 230–31
    to storytellers, 231
    tips on, 231
Little stories, 82, 83–84, 190
"Loafing and inviting the soul,"
        53–57, 58
    family stories and, 100
    and thinking or feeling backward,
        59–64

McGrath, Patty, 210
Martin, Rafe, 111
Marvin, Lee-Ellen, 207
Meaning(s)
    abstract, 104–9
    creating, in story development,
        14–18, 31–32
    stories as transmission of, 53
Meetings with Remarkable Men
    (Gurdjieff), 179
Mellon, Nancy, 28
Memories
    childhood, incorporating into
        stories, 49–53
    childhood, recovering, 53–57,
        58–64
    connecting, 59, 67
    floorplan sketches and, 111–12
    preservation of, 30, 34
Memorization as aid, 173
Memorizing stories, 170, 218. See
    also Embodiment of story
    versus embodiment, 169–73,
        178
Memory. See also Remembering

developing through storytelling,
        28–30
    as "story-based," 41
    storytelling necessary to, 16
    triggering, 67–69, 73
Memory legwork, 93–94
    for family stories, 98–103
Memory work
    focusing of attention, 60–64
    "loafing and inviting the soul,"
        53–57, 58
    thinking and feeling backward,
        60–64
Men and estrangement from feelings,
        60–61
Mindfulness, storytelling, 27–28
Moralizing in stories, 105
Moviemaking, mental, 81, 83, 110,
        175
Movies, 232
Museletter (newsletter), 207
Music from childhood, 94–95, 232
Myerhoff, Barbara, 177
Myths, 6, 80, 188

Nachman, Rabbi, 135–36
Narrative therapy, 41–42
National Storytelling Association,
        209, 210, 240
Newton, Isaac, 128
Newton model of creativity, 128
Notebook keeping, 229
Novak, Michael, 106–7

Observing experiences for stories. See
    Storystalking
Occasions for storytelling, 181, 182
Odin, myth of, 38, 40
Opportunities for storytelling. See
    also Contexts for storytelling
    in community, 207, 208–10, 214
    in family, 197
    at work, 201–3

Pacing, 159, 163, 184
Pauses, planned/unplanned, 164
Pennington, Lee, 65–66

Perception
    childhood influences on, 49, 52
    stories and, 9
Perkins, John, 70–71
Personal stories. *See* Stories, personal
Personal storytelling. *See* Storytelling, personal
Photographs, 96–97
Picasso, Pablo, 24
Pictures, 96–97, 110–12
Pike, Larry, 203
Place, sense of, 112–13
Plot development, 137–45
    controlled versus fluid, 139–40
    formal, 152–53
    four-point dramatic pattern, 141–42
    key scenes and, 140–44
    overconcern with, 138–39
    storyboard for, 146–47, 152–56
    in stream metaphor, 137–40
    three-circle organization, 143, 144–45
Pollack, Rachel, 70
"Portrait gallery" narrative, 140–41
Postures. *See* Body language
Practice of the Wild, The (Snyder), 113
Preparation of listeners, 183
Proust, Marcel, 234
Psychotherapy, 17, 19
    life review work in, 84
    narrative, 41–42
    premise of, 41
Public speaking, fear of, 215

Questions
    generating, 99, 100
    from listeners, 220
Quindlen, Anna, 42–43

Rapport, 186–87, 219
Reconnecting with inner storyteller, 45–46
Rehearsing stories, 175, 177
Relaxing, 53–57
    rituals to aid in, 56

Remembering. *See also* Memory
    embodiment and, 169–70
    pauses for, 164
    spiritual aspect of, 38–39
    and story-knowing, 38
Repetition in stories, 162–63
Research. *See* Memory legwork
Response, lack of, 221–22
"Restorying," 78–81
Rituals, 56, 72
    to aid relaxation, 56
    cultural, lack of in U.S., 29
    for family storytelling time, 197–98
Robards, Jason, 135
Roethke, Theodore, 129

Satirical allusion, 162
Secrets, sharing, 4
Seed story, 77–78
Self. *See also* Inner self
    talking out story to, 127–36, 137
    trust in, 132
Self-denial, 18
Self-talk, 216
Senses, appealing to, 160
Sensory images, 107–8, 234
Shank, Roger C., 41
Sharing personal stories, 107
    generating audiences for, 189
Simms, Laura, 21
Sisyphus model of creativity, 128–29
Sketches
    of floorplans, 111–12
    for storyboard, 146
Small-group movement, 209–13
Smells, 234
Snyder, Gary, 113
Spontaneity in storytelling, 132–34, 139–40
Starting-point situation, 142
Stone, Elizabeth, 95
Stone, Richard, 43, 206
Stories, personal
    abstract meanings of, 104–9
    adaptable, 157–58, 170
    big, 82–83

    broad categories of, 82–84
    characteristics of good, 104
    combined with traditional stories, 115–19
    enlivening, 157–65
    importance of telling our own, 17–18
    inducing/deducing, 107
    length of, 144
    little, 82, 83–84
    making memorable, 8
    as memorable, 30
    observing experiences for, 121–24
    plotting development of, 137–45
    sharing, 107
    traditional stories within, 115–17, 162
Stories, traditional, 5–6
    combined with personal stories, 115–19
    within personal stories, 115, 162
Storyboard, 146–56, 174
    defined, 146
    example of using, 147–56
    methods, 146
    sketches for, 146
    written, 146, 153–56, 174
Storybuilding questions, 27
Story-developing process. *See also* Key scenes; Plot development; Vocalizing story ideas
    creating meaning in, 14–18, 31–32
    creativity in, 16, 21–24
    therapeutic nature of, 17
    vocalizing in, 127–36
Storygifting, 209
Story ideas
    memory legwork and, 93–94
    restorying, 78–81
    translation options, 77–80
    triggering, 235–39
Story-knowing, 38
Story prospects
    alertness to, 121–24
    developing sensitivity to, 121–24
Storystalking, 121–24
    defined, 121

Storytellers, natural-born, as
misconception, 171–72
Storytelling, personal. *See also*
Stories, personal
as alternative to ordinary talk,
19–20
benefits of, 13–30
connecting to others through,
18–21, 32
dynamic equilibrium in, 19
embodiment of story and, 169–73
feelings derived from, 9
fluidity important in, 139
impact of, on listener, 180
lack of self-involvement in, 20
magic of, 226–27
memory and, 16, 28–30
memory legwork and, 93–95
plot development and, 137–45
primary purpose of, 19
versus psychotherapy, 17, 19
spontaneity in, 139–40
therapeutic value of, 17
Storytelling (magazine), 203
Storytelling and the Imagination
(Mellon), 28
Storytelling World (magazine), 241
Story types, Elizabeth Ellis's, 85
Subjectivity, 224
fear of, 22
in storytelling, 23, 24, 53

Talking out story to self, 127–36, 137
Tape recording, 230

Taylor, Daniel, 21
Telephone, turning off, 198
Television, 196, 232
Tell Me a Story (Shank), 41
Thinking or feeling backward, 60–64,
66–67
Time, 66–67
factor, 144, 176–77
and place for storytelling, 181, 182
Timelines, parallel, 92, 93
Torrance, Jackie, 208
Travers, P. L., 45
Trigger. *See* Memory, triggering
Trusting oneself, 132
Truth, meaning of, in personal
storytelling, 23–24
Turning points
in drama, 142
personal, 89–92

Uniqueness, 65–66

Van der Post, Laurens, 22
Vertical thinking, 92
Visualization
creative, 234
of inner storyteller, 46–48
Vocal art, storytelling as, 134–35
Vocal guidelines, 183–88
Vocalizing story ideas, 127–36
story development through,
130–32
Vocal tones and style, 159, 163,
179–81, 183–86, 187–88

Voice, 179, 180
making most of, guidelines for,
180–81, 183–88
normal tone of, 183–84, 230

Walljasper, Jay, 54–55
Ward, John, 204
Western culture
lack of intimacy in, 44
lack of storytelling in, 29, 43–44
White, Michael, 42
Whitman, Walt, 54
Wiesel, Elie, 37
Windham, Kathryn, 6, 209
Word and Image (Jung), 132
Work, storytelling at, 191, 201–5
activities calling for, 201
adapting stories for, 193
benefits of, 201–5
contexts for, 201–3
creative thinking and, 203, 204
humanizing work and, 202
job-appropriate personal stories
and, 201–2, 203
selecting stories for, 201, 203,
204
team-building and, 204

Yellow Moon Press, 240

Zeitlin, Steven, 196
Zen Buddhism, 123, 159
tales, 85–86, 224–27

ABOUT THE AUTHOR

Jack Maguire is a storyteller, writer, and workshop leader living in New York's Hudson River Valley. Among his many publications are: *Creative Storytelling*, *Your Guide to a Better Memory*, *Care and Feeding of the Brain*, *Night and Day: Use the Power of Your Dreams to Transform Your Life*, and *What Does Childhood Taste Like?* He is a board member of the Visions Story and Art Center based in Poughkeepsie, New York, which sponsors the annual Hudson Valley Storytelling Festival. Performances and workshops are arranged through Tale Trails, Inc., 17 South Chodikee Lake Road, Highland, NY 12528.